Paul Cowan

AN ORPHAN
IN HISTORY

One Man's
Triumphant Search
for His Jewish Roots

Afterword by Rachel Cowan

JEWISH LIGHTS Publishing
Woodstock, Vermont

An Orphan in History:
One Man's Triumphant Search for His Jewish Roots

2002 First Jewish Lights Edition
© 1982 by Paul Cowan
Afterword © 1989 by Rachel Cowan

Originally published in 1982 by Doubleday & Company, Inc.

Library of Congress Cataloging-in-Publication Data
Cowan, Paul.
An orphan in history : one man's triumphant search for his Jewish
roots / Paul Cowan ; afterword by Rachel Cowan.
        p. cm.
ISBN 1-58023-135-7 (Paperback)
1. Jewish way of life. 2. Judaism—United States. 3. Cowan, Paul. 4. Journalists—New York (State)—New York—Biography. 5. Jews—New York (State)—New York—Biography. 6. New York (N.Y.)—Biography. I. Title.
BM723 .C68 2002
296'.092—dc21

                                    2002010343

10 9 8 7 6 5 4 3 2 1

Manufactured in the United States of America

Published by Jewish Lights Publishing
A Division of LongHill Partners, Inc.
Sunset Farm Offices, Route 4, P.O. Box 237
Woodstock, VT 05091
Tel: (802) 457-4000   Fax: (802) 457-4004
www.jewishlights.com

Dedication

I have a mystical belief that books echo back and forth through the generations. So this is dedicated to:

the memory of my parents, Pauline Spiegel Cowan and Louis G. Cowan;

to my uncle Modie J. Spiegel and the memory of my grandfather Jacob J. Cohen;

to my wife, Rachel Cowan;

to my children, Lisa Cowan and Matt Cowan;

to my teacher, Rabbi Joseph Singer.

Foreword

An Orphan in History is my story as an American Jew. I have spent years retrieving the religious and cultural legacy which had evaporated, in my family, under the pressure of assimilation. But, with only slight variations in personal and cultural details, it could be the story of Frankie Ruggio, whose grandfather spoke Italian and was named Dante; or of a midwestern computer technician named Peter Holmes, whose Scandinavian-born grandfather was a fisherman named Per Hansa; or of Joe Martin, whose father, José Martinez, was a highly skilled cigar maker from Havana. In a way, it is the story of millions of immigrant families who left the economically and culturally confining Old World towns where they were raised, and paid for the freedom and prosperity this country offered with their pasts.

At first, it must have seemed like a marvelous bargain. For most of the twentieth century, melting-pot America was like the pot of gold at the end of history's rainbow. In this land of limitless possibilities, one's past seemed to be an encumbrance: something that was filled with atavistic superstitions, that was anathema to enlightened people, that presented an obstacle to personal progress.

But now, America's power is waning; we are living in a post-Copernican age, where we are no longer the center of the world. The country no longer seems to promise my generation—or my children's—the degree of social or physical mobility it promised my parents and grandparents.

As a result, many people who might have once explored the nation's physical or economic frontiers are journeying inward: they are Kit Carsons of the soul. Some adopt creeds that are new to them—Eastern religions, or an all-embracing born-again Christianity. But many, like me, seek to synthesize their Old World heritage with the America that has shaped their consciousness.

In many cases, they travel or seek to recapture their pasts by the use of new tools of genealogical research that have proliferated since Alex Haley published *Roots.* Those techniques help provide the information, the textures of experience, which transform an ethnic label into a distinct, three-dimensional identity. But they don't provide the spiritual nourishment which is, at last, the thing most of us yearn for.

Sometimes a seeker encounters a person who embodies the faith and the history he craves. That can happen as an apparent accident—Carlos Castañeda describes his involvement with Don Juan as such. It can result from the kind of search Alex Haley made when he voyaged to the African country of Gambia, and then to the town of Juffure, where he met a *griot,* an old man, a storyteller, who told him about his ancestor, Kunte Kinte.

My own friendship with Rabbi Joseph Singer, my teacher, is the result of my father's guidance, my journalist's luck, my own planning. That relationship still contains a large element of mystery. For, like most transmitters of faith, Rabbi Singer's power resides in the part of his personality that has withstood the lures of twentieth-century rationalism, and therefore preserved what is most compelling about traditional Judaism.

Of course, like most seekers, I have had to find my own way into faith. It is a voyage that never seems to end. That is why, as some readers will note, I have been vague about some details of ritual observance which seem to grow more important to me from one year to the next.

I am describing a journey, not the landscape of the destination. This is an account of my effort to recover my ancestral legacy— through journalism and politics, by uncovering the details of my family's past and becoming involved with the religion I inherited, and by accepting the emotionally difficult realization that life defies reason: life unfolds unpredictably; it contains treasures and sorrows that none of us can foresee. I hope the story of my search will help other orphans in history find their way home.

Acknowledgments

I have interviewed hundreds of people for this book. Some are quoted by name; some wish to remain anonymous; most will recognize the nuggets of personal or historical insight they furnished.

In a few cases—those of my antagonists at Choate and some former girlfriends—I have disguised names. In some others, I have drawn from material I originally obtained for my book *The Making of an Un-American* or for my *Voice* articles.

I do want to acknowledge some people by name.

My brother Geoff and my sisters Holly and Liza have talked with me about this book since I began to write it—sometimes on a daily basis. At times, I've felt that I've interrupted their productive present lives with my obsessions about the past. And sometimes we have all been struck by the contrast between my personal past and our collective one, for these interpretations of the family and childhood we shared are mine and don't necessarily reflect their experiences or their points of view.

I want to thank my uncle John Spiegel, psychiatrist and social scientist, an unfailingly perceptive man whose insights have helped me enormously with this book.

Charles B. Bernstein, a Chicago-based lawyer and genealogist, has provided miracles of research which saved me years of work and helped me clear up scores of puzzles with quotes from crucial, almost unobtainable, documents.

My mother's friends Edna Lerner, Anne W. Simon, Leah Weisner, Judy Rosenwald, and Mimi Siffert have afforded invaluable insights, as have my father's friends Stan Kaplan, Joseph Lash, Milton

Krentz, and Selma Hirsch. Of course, I take full responsibility for the portraits that emerge.

Some of my uncles, cousins, and aunts are mentioned by name, others are not. Originally, I guess, I sought to interview them largely in order to obtain information. But, for me, the enduring benefit of these contacts has been the increasingly deep sense of family—and the importance of family—they have afforded me.

My great-uncle Abraham Cohen, who was extremely helpful to me, died in May 1981. I wish that he could have lived to read this book.

Ken McCormick, Senior Consulting Editor of Doubleday, and Susan Schwartz, my editor, have taken an extraordinary amount of time to discuss this project with me, and to read what I wrote as soon as it was completed. Their opinions and encouragement helped me through some very difficult times.

My very good friends Rabbi Wolfe Kelman and Jacqueline Gutwirth both read a slightly earlier version of this manuscript, and made invaluable corrections and changes. My sister-in-law, Connie Egleson, has been an extremely helpful reader.

My agent, Amanda Urban, has given me frequent good advice and, more important, thrilled me at a moment of self-doubt by understanding this book in the exact context I meant it to be read.

I know it is unusual to dedicate a book to one's spouse, and then to acknowledge her. But my wife, Rachel, reads and rereads everything I write; she is the editor and friend I trust most. She is midwife to almost all my ideas and words.

Of course, in the end, much of a book like this must be largely speculative, and the guesswork is mine. Since many of the figures are dead, I can only hope I have interpreted their actions fairly and accurately.

PART ONE

PART ONE

1

For more than four years now, I have been embarked on a wondrous, confusing voyage through time and culture. Until 1976, when I was thirty-six, I had always identified myself as an American Jew. Now I am an American and a Jew. I live at once in the years 1982 and 5743, the Jewish year in which I am publishing this book. I am Paul Cowan, the New York-bred son of Louis Cowan and Pauline Spiegel Cowan, Chicago-born, very American, very successful parents; and I am Saul Cohen, the descendant of rabbis in Germany and Lithuania. I am the grandson of Modie Spiegel, a mail-order magnate, who was born a Reform Jew, became a Christian Scientist, and died in his spacious house in the wealthy gentile suburb of Kenilworth, Illinois, with a picture of Jesus Christ in his breast pocket; and of Jacob Cohen, a used-cement-bag dealer from Chicago, an Orthodox Jew, who lost everything he had—his wife, his son, his business, his self-esteem—except for the superstition-tinged faith that gave moments of structure and meaning to his last, lonely years.

As a child, growing up on Manhattan's East Side, I lived among Jewish WASPs. My father, an only child, had changed his name from Cohen to Cowan when he was twenty-one. He was so guarded about his youth that he never let my brother or sisters or me meet any of his father's relatives. I always thought of myself as a Cowan— the Welsh word for stonecutter—not a Cohen—a member of the Jewish priestly caste. My family celebrated Christmas and always gathered for an Easter dinner of ham and sweet potatoes. At Choate, the Episcopalian prep school to which my parents sent me, I was often stirred by the regal hymns we sang during the mandatory chapel service. In those years, I barely knew what a Passover seder was. I didn't know anyone who practiced archaic customs such as keeping kosher or lighting candles on Friday night. Neither my parents nor I ever mentioned the possibility of a bar mitzvah. In 1965, I fell in love with Rachel Brown, a New England Protestant whose ancestors came here in the seventeenth century. It didn't matter the least bit to her—or to me—that we were an interfaith marriage.

Now, at forty-two, I care more about Jewish holidays I'd never heard of back then, Shavuot or Simchat Torah, than about Christmas or Easter. In 1980, fifteen years after we were married, Rachel converted to Judaism, and is now program director of Ansche Chesed, a neighborhood synagogue we are trying to revitalize. Our family lights Friday night candles, and neither Rachel nor I work on the Sabbath. Since 1974, our children, Lisa and Matt, have gone to the Havurah School, a once-a-week Jewish school we started, and at fourteen and twelve they're more familiar with the Torah than I was five years ago. They are very thoughtful children, who have witnessed the changes in our family's life and are somewhat bemused and ambivalent about them. There is no telling whether they'll follow the path we have chosen. But that is true of all children. This past September, Lisa undertook the difficult task of learning enough Hebrew in six months to chant a full Haftorah (a prophetic text) at her bat mitzvah at Ansche Chesed. That day I was as happy as I've ever been in my life.

By now, I see the world through two sets of eyes, my American ones and my Jewish ones. That is enhanced, I suppose, by the fact that my father, who was once president of CBS-TV, who produced "The Quiz Kids," "Stop the Music," and "The $64,000 Question," and my elegant mother, an ardent civil-rights activist, moved easily through all sorts of worlds. Even now, as a journalist, I want to be at once a versatile American writer like James Agee or John Dos Passos and an evocative Jewish one like Isaac Bashevis Singer or Chaim Potok. Sometimes it makes me feel deeply conflicted. Sometimes it makes my life seem wonderfully rich and varied. I do know this: that my mind is enfolded like a body in a prayer shawl, by my ancestral past and its increasingly strong hold on my present. Scores of experiences have caused me to re-create myself, to perceive a five-thousand-year-old tradition as a new, precious part of my life.

I am not alone. Indeed, I believe my story, with all its odd, buried, Old World family mysteries, with its poised tension between material wealth and the promise of spiritual wealth, is the story of much of my generation, Jew and gentile alike.

It is also, of course, the story of a faith—Judaism—which remained a powerful force in my family despite my parents' outwardly assimilated lives. I have a brother, Geoff, forty, and two sisters, Holly, thirty-eight and Liza, thirty-four. Right now Holly and I are more religiously observant than Geoff or Liza. But the four of us all live lives whose Jewish flavor would have been unimaginable to us when we were young. I know that, for my part, I am reacting to the rootlessness I felt as a child—to the fact that for all the Cowan family's warmth, for all its intellectual vigor, for all its loyalty toward each other, our pasts had been amputated. We were orphans in history.

More important, I think, we were reacting to strong messages both our parents were sending—messages that made us feel a duty and a desire to find a way back home. When I was in grade school, my mother's ideas influenced me more directly than my father's. Polly was an active, attractive person—the only woman I've ever known who cared as much about elegance as she did about social justice. Her cool organizational style and dazzling smile left a lasting impression on everyone she met. But underneath it all, she felt a passionate turbulence about her background that left a deep impression on me.

Polly, whose German-Jewish family had come to America in 1848, was haunted by the Holocaust. Sometimes she became obsessed with small details that reminded her of that era. When I was a little boy, if my hair flopped down over my eyes, she would tell me I looked like Hitler and insist that I brush it back. Until I was in my mid-teens in the 1950s, she never permitted me to walk through the Yorkville section of New York, since the Nazis had once been strong in that German-American neighborhood. Those rather quirky attitudes blended in with the certainty—which she repeated as a litany—that even in America, even for wealthy Jewish merchants like the Spiegels or successful show business people like the Cowans, outward prosperity, apparent mobility, had nothing to do with real security. She and my father sent me to fine schools, which prepared me to become part of the American elite. She seemed to agree when my father urged me to get a Ph.D., but in quieter conversations, when we were shopping together or talking late at night, she'd insist that I learn a trade—not a profession, but a trade—since she secretly believed that one day we'd have to leave all our goods and money behind and flee to some strange foreign land, where my survival would be insured by a skill that didn't depend on language.

But her feelings about the Holocaust also imbued her—and us—with a secular messianism: a deep commitment to the belief that we had a lifelong debt to the six million dead. We could repay some of it, she always insisted, by fighting anti-Semitism wherever we encountered it. Furthermore, she believed that our history of oppression obliged us to combat all forms of injustice. Because of her influence, most of our family was involved in the civil-rights movement, particularly in the Mississippi Freedom Summer in 1964. Geoff and I registered voters in the Delta and Vicksburg. Polly organized groups of northern black and white women to spend time in the state's segregated communities, arranging covert integrated meetings. Holly sent out a newsletter about the Summer Project. Lou, frightened for us but proud, used all the influence he'd acquired as a television executive and confidant of politicians to keep us out of trouble and promote our causes.

There was no doubt in any of our minds that we were risking our lives to achieve the very American goal of integration because our kinsmen had been slaughtered in Lithuania, Poland, and Germany.

But it never occurred to me, back then, that my mother's intense, sometimes reverent, sometimes frightened feelings about the six million would leave me with a thirst for the inner details of the faith she knew nothing about, whose name she wanted me to defend.

In retrospect, I realize that my father must always have half hoped that I would develop that thirst. Indeed, he promoted it toward the end of his life, when he was in his sixties and I was in my thirties. But as I was growing up, I thought he wanted to divorce himself forever from the religious world he'd known as a boy in Chicago. He never talked very much about his father, Jake Cohen, but the few details he did divulge portrayed my grandfather as a cruel man: harsh and nasty toward his wife, Hetty Cohen (whom my father adored), subject to inexplicable rages that would occasionally cause Jake to order his son Lou to sleep on the kitchen floor. Sometimes Jake would leave his wife and child and work, with no explanation and no warning, so that he could attend a boxing match in Detroit or New Jersey. Incredibly, he seemed to begrudge his only son all his teenage triumphs. He never came to see Lou compete in track and field championships. When Lou was elected president of his high school student council, Jake looked at him mockingly and asked, "Why did they choose you?"

Lou felt that he had been saved from Jake Cohen by his mother's bachelor brother, his uncle Harry Smitz (whom Lou always called Holly). He liked to tell an anecdote that illustrated the contrast between those relationships. When Lou was a high school senior, his track team won a city championship. But Lou didn't receive any awards. When he came home that night, very upset, Jake Cohen asked him, "What made you think you deserved to win anything?" Holly Smitz had a medal he always wore on his watch. He gave it to his nephew and said, "That's your award."

Lou called or visited his mother almost every day of his adult life. I remember him weeping for hours when she died in 1949.

He rarely saw Jake Cohen. He did send him seventy-five dollars a week and I recall his telling us, with irritation in his voice, that Jake, destitute, was always nagging him for more. Jake died in 1950. I can't remember my father mentioning that fact.

Once, when I was a boy, my father told me that he recalled the Yom Kippurs he went to synagogue and watched Jake Cohen weep and beat his breast to atone for his sins. Then, after services, Lou would walk home with his parents and the rest of the huge Cohen clan and listen, appalled, as they fought over status and money; as they gossiped cruelly about siblings who weren't there. That wasn't religion, my father would tell me angrily. That was hypocrisy.

Now, though, as I review my childhood, I remember random words and gestures which hinted that my father had emotional roots in the world the Cohens inhabited—roots that flowered into ideas and activities late in his life.

He was a distinctly Jewish-looking man, while everyone else in our family was ethnically indistinguishable. He was about six foot two inches and always overweight. My mother would glance fondly at his slightly soft body, talk wryly about the incredible amount of worried attention he lavished on us, and tell her children that her husband was our real Jewish mother. He had a large nose (my mother would occasionally touch my small one and tell me she was glad it wasn't big like his), and a quick, ready smile, an eager way of listening that made people realize at once that he was alert to every nuance of their mood. I have a childhood memory of watching my father move from table to table at the show business hangouts like Sardi's which he frequented because of his job, working the room like a skilled politician. He made everyone he met feel singularly important, looking at them continuously, never gazing off to see if a more powerful person was somewhere else in the room. He communicated warmth through his attentive silences, through his ability to reach out and touch people fondly, not sensuously or aggressively. And he was always ready with a compliment; when he introduced his friends to each other, he always seemed to be orchestrating what was best in them. He was protective, not threatening.

Sometimes, slightly self-mockingly, he'd use one of his few Yiddish words to describe his behavior to my mother. He had *shmeicheled* (buttered up) someone. But he was doing himself a slight injustice. For though he could be cunning about people's strengths and weaknesses, he rarely let himself dwell for long on their flaws. At dinner he'd often tell us that some friend, some colleague, was "a darling man"—that was his favorite expression. He wooed people, but rarely considered that they might have self-serving reasons for staying inside his orbit. He *shmeicheled* with love.

I have been writing about his public persona. But inside the family, there were other, more intimate ways that Louis Cohen's ethnic past revealed itself through Louis G. Cowan's cosmopolitan present. For example, I always knew that he didn't like to eat pork, but I believed my mother's teasing assertion that he was displaying a silly, endearing superstition akin to his belief that if you had bubbles in your coffee you'd get rich. But when I remember the involuntary look of disgust that sometimes passed over his face when we had pork chops for dinner, I think that his reflexive aversion to the meat that's forbidden to religiously observant Jews might have provided a glimpse of tangled, powerful feelings he was unable to express openly—unable, perhaps, to express to himself.

On Sundays, when I was a boy, he would often take the entire family down to the Lower East Side, which was still a predominantly Jewish neighborhood. Our ostensible mission would be to buy some bagels and lox and challah. But we could have gone around the corner to do that. He would spend delighted hours lingering on those crowded, noisy streets, exploring the small stores, watching the transactions, usually in Yiddish, between the shoppers and the storeowners, who wore yarmulkes and stroked long gray beards as they talked. Back then, I thought my father liked the neighborhood because it was quaint, or because he had an insatiable curiosity for new faces, new ideas. It never crossed my mind that the place might evoke memories for him. But now I recall that, as we walked back to the car, we'd pass signs with Hebrew letters and my father, whose verbal memories of his religious childhood were so sparse and bitter, would remark with pleased amazement that he hadn't studied Hebrew for thirty years but he still could read the language. Back then, it never occurred to me to ask him why he had studied Hebrew. Now I wonder what sort of associations were tumbling around in his brain.

When I told my parents I planned to marry Rachel, I regarded the fact that she wasn't Jewish as a casual, interesting detail. I was astonished to see how unsettled my father became. Later he came to love her so much that her background didn't matter to him at all. But the memory of the quick stab of pain that crossed my father's face when I told him my good news is one I'll always carry.

It helps me understand another scene that has troubled me. Christmas was an important event in our house. My mother used to start shopping in mid-November, working from the master list

she composed each year of relatives, friends, and business associates who required presents. Geoff and I had an annual date to ca-
vort up and down Fifth Avenue just before the holiday, caroling to
startled passersby, buying our parents gifts like mynah birds or a
long-stemmed Sherlock Holmes pipe when we couldn't think of
any useful presents. Every Christmas Eve, my father would sit down
in the small, cozy study where we gathered, open up *A Christmas
Carol,* and try to sustain our interest in the story we all knew by
heart. We drifted away, one by one, to wrap up our presents and put
them under the tree. He would always laugh—our inattention was
a family tradition—but with the tone of martyrdom in his voice,
which suggested there was some emotional turbulence he was
fighting to conceal. Now I realize that Christmas wasn't his holiday
any more than pork was his food, though he loved the day as a
chance to shower gifts on his wife and children. How could Jake
Cohen's son have felt completely comfortable on Christmas Eve?
The expression on his face must have reflected the sense that, on
such occasions, there was a hidden but unbridgeable cultural gulf
between him and the Jewish-WASP family he adored.

I don't want to make Louis Cowan sound like the passive victim of
forces he could not control. On the contrary, when I was growing
up he wanted nothing so much as to blend in with the cosmopolitan elite. I think that when he was president of CBS-TV, he
felt he had found the assimilationist utopia he'd always been seeking right there in the boardroom.

He wanted me to go to Choate, especially when my teachers at
the progressive Dalton School—which boys had to leave in eighth
grade—told my parents that I'd never get into a good college unless
I was forced to acquire decent study habits. Once I was rejected at
Exeter, his persistence overrode my mother's feeling that, at a church
school, I'd encounter a sustained psychological version of the physical dangers she feared when she told me not to walk through
Yorkville. My father wanted me to become friends with upper-class

WASPs so that I could function in their world with the kind of ease he wished he possessed. The strategy backfired completely.

For the first two years I was at Choate, 1954 and 1955, I felt I was walking through a human minefield of anti-Semitism. Later, when I was more self-possessed and poised, the bigotry that so many people there displayed disgusted me so much that I decided I never wanted to become part of their crowd. That attitude reinforced the voice that was already in me, urging me to identify as a Jew.

I entered Choate when I was thirteen, bar mitzvah age. If I didn't know much about synagogue life, I knew even less about church life. I remember the first few times I attended the mandatory nightly chapel services. All the worshipers knew what hymns to sing. Was there a sort of spiritual telepathy that united them? I was a very scared young boy—awed by the easy suburban grace of my classmates, who seemed far more self-assured than the wealthiest assimilated Jews I had known in New York. I certainly didn't want to betray my ignorance by asking dumb questions. So it took me a very bewildered week to realize that the numbers tacked onto the church's pillars referred to the little red hymnal in front of me.

Sometimes for me that Choate chapel was a magic place. I loved the musty smell of the old wooden pews, especially on rainy days. The hymns became so important to me that I memorized dozens of them. Perhaps some, like "Onward, Christian Soldiers" and "Glorious Things of Thee Are Spoken" (which had the same melody as "Deutschland Über Alles") should have bothered me. They didn't. They awed me. So did the sight of my classmates receiving confirmation from the bishop of Connecticut, who looked majestic in his white robe and deep purple stole, with a miter in his right hand. Once in a while, usually as exams approached, I would go down to chapel for morning services, which weren't mandatory. I'd drink the grape juice and eat the wafer that symbolized communion. In a way it was superstitious. Choate's God was the only one I knew, and I figured that if I appeased Him I'd get good grades on my exams. But I knew I was also a very lonely boy, who needed to be-lieve in a Supreme Being to ease my relentless fear.

There were about twenty-five Jewish kids out of the five hun-dred students at Choate. Most of them had more religious training than I, and they experienced flashes of guilt, not moments of ex-hilaration, during the high points of the Episcopalian ritual. On Holy Days like Rosh Hashana and Yom Kippur—whose meaning I knew, but never connected to my own life—some of them would disappear from chapel—and often from school—to participate in ceremonies I couldn't quite imagine.

One of them, Joel Cassel, had spent his first thirteen years in a Jewish community in Waterbury, Connecticut. We were friends, but we never once discussed our backgrounds or our feelings while we were at Choate. Long after we had graduated he told me that his family had kept kosher back in Waterbury, that he had had a Conservative bar mitzvah, that he'd been president of his syna-gogue's youth group. His father, like mine, had sent him to Choate because the school seemed like the gateway to the American dream, but his father's ambition didn't ease Joel's sense of dis-placement. Outwardly, he was a tough, funny kid. I envied him his ability to win friends by making our classmates laugh. But inwardly he must have hurt terribly.

The chapel services were the focus of his pain. My favorite hymns, like "Onward, Christian Soldiers," offended him so much, he told me in later years, that every single night, while the rest of us were reciting the Lord's Prayer or the Episcopalian litany, he would ask God to forgive him for being in chapel at all. He'd promise God that "If I say Christ, I don't mean it—believe me."

Every night, as the service ended, the school's headmaster would bid us to pray "through Jesus Christ, our Lord." After Yom Kippur in our junior year, the Christian words seemed so offensive to Joel that he decided to push his mood of repentance into action and defy the blessing directly. He refused to bow his head in prayer. The small symbolic revolt excited all the Jews at Choate. We met once, decided that none of us would bow our heads, and called ourselves "the Wallingford Jew Boys." It was the kind of act that would have appealed to my mother—and did appeal to the moralistic, wrathful Polly Cowan in me. I remember holding my head high those nights, feeling an incredibly strong surge of tribal loyalty that I'd never before experienced.

Our action clearly threatened the Reverend Seymour St. John, the headmaster. One night he gave a sermon insisting that if he went to a mosque he'd take off his shoes; if he went to a synagogue he'd wear a skullcap. "When in Rome, do as the Romans do," he admonished us. (None of us had the knowledge or the wit to point out that his Anglican forebears hadn't exactly followed that advice.) In only slightly veiled terms, he threatened to expel anyone who insisted on keeping his head upright. Our revolt collapsed instantly. We were isolated and vulnerable once again. Since none of us had the courage to exchange stories of the anti-Semitism we had experienced, each of us felt we were being tormented because we were personally deficient.

Wade Pearson lived next door to me during my first year at Choate. Night after night he would come into my room and lecture me about how pushy and avaricious Jews are. Did I think the character Shylock came out of Shakespeare's imagination? Did I think Fagin was a pure invention of Dickens'? No, they were generic types. I—and my kind—were just like those forebears. During those sessions, Wade's friend Chip Thornton, a fat kid who was reputed to be a great wit, would add mirth to our literary talk by calling me "the traveling muzzy" because of my acne, or making jokes about "the mockies"—a term for Jews I had never heard before.

Lester Atkins, a loutish kid who sat behind me in junior year math class, used to clamp his feet so tightly against my jacket that if I leaned forward to answer a question I'd wind up with an unmendable rip. One day he snatched my geometry book. He gave it back to me at the end of class, though he didn't tell me he'd written me a message. That night I went to my teacher's apartment to ask for help with homework. The teacher pointed to a carefully-lettered sign that had been inscribed on the upper right hand corner of the page we had been working on that day. Had I written it myself? he asked. FUCK YOU, YOU KIKE, it said.

Then there was Ned the Gimp, as he called himself, who used to limp into the common room of the dorm where we all lived one summer, and greet me with the thick, mocking Yiddish accent he had lifted from Mr. Kitzel on the old Jack Benny show. The other kids thought the routine was a riot. I know that Joel Cassel, who had been toughened by the years he had spent as one of the few Jews in the public schools of Waterbury, Connecticut, would have found some way to neutralize the Gimp with banter. I couldn't do that. Usually I'd laugh nervously, hoping that my acquiescence would allow me to blend into the gang that seemed so menacing—until the next day when the Gimp's onslaught would resume. By then, I'd read *The Sun Also Rises*. I had the terrible feeling that I was the reincarnation of the long-suffering Robert Cohen. That was reinforced when a friend of mine asked me why I was so passive when the Gimp was around. Oddly, my friend's well-meaning question hurt me even more than the Gimp's insults. For it convinced me that all the kids at Choate saw me as Robert Cohen: helpless and weak-willed: a prototypical defenseless Jew.

I never told my parents about the anti-Semitism I experienced at Choate. I never told anyone. I felt guilty about it, as if I were personally responsible for my plight. Each autumn they had a Fathers' Weekend at the school. Lou, still rising in the media world, was his usual *shmeicheling* self, charming the teachers with his personality, trying to cement our relationship to the school by donating a complete set of Modern Library books. I felt very much in the shadow of this energetic, self-made, successful man. I didn't want to take the risk of describing my problems, for that might make him feel that his oldest son was a failure. Besides, what could he—or Polly—do about the anti-Semitism? Complain to the headmaster? I didn't want them—or anyone—to wage my fights for me. I was very impressionable back then. In sermon after sermon, the Reverend St. John told us that Choate was a place where you took responsibility for yourself. You went "the extra mile" if you had a problem. I accepted that view. It seemed unmanly to complain.

For nearly three years, I'd lie awake every night, fantasizing about ways to escape from the school. Then I realized I didn't want to leave in what I considered disgrace. So I'd fantasize ways to impress the bigots, ways to leave with dignity.

I actually did impress them. By senior year, I was a big shot on the newspaper, the literary magazine, the debate society. I'd found a special motley substratum of bright, wacky friends—my working-class Italian roommate, who was there on a science scholarship; the son of Spanish immigrants who lived in Wallingford, where Choate was located; a very poetic jazz musician; a brilliant, worldly exchange student from Switzerland. We created a fantasy world for ourselves which mocked the real world in which our classmates lived. For example, after vacations, dozens of kids would boast about visiting two New York whores, Gussie and Sally. My roommate and I named our goldfish Gussie and Sally. In New York we'd crash the society dances, and puzzle the serious preppy girls with questions about where we could stable the polo ponies we had just brought up from Panama. At Choate, one dance weekend, we organized a folk sing where my date—about whom I'd written a very romantic story in the school literary magazine—was the star. Our classmates flocked to that, not to the formal events which the school had organized. By senior year we were bright enough and lively enough to seem quite glamorous. We had succeeded on our own terms.

But those successes created a new set of problems. Now kids who wanted to befriend me often made a conscious effort to disassociate me from other Jews. Hans Peterson, a bookish lacrosse player, came from Long island. The Jews were taking over his home town, he would inform me, and I should know their true nature. They were loud and money-minded, bad-mannered and aggressively sarcastic. Of course, I was different: I was soft-spoken, well-read, with a taste for parody and fantasy. At least, that was his explicit message. His implicit message was that I bore direct responsibility for his new neighbors.

In my senior year, Sidney Konig, a younger Jewish kid on my corridor, was the new target of abuse. I didn't really like him. He was so whiny, so defensive, so obviously Jewish-looking, that I secretly believed he deserved the treatment he was receiving. Still, I became his ally. As seniors, my Italian roommate and I wielded power over the other kids. We'd punish anyone who mistreated Sidney.

Why, I wonder now, could I debate Hans or defend Sidney with a degree of aggressiveness I could never display when the Gimp was teasing me? My answer makes me a little uncomfortable.

It stems from my mother's insistence that in the presence of anti-Semitism I should always announce I was a Jew. What a curiously mixed message that was! For years, I thought it simply contained the willed bravery of her *noblesse oblige*. But now I realize that there was an unmistakable, slightly disdainful pride in her sense that, with my Welsh name, my brown hair, my thin nose, I could "pass" for whatever I wanted. I could be free in America, not wed to any ghetto.

So, in her opinion, as a totally assimilated Jew—or, rather, as a Jew who could escape whenever I wanted—I was supposed to remember the Holocaust and defend my less fortunate kinsmen, the Sidneys, the Jews who were moving into Hans's town on Long Island, in just the same way as I was supposed to defend the blacks.

In grade school, it never occurred to Polly—or to me—that I might be the Jew who needed defending. I wasn't prepared for personal abuse. When it came I was paralyzed with confusion and surprise. And I was paralyzed with the feeling that it was both self-demeaning and gauche to fight back.

My four years at Choate shattered the illusion Polly had helped implant. And they reinforced her equally strong, completely contradictory assertion that a Jew in any profession, under any name, was subject to attack.

After the four years at Choate, I could never pretend that I was and wasn't Jewish: that I could be part of a family which fought oppression in the name of the six million, and yet remain personally unscarred by anti-Semitism. I couldn't hide, except by surrendering my Jewish identity completely. Neither Wade nor Lester the Lout nor Ned the Gimp cared at all whether my name was Paul or Saul, Cowan or Cohen; whether I went to chapel or synagogue on Yom Kippur; whether I bowed my head and said an Episcopalian litany or held it high and recited the Shema. Either way, I was a Shylock, a Mr. Kitzel, a kike.

Once I'd been through that experience, my mother's message about the six million became, perhaps, the single most important fact of my life. For, though I didn't begin to understand the consequences of my feelings for decades, I knew from then on that it was unthinkable that anyone would ever separate me from my tribe.

It was at Choate that my fascination with my grandfather Jacob Cohen began. At Dalton where I lived in an assimilated world of liberal, tolerant peers, he seemed like an oddity, a cruel man who had caused my father great pain, but who bore little connection to me. But at Choate, where I was an outsider, my identity as Paul Cowan, the son of a TV producer and a mail-order heiress, sometimes seemed like a disguise.

As a result, I began to dwell on the fact that I was the grandson of someone named Cohen: an Orthodox Jew, an impoverished used-cement-bag dealer from Chicago. Of course, I had no idea of what an Orthodox Jew was or what a used-cement-bag dealer did. But I wanted very much to know. So gradually, imperceptibly, while my teachers at Choate praised me for adapting so well to the school's environment, I began to feel impelled to search for a link between Jake Cohen's world and mine.

My father was the only link, but he was rarely willing to talk about the past. So I remember very clearly the night he sat up with Geoff and me in the small, book-lined study of our apartment, eating ice cream while he reminisced. He began by describing his early days as a public relations man in Chicago, where he'd handled accounts like the Aragon and Trianon ballrooms, where he'd publicized bandleaders like Kay Kyser, Wayne King, and Ted Weems. I loved those stories, loved the gritty feel of the streets in Chicago's uptown section where he'd worked, loved the fact that my father, now so at home in the CBS boardroom, had once earned about half his money as the owner of Riverside Roller Rink in Chicago. In the shank of that intimate night, I asked him to tell us more about the Cohen family.

Where, in Eastern Europe, did the Cohen family come from? He said he didn't know. Then he added, "They weren't really Cohens anyway. I guess you boys don't know this, but Cohens are supposed to be part of the Jewish priestly caste. They had some other name in Europe, but they thought that America was one gigantic Jewish community, so they changed their names when they came here so that people would think they were important."

When Geoff was in college, he used the anecdote in one of his most important examinations to sum up the complete uprooting most immigrants underwent in America. When I heard Malcolm X say he'd dropped his original name because it was a slave name, I felt the angry black man was speaking for me. For America—or, at least, Americanization—had robbed my family of its name, its identity.

Geoff and I never discussed my father's story until we were in our thirties. Then we discovered that the rift between our ancestors in Europe and the Cohens in Chicago, between Jake Cohen and Lou Cowan, had been echoing in our psyches throughout our adult lives.

I tried to search for my grandfather's identity when I was in graduate school at the University of Chicago—in the Hyde Park area of the city, where the Cohens had lived. I often found myself chatting with elderly Jewish shopkeepers, asking them whether they had known Cohen, the used-cement-bag dealer. I think I imagined a wizened old man who carried used cement bags under one arm, a battered copy of *Ring Magazine* under another, and spoke with a faint Yiddish accent. I never met anyone who knew him.

By the time I was in my thirties, the Judaism that was the subtext of my childhood had emerged to form an increasingly close bond between my father and me. By then, I was a professional journalist, a staff writer for *The Village Voice*. In 1972, I set out to write a short nostalgia piece about the Jewish socialism that had once flourished on New York's Lower East Side, and discovered that there were tens of thousands of old, mostly Orthodox, Jews in the neighborhood, who lived at the poverty level of three thousand dollars a year. I wrote about them in a long article called "Jews Without Money, Revisited." More important, I felt an unexpected attraction to their world. In a way, of course, the project was a continuation of my search for Jake Cohen. I remember imagining him in the basement shuls where I spent some of my time.

A few years later I spent an afternoon in the Munkaczer tallis (prayer shawl) factory, a few blocks away from the stores and old synagogues that used to enthrall my father on those Sundays when we searched for bagels and lox on the Lower East Side. David Weiderman, seventy-two, born in Hungary, was weaving the garment on a clattering fifty-two-year-old mechanical loom. His father, who had taught him the trade, died in Hitler's Europe. Now Weiderman, isolated from his past in that small, noisy store, tried to uphold the tradition of careful religious craftsmanship he had learned as a boy. His prayer shawls were made out of pure Turkish wool. He was scornful of the cheap, mixed tallisim, imported from Israel, made of wool diluted with rayon. "Let the others do it the way they want," he said. "It's not my business. I'll do it the way it has always been done."

How proud he was of that ancient trade! For a moment I saw him as the guardian of an irrecoverable past.

That night I described David Weiderman to my father. I thought he would be mildly interested. To my astonishment, he was fascinated. The next morning he called me. He'd been thinking about the tallis maker all night. Why didn't I try to recover the past I had glimpsed in his store by writing about Orthodox Jewish craftsmen?

I couldn't, I said. The gray-bearded old sages I had seen on the Lower East Side seemed unapproachable. They reminded me of my assimilation, of my ignorance of the basic Hebrew blessings, of most holidays that marked the cycle of my ancestors' years. Besides, some were bound to know that I had married a gentile. I'd mentioned that fact in "Jews Without Money, Revisited." I didn't want to argue with them about my personal life. I feared they would treat me as an irretrievable outcast, or insist that I embrace their ways. No, I told my father. Their world was off limits to me.

But he was relentless. Every week or two he would remind me of the valuable spiritual adventure I was passing up. He would repeat his idea for a book with a greater degree of eagerness than I'd ever heard in his voice. I would recite my list of disabilities and change the subject.

If he was relentless about my Jewish present, I was relentless about his past. One night in 1975, when he was in his mid-sixties and I was in my mid-thirties, I spent an hour in the living room of the apartment of the Westbury Hotel, where he and my mother moved after all four of us children had left home, begging him to tell me the names of his Cohen kin. Grudgingly, he consented. To my surprise, he not only knew their names; he knew their occupations and the dates they had died.

He said I had one living great-uncle, Abraham Cohen, a former Republican alderman who had represented the district adjacent to the University of Chicago. The news excited me. I told him I wanted to meet this Abraham Cohen the next time I was in Chicago. I was sure I could protect my father by disguising my name and pretending I was a graduate student writing a Ph.D. thesis on Jews in American politics.

"No," he said, "don't do that. The Cohens will only hurt us. They'll ask us for money." His fear didn't make any sense to me. Our names were in the phone book. Besides, the Cowans weren't exactly a private family. If my mother and father weren't making news, my brother or I were writing it. Anyway, Jake Cohen had been dead for more than twenty years. How could one of his brothers hurt us?

Still, I obeyed my father's request. He'd had cancer and three heart attacks. I didn't want to risk stirring up memories that might kill him. But we did agree—tacitly at first, then quite openly—that when he died I'd do everything possible to uncover his missing past—and mine.

By 1976, Rachel and I were fasting on Yom Kippur. When I told my father that, he answered that were he in better health, he would join us. He had fasted every year until he was thirty, he said. I was thirty-six at the time. In all our conversations about Judaism, he had never told me that simple fact.

That Yom Kippur we talked of other Jewish traditions. A few weeks earlier I had heard of a Jewish law which says that all holy books must be buried, for to throw them out is to profane the name of the Lord. My father believed that all books were sacred. That day he told me a friend of his had searched through the Talmud and found the wording of that injunction. He planned to have it printed in specially designed letters. Then he wanted to frame it and hang it up in his office, next to his treasured copy of the First Amendment.

He never got to do that. Early in the morning of November 18, 1976, my parents' apartment at the Westbury Hotel caught on fire. They both died in their sleep.

The fire was headline news. So when I wasn't visiting the precincts of death—the police station, the funeral home, my parents' blackened apartment—I was answering condolence calls. Most were from friends. But one was very strange.

It came from a man named Bert Lazarus, who lived in Chicago but happened to be in New York on business. He said he was a cousin of my father's, on the Cohen side. In a soft, hesitant voice, he said that he had to catch a plane during the funeral. Could he come to the reception before it and pay his respects?

Lazarus was wearing a long black coat when he entered the reception room at Campbell's Funeral Home. He had chalk-gray hair and deep-set blue eyes.

Geoff and I were standing next to each other when he came in and introduced himself. After a brief, embarrassed pause, Geoff asked the question that haunted us both. What was our true family name?

Lazarus paused, surprised by the question, unsettled by Geoff's intensity.

"Why, it's Cohen, of course," he said in his soft voice. "Your great-great-grandfather Jacob Cohen was a rabbi in Lithuania."

"Where in Lithuania?" I asked.

"A town called Lidvinova. He must have been a very fine man. The oldest Orthodox synagogue in Chicago is named after him."

He hurried away a few minutes later. What a strange gift Lazarus had inadvertently brought. He had given us our identity at the moment of our parents' death.

In the weeks after the fire, I became determined to honor what had turned out to be my father's last wish—to write about Orthodox craftsmen. I was lucky to find a guide to their world—Rabbi Joseph Singer, sixty-four, born in Poland to a family of rabbis, the tenth-generation descendant of Gershon Kitover, brother-in-law of the Baal Shem Tov, the founder of the Hasidic movement.

Did Lou guess that I'd find such richness in Rabbi Singer's world? Did he realize that, as I immersed myself in it, I would come to identify with the Jewish community—warm, quarrelsome, and difficult as it is, and claim its traditions as my inheritance?

As soon as I began to meet people who made that religion seem attractive, I was faced with a clear choice—a choice, indeed, about history, though I never knew how to articulate it until my sister Holly furnished the words. Should I explore Judaism, the real, living link with my ancestors and the six million? Or should I reject it, and be another conscious participant in the obliteration of five thousand years of history?

Put that way, of course, it wasn't really a choice. Maybe my parents' Judaism lacked content, maybe it was laced with ambivalence. But there was such a deep wellspring of pride at the core that everything else seemed relatively unimportant. I loved Polly's secular messianism. I missed the part of Lou that had perished in America. I have come to realize that my challenge is how to recover Saul Cohen, how to enter the religious world that would once have been his by inheritance, without relinquishing Paul Cowan and the America he loves.

2

Once in my search for my patrimony, I asked my father to forget the wounds the Cohen family had inflicted on him, and tell me about some memories he treasured.

He was willing to do that. He said he had admired his immigrant grandfather Moses Cohen, a scrap-iron salesman who spoke seven languages and spent his spare time in his family's Hyde Park apartment, reading secular writers like Goethe and Tolstoy or studying the Talmud. Ordinarily, Moses isolated himself in a special book-lined corner of his living room, ignoring the noise that came from his seven sons and three daughters. Lou used to feel flattered that the reserved, rather dandy old man—who usually wore a suit, a bowler hat, and sported a pince-nez—answered his questions about books more readily than his sons' questions about their careers. According to Bert Lazarus, Moses was the most promising son of Rabbi Jacob Cohen, the Lidvinova *rav*. From the time he arrived in Chicago, in 1881, pious Jews, especially those who spoke only Yiddish, sought him out in the shul, or on the street, or in his home, asking him to resolve a religious debate, or to explain some puzzling aspect of Chicago's English-speaking world. Two of his sons, Jacob, the eldest, and Leopold, the fourth boy, were quite religious. But they didn't share Moses Cohen's taste for books. So he doted on my father, his oldest grandson, who plainly had the intelligence and self-discipline to carry on the family's proud tradition of piety and scholarship.

My father also recalled a pleasant time he'd had with Jake Cohen. Once, he said, when his mother was on a trip, he spent a marvelous weekend with his father. Whatever his flaws, Jake always possessed an immigrant's wonder at the things most second- and third-generation Americans take for granted—he loved professional sports, loved restaurants that offered a wide variety of foods, loved cars, railroad trains, and movies. During those few days, he let his son see Chicago through his eyes. Jacob and Louis ate out, three meals a day, at restaurants where Jake was on back-slapping terms with dozens of patrons. The two Cohens spent much of their time at vaudeville shows. That weekend Lou felt more affection for his dad than he ever had or ever would.

Those two memories contain themes that echo through my father's years. For, though he was deeply loyal to his mother's ambitious German-Jewish family, the Smitzes, he couldn't bring himself to heed their deepest wish: that he graduate from the University of Chicago Law School and enter into partnership with his increasingly successful uncle Holly. He tried a pre-law course when he was an undergraduate at the University, discovered that it bored him thoroughly, and decided to become a public relations man. His most prominent clients, the ballrooms, the bandleaders, came straight from the vaudeville houses he and his father had visited on the one pleasant weekend they shared.

When Polly was pregnant with me, Lou, still a public relations man, yearned for a bright child who would be normal, not obnoxious, who would add luster to the family name with his scholarship. Well, so do many parents. But my father used his mood as a metaphor for a new form of mass entertainment: that was his show business genius.

His prayer for his child became the premise of "The Quiz Kids," which combined Moses Cohen's love of learning and Jake Cohen's fascination with American razzmatazz—professional sports and vaudeville. The show sustained a veiled, secularized version of the scholarly tradition Moses Cohen cared so much about. It made Louis G. Cowan—as my father called himself by then—a famous man.

It made bright children like Joel Kupperman, Richard Williams, Harve Bennett Fischman, and Ruthie Duskin into culture heroes for an entire generation. During the 1940s and 1950s, millions of Americans between five and sixteen longed to be Quiz Kids. In their fantasies, they were participants in my father's radio show. By creating it, he helped whet the intellectual appetite of an entire generation.

Why, I often wonder, can't I feel a simple pride in my father's show business triumphs? Why am I compelled to place his worldly success in the context of his ethnic background? For that matter, why have I always been so much more interested in learning about the one Eastern European grandparent I didn't know than in hearing stories about the German Jews, the Spiegels, the Smitzes, and the Strauses, the fascinating, successful grandparents, uncles, aunts, and cousins who were almost like an extended family? Geoff and Holly and Liza were mildly curious about Jake, but none of them shared my intense desire to discover more about the Cohen family. Did my idiosyncratic preoccupation have something to do with my role in the family? After all, Lou, an only child, was the eldest son of an eldest son. I was *his* eldest son. That fact contained immense power. It set off a depth charge in my consciousness. If he could sever his relations with his father, I wondered, was there something in the recesses of his mind—or mine—that would permit the same thing to recur in my generation?

I felt I had to understand the rift between my father and my grandfather. Ironically, I could only begin to understand one of the most important facts of my father's life after he died. For it was Bert Lazarus' coincidental appearance at the funeral home that led me to the Cohen relatives I had always wanted to meet. As I talked with them, I became aware of a mystery I felt compelled to solve.

It was defined for me by my cousin Saul Cohen, fifty-five, the president of the Leeco Steel Company, successor to the scrap-iron yard Moses Cohen had founded nearly a century ago. On a lovely summer afternoon in 1978, Saul told me a story that made me weep.

In the 1940s, Louis Cowan had moved his family to New York, where he was working for the Office of War Information. Though he rarely saw Jake, he was sending him a stipend of seventy-five dollars a week. Nevertheless, Jake used to go to his son's Chicago office to demand more money. That angered Lou. The occasional personal confrontations between the two men filled my father with rage.

On more than one occasion, Jake asked his prosperous younger brother Leopold—Saul's father, who was then the owner of the steel

yard—to loan him enough money to travel to New York. I remember
my father's once telling my mother that Jake had come to ask for
money again.

But Saul, twelve years older than I, perceived his uncle's journeys
differently. "Jake went to New York to see his grandchildren," he said.
"He used to stand outside your apartment waiting to get a glimpse of
you. He followed you on the streets. He saw you many, many times."

Other members of the Cohen family had already told me about
Jake's unabated pride in his son. He used to clip every newspaper
article about Lou. Often, he'd make a point of listening to "The Quiz
Kids" or "Stop the Music" with friends or relatives so that he could
boast about his boy. On occasion, he'd interrupt dinner-table conversations with speculations about his grandchildren. Sometimes
his voice sounded deeply pained. Everything I'd heard about Jake
Cohen's later years convinced me that Saul's story was accurate but
I couldn't accept the view of my father it implied. The Lou Cowan
I knew was an almost compulsively generous man with an unfailing
interest in other people. Lou had always told us about his daily visits to his dying uncle Holly. As a child, I'd sat, reading, in our New
York apartment while he telephoned his mother in Chicago almost
every day and engaged her in long, loving conversations. His example made it natural for me to visit him or call him every few days
during his seven-year battle with cancer and heart disease. Cruel as
Jake might have been, I couldn't understand why my father had denied him the chance to meet his grandchildren.

There was another dimension to my confusion. Was there a connection between Lou's attitude toward Jake and his lifelong refusal
to discuss the details of his religious upbringing? A childhood friend
of his, Joe Berkenfield, now a real estate developer in Shaker Heights,
Ohio, described an event which convinced me that there was.

Joe Berkenfield said that he could never forget the Thursday in
mid-December, 1922, when Louis Cohen told him that his bar mitzvah—an Orthodox bar mitzvah—was scheduled for the next Saturday, the Shabbos in the midst of Hanukkah. Berkenfield was
astonished. Their neighborhood, on Michigan Avenue in Chicago,
was a thoroughly Americanized place. It was an environment

where men and boys were still furious at the 1919 Black Sox scandal—during which legendary White Sox baseball players like Shoe-
less Joe Jackson had conspired to throw the World Series to the
Cincinnati Reds—and utterly indifferent to the Talmudic discussions that Moses Cohen and his friends conducted with such vigor.

Until that day, Berkenfield had never even heard of a bar mitzvah.
He and his friends were all confirmed at Chicago's ultra-
Reform Sinai Temple, where rabbis preached in English to a silent
congregation, where Sabbath services were held on Sunday to let
business people keep their stores open on Saturday. Besides, he and
Lou Cohen were inseparable. How could his closest friend have
gone to Hebrew school without his knowing it?

On a chilly Saturday morning, December 16, the twenty-eighth
of Kislev, the two boys walked a mile from Lou's house to the synagogue on Forty-seventh Street and St. Lawrence Avenue. When
they arrived, rather early, they found only a handful of men present,
uttering sounds Berkenfield found unintelligible.

"What are they doing?" he asked Lou Cohen. Lou smiled, and—
with a familiarity that encompassed Berkenfield's background and
the background of the men in the shul—he said, "That's called *davening* (praying). These are early-morning services. Just make some
noises in a singsong voice and they'll think you're davening, too.
They won't pay attention to us, anyway."

The two teenagers waited for about half an hour while the men
finished their prayers. Then the main service began. In the midst of
it, Lou walked up to the *bimah* (the platform in front of the ark
where the Torah is kept) and, in unstumbling Hebrew, read from the
Torah and from the book of Zechariah, the prophetic portion for
the day. *Sing and rejoice, O daughter of Zion; for, lo, I come and
will dwell in the midst of thee, saith the Lord.* Afterward, Lou and
his parents, his uncle Holly and his grandmother Tillie, joined the
whole huge Cohen clan and went downstairs for a *kiddush* (a post-
service blessing over the wine, which is usually followed by a cele-
bratory meal). That night, Moses Cohen gave his grandson, Louis
George—or Leibel Gershon, as he had been called at the Torah—a
lavish party to celebrate the fact that today he had become a man.

According to Bert Lazarus, Moses was so proud of his oldest grandson, the bar mitzvah boy, that he hired a small fleet of chauffeur-driven cars and dispatched them to Jewish neighborhoods throughout Chicago to bring every Cohen relative to the event.

None of Lou's friends on Michigan Avenue—including Joe Berkenfield—remembers knowing about the party. Except for Joe Berkenfield, none of them remembers knowing about the bar mitzvah.

My father never mentioned it to his children either, even after my sister Holly and I became interested in religion, even after we both decided, in our separate ways, that we wanted our children to have Jewish educations. We never connected random details like my father's knowledge of the Hebrew alphabet to anything concrete that had happened in the past. Now, I assume that he had studied Hebrew formally, rigorously, in order to read from the Torah fluently. But even in 1976, when my father was urging me to write about Orthodox Jews, when he told me he had fasted on Yom Kippur, it never occurred to me to ask him if he'd had a bar mitzvah.

But he was keeping something even more interesting from me. During all the years he claimed to be ignorant of his roots, he had to know that he was the great-grandson of Rabbi Jacob Cohen. Bert Lazarus, who was at Lou's bar mitzvah, remembers that Moses Cohen, the family patriarch, was honored with the first *aliyah:* he was the first person to bless the Torah. Traditionally, only *Kohanim* (descendants of the priestly caste) receive the first *aliyah*. When Moses was called to the Torah, he was introduced by his full Hebrew name, Moshe ben Yaakov ha-Kohen, Moses, son of Jacob, the priest.

Lou Cohen, who could joke about the *daveners,* who knew enough Hebrew to read from the Torah, must have understood those words and recognized their significance. I think that if he had lived longer, he would have described his bar mitzvah and the family history behind it to me. The week he died, he mentioned his bar mitzvah to his friend Selma Hirsch, Associate Director of the American Jewish Committee. That seems to have been the first time he discussed the ceremony with any of the friends he made as an adult in New York. Plainly, he was regaining pride in his religious past.

But why had he felt obliged to conceal so much for so long? As I thought about that question, I became convinced that his silence was the result of his tortured relationship with Jake, not his feeling about Judaism. What was the source of those feelings? What had happened in the Cohen household? How had Jake, whom Saul loved, managed to wound Lou so deeply?

To solve that mystery, I knew I had to delve into the past. The rift between Lou and Jake had to have roots in Lidvinova, their ancestral home. I wanted to go there, to see it, even though the Jews who once lived there, who might have provided clues to my father's family's troubled history, had either emigrated or perished in the Holocaust. But the Lithuanian government had put the segment of the country that includes Lidvinova off-limits to tourists.

Instead, I spent a month reading about that area of Lithuania in the Jewish room of the New York Public Library, and interviewing people who had been raised there. Its history was fascinating. In the mid-nineteenth century, Lidvinova was a tiny town, three hours by wagon from Kalvarija, Marijampol, and Suwalki, larger cities. But it was close to the German border; it was not the kind of culturally isolated place that appears in the works of Isaac Bashevis Singer and Sholom Aleichem. In the 1850s and 1860s, Jews from that region frequently traveled across the border as peddlers or merchants, smugglers or capitalists. Many knew the language of commerce—Russian or Lithuanian or German—as well as their native Yiddish.

Inevitably, they met people and read books with relatively modern ideas. Rabbi Jacob Cohen had an especially wide range of contacts throughout the border area, for he was a *maggid* (an itinerant preacher), who traveled from town to town delivering sermons or explications of the Torah after the evening prayer.

Although a few Lithuanian Jews achieved financial success where they lived, most knew that their social and economic mobility was still limited. For instance, many state-run secondary schools required that there be eight or ten Christian children for every Jewish one. As a result, many Jewish parents, including poor ones, put three or four Christians through school in order for their own

youngsters to get an education. There were no universities in that
area of Lithuania, and only a handful of very wealthy Jews were able
to obtain permission for their offspring to study in cities like
Moscow or Petrograd, where Jews were forbidden to settle. It was
hard for most Jews to get an education or find employment that was
commensurate with their intelligence or their sophistication. They
were part of a very early revolution of rising expectations.

In the 1860s, about twenty years before the great Jewish migra-
tion from Eastern Europe, many of the most talented, ambitious
people from Lidvinova, Kalvarija, and Suwalki decided to escape
the confines of their cities and towns by coming to the United
States. Many of them spoke German. Many were acquainted with
the smugglers in their region, who taught them how to sneak
across borders if they had to. They had no trouble making themselves understood in the port cities of East Prussia. The process of
leaving home, voyaging through unfamiliar territory, and boarding
a ship didn't seem particularly threatening to them.

Most of the Lithuanians remained in New York. But by the mid-
1860s, a handful of Lidvinovans became the first substantial group
of Eastern Europeans to settle in Chicago. They arrived with a Sefer
Torah, a handwritten Torah scroll, which Rabbi Jacob Cohen had
given to a man named David Zemansky just before he left for America. Zemansky treated the scroll with enormous care. On the ship
to New York, and later on the train to Chicago, he wouldn't let the
Torah out of his hands for fear that it would touch something that
would profane it. At first, the Lidvinovans put the precious scroll in
Zemansky's house and conducted services there. Then, when there
were too many of them to fit into a home, they purchased a building, placed Rabbi Jacob Cohen's Torah in the ark behind the
bimah, and established Chicago's first Orthodox synagogue, Beth
Hamedresh Hagodol. They worshiped just as they had worshiped
in Rabbi Jacob Cohen's shul in Lidvinova.

In 1867, Moses Cohen's brother-in-law Abraham Lieberman
came to Chicago. According to Bert Lazarus, he and several of his
friends from Lidvinova got their start in the aftermath of the great
Chicago fire of 1871. Among the tons of scrap iron they salvaged

from the fire, they found some safes. They kept the valuables the safes contained, and sold the metal as scrap.

In 1881, Abraham Lieberman sent enough money back to Lidvinova to bring his sister Anna, her husband Moses Cohen, and five other members of their extended family to Chicago. He immediately gave the eighteen-year-old Moses the job of business agent in his scrap-iron yard.

Despite his youth, Moses was able to navigate the unfamiliar American world with extraordinary skill. As a Cohen, he had status; he acquired business connections through the Liebermans. In addition, he was an extremely hard worker. He would rise at daybreak to recite the morning prayers, then walk to the Liebermans' scrap-iron yard, five miles from his house, so that he could save money on carfare. When he got home, at seven or eight, he always made a point of studying English. Once he learned the language, he became an even more effective salesman. As a rabbi's son, he had developed a confident, commanding manner. He loved to talk about the books he had read. He fascinated his customers—Jews and non-Jews alike—with his discussions of Torah and of literature.

He was determined to build up his own business. At night, after his English lesson, he'd often leave home to collect scrap iron. He stored the metal in his back yard, and sold it to peddlers at wholesale prices. Most of the peddlers were Jews from the more remote areas of Eastern Europe who had arrived in the 1880s and 1890s. To such people, he was already a merchant: an American success.

The newer Eastern European immigrants often asked Moses for religious advice. Many of them had great trouble in reconciling the strict Orthodox Judaism they had known as children with the freewheeling, hurly-burly atmosphere of Chicago, where Jews as well as Christians seemed to care more about money than piety. These were men and women who not only refrained from working on the Sabbath and were punctilious about dietary regulations, but also saw each microscopic detail of life in Jewish terms. For example, many of them didn't date the letters they wrote back home by the Common Era month or even the Jewish month, but by the day following the portion of the Torah that had been read in synagogue that Saturday. Many couldn't remember that in America the custom was to celebrate birthdays according to the Roman calendar, not the Jewish one. Many of their children never really knew when their own birthdays were. In their Jewish and secular lives, they were cut loose from the moorings that had anchored their people for centuries by an American culture that was fraught with religious problems and economic possibilities.

Sometimes, in their writings, they sounded desperate. Some congregants of Beth Hamedresh Hagodol wrote a plaintive article in a Yiddish-language newspaper describing "shameful deeds" like "the many disruptions and troubles that were caused between families and within small congregations by men who call themselves rabbis, who for the sake of a few dollars will divorce a husband who is in America from a wife in Poland, which brings misfortune and ruination to helpless, innocent children. And these self-styled rabbis for the sake of a few dollars . . . authorize men to be *shoctim* [ritual slaughterers] who know nothing of *shechita* [the laws of killing animals according to kosher standards]." Within a very few years, many of these Jews came to rely on Moses Cohen, the rabbi's son, the prospering businessman.

Ever since he had arrived in Chicago, Moses had dreamed of going into business with his oldest male child. In 1899, he took a step toward achieving that dream. He bought his own scrap-iron yard on Prairie Avenue. He called it The Union Iron Company until 1902, when he made Jake his partner, and changed the name of the business to Moses Cohen and Son.

Jake quickly disappointed him. He—not his father—was unable to adjust to America. Moses, the *maggid*'s son, the multilingual immigrant from a border area, was experienced in adapting to whatever culture he entered. Jake, born in 1882, a year after his parents arrived in America, was reared in Chicago's Jewish ghetto by a very young, Yiddish-speaking mother. He was overwhelmed by his father's self-confident manner. The America that lay outside the boundaries of his very narrow world beckoned him. He would skip work for days at a time, his brother Abraham, the Republican alderman, told me. "He'd go anywhere there was a championship fight. Or he would hop on a train and go to Warm Springs for the baths. He never told my father where he was going. When he got back my father would be furious. The two of them would scream at each other for hours at a time. Then they would quit talking to each other for days. Jake didn't mean to do it. In his way, he was a wonderful man. But he took all the money he and my father earned and spent it on himself. He didn't leave anything for the business. Soon he and my father went bankrupt." That was in 1910, the year after Louis Cohen was born.

For Jake, the ghetto was confining, but Judaism was not. He practiced it faithfully. He could read the Eighteen Benedictions, which a pious Jew recites three times a day, in such rapid Hebrew that his fellow *daveners* named him the "freight train." Though he loved to eat out, he never mixed meat with milk. He was careful to heed the special rules that apply to the *Kohanim*. For instance, he never went into a synagogue for a funeral or into a cemetery for a burial, since the Torah says those acts make a priest unclean.

Had he lived in Lidvinova, his ancestry, his involvement with religion and his position in the family would have been enough to guarantee him a good match and a great deal of respect. If he lacked a head for business, his wife, his siblings, and his children would have provided him with enough money to spend his days in the village's study house, learning Torah. But in Chicago few people cared about those Old World traditions. Jake Cohen was a displaced religious aristocrat.

When Moses Cohen and Son went bankrupt, Jake lost the respect of his scholarly, hard-working father. His brother George, two years younger than he, and an apparent prodigy, graduated from the University of Chicago Law School in 1908. Mandel, the next oldest, became a doctor. By 1913, Leopold, the fourth brother, who loved shul with the same intensity that Jake did, had gone into the scrap-iron business and regained the old accounts. What was once Moses Cohen and Son now became the Leopold Cohen Steel Company. Moses, who wanted as much time as possible to study Torah and Talmud, was made its superintendent. As far as he was concerned, Leopold had satisfied the same family and business obligations Jake had squandered. And he had satisfied them while maintaining his commitment to Orthodox Judaism. So, in the end, Jake was not only a displaced aristocrat. More tragically, he was a displaced eldest son.

Jake was a ravishingly handsome man, not the wizened, Yiddish-speaking salesman I had imagined when I was a graduate student at the University of Chicago. In his twenties, when he was courting my rather plump grandmother Hetty, he was tall and slender, with sultry, slightly moody blue eyes, and jet-black hair. He filled out as he grew older. In a photo that was taken in 1925, when he was forty-three, he seemed to have the poise and the energy to be the head of a giant corporation.

He and Hetty had been married for two years when Moses Cohen and Son went bankrupt. The financial disaster highlighted a tension which had always been inherent in their relationship. For Hetty's mother, Tillie Smitz, was a secularized German Jew who had always felt a reflexive distrust for the religious, Yiddish-speaking, Eastern European Jake Cohen. His failure deepened that distrust. Of course, it disturbed Hetty, too. Perhaps she had been mistaken to marry him. Perhaps her mother's judgment was right.

Then Jake made a temporary recovery. He founded a moderately successful business of his own, the Jerome Trading Company, which operated out of a warehouse near the Loop. In those days, used cement bags, the product he sold, were in constant demand. Every year, they were filled with sand or gravel and used to build dikes along river banks to prevent floods.

People who lived near Jake, Hetty, and Lou Cohen on Michigan Avenue in the 1920s remember them as a prosperous, happy family. They had a spacious apartment in a sturdy yellow brick building across the street from a park. Lou's childhood friends still have pleasurable memories of the meals of gefilte fish, noodle kugel, matzo-ball soup, roasts, and chicken that my grandmother Hetty used to prepare for her husband and son. According to Joe Berkenfield, Jake, who loved cars, used to buy a new Studebaker every year during the 1920s. He used to take his wife, his son, and their friends on special outings, where they would buy candy and ice cream, or shop for the antiques Hetty collected or the knick-knacks Jake loved.

Still, the tension between Jake and Hetty persisted. Indeed, the conflict between the Cohens and the Smitzes may have been impossible to avert. For Tillie Smitz's attitude toward Jews like her son-in-law was typical of her culture and her social class. At the turn of the century, Eastern European Jews and German Jews harbored deeper suspicions toward each other than either group did against gentiles. The conflict manifested itself as soon as the first Lithuanian Jews arrived in Chicago. Many of the Jews who had already settled there, immigrants from the Rhineland near France, had been influenced by modern trends in European culture while they were still in Germany. In the United States, they were proud of their ability to live in the same way as their fellow Americans did. They were embarrassed to be identified with the Zemanskys, the Liebermans, the Cohens, who spoke to each other in Yiddish (which Germans dismissed as "the Jargon"), who were strict in their observance of the Sabbath, who usually covered their heads on the streets. It was the German Jews, not the gentiles, who coined the word "kike." (The term seems to be from the Yiddish word *kikela,* the circle illiterate Jews made when they signed immigration papers in America.) They wanted the Eastern Europeans to be known as Slavs or Poles, not Jews. In 1881, in the Illinois *Staatszeitung,* a newspaper for German gentiles and German Jews, a Jewish lawyer named Adolph Moses derided his Russian counterparts "whose cultural standard is still Asiatic. . . . They are mendicants in Europe and peddlers in America."

Outwardly, by the turn of the century, the ethnic lines had become a little blurred. Lithuanian Jews like the Liebermans and the Cohens, who had made some money and achieved a degree of Americanization, began to mingle with middle-class German Jews like the Smitzes. But conflicts were almost inevitable when relationships became intimate. In America—where freedom of choice was the norm—every detail of personal life could become an emotional battleground. Did a couple observe the dietary laws? How strict were they about the Sabbath? How committed were they to synagogue or prayer? How much Jewish education would they give their children? Did the German partner care that a marriage to an Eastern European spouse would almost certainly cause the couple to be banned from the German-Jewish country clubs and social clubs? In the end, those religious and social tensions played as large a role as the financial ones in tearing Jake and Hetty's marriage asunder.

Hetty was dominated by her mother, Tillie Smitz, who had been widowed when Hetty was two and Holly was six months old. The fact that she had to start her own business, a millinery store, in Chicago's rough-and-tumble commercial world made her tougher and more resourceful than most women of her generation. In her store, she met many of the German Jews whose fortunes were already established by the beginning of the twentieth century: the Rosenwalds, who owned Sears, Roebuck; Henry Homer, the first Jewish governor of Illinois; members of the Pick family, which founded the Pick hotels. As she listened to them describe the lush suburbs where they were beginning to settle, she became increasingly ambitious for her family and particularly for her only grandchild, Louis. She would use all her wiles to combat anyone—including Jake Cohen and his family—who threatened his success. And she sought to indoctrinate Lou with pithy, Horatio Alger-like maxims. She repeatedly told him, "Tell me who you go with and I'll tell you who you are." In other words, he'd become important if he chose socially prestigious friends. Soon, her admonition became a reflex with him.

As Hetty Cohen was dominated by her family, so Jake felt a blood loyalty to the Cohen clan. No amount of pressure from the Smitzes could destroy it. The Cohens had their religion and their shared pride in their rabbinic past. They revered Moses, and adored their mother, Anna. They felt as much disdain for the kind of watered-down Judaism and studied orderliness that seemed to characterize the Smitzes as the Smitzes felt for the Cohens' Orthodoxy and the constant hubbub that pervaded their crowded household.

Moreover, the ten Cohen children—especially the boys—knew they needed each other for protection against a hostile world. For Chicago, in those days, was filled with the kinds of anti-Semitic gangs James Farrell described in his *Studs Lonigan* trilogy. Though Lou Cohen and his friends on Michigan Avenue got into a few brawls with them, they usually made a point of avoiding them on the street. But the Hyde Park Cohens, a little older, were tough and aggressive. Often, they spent their spare time in the basement of their apartment, working out with boxing gloves, a punching bag, Indian clubs so that they could stave off their enemies. Sometimes they would spar with each other or chortle over fights they had won on the streets. That was especially true of Leopold and Abe, who became classy enough boxers that they could earn twenty-five dollars a night at practically any ring in the city.

The Cohens were verbally tough, too. The boys, including Jake, often razzed people instead of talking to them. On occasion, they would cross the line from playfulness to hostility if an outsider couldn't defend himself.

And to some of them, Lou Cohen was an outsider: a Smitz, not a Cohen. That cultural difference was heightened by Lou's appearance. When the family gathered at Moses Cohen's house, Hetty often dressed him up in a Little Lord Fauntleroy suit and white socks that stretched to his knees. She often called her son "my little pigeon." Some of Jake's younger brothers and sisters, who thought the boy was pampered, would use the loving nickname as a form of derision. They would taunt the "pigeon." When they saw that Lou, strong and sturdy, a track star in grade school and high school, had some deep-seated belief in courtesy—or some secret fear—that prevented him from talking back or fighting back, they picked on him still more. I know how hurt my father must have been. Once I asked him to describe a typical night at the Cohen house. He began to imitate his relatives intoning his name, "Louie, Louie, Louie," as if the shrill, nasty tones he had heard in their voices had whittled his ego to shreds.

Still, despite the ceaseless conflict between the Smitzes and the Cohens, Jake and Hetty lived together until 1930, the year the

Jerome Trading Company ceased to function. In an era when divorce was still a scandal, they'd spent years trying to adjust to each
other's cultural demands without making any substantial changes in
themselves. But their personalities and their worlds were too different for any compromise to occur. Lou was caught in the crossfire.

For years, Hetty Cohen, a jolly, expansive woman with scores of
highly assimilated Jewish friends, made a cheerful effort to spend
time in her husband's religious environment. She would accompany him to Shabbos meals at the Lazaruses' and the Liebermans'
as well as the Cohens'. She would sit in the balconies of the Orthodox synagogues he attended. She would prepare him the Jewish foods he liked. According to Jake's younger brother, Abe
Cohen, who knew her best when he was attending law school, she
was very friendly to Jake's family, even ironing Abe's shirts on occasion. Sometimes, when Abe was broke, she went out and bought
him new clothes. But her willingness to accept Jake's religion and
his relatives was more than a way of exercising her wifely duty. It
was part of a complicated trade-off, based on a wistful hope that
she could involve Jake in her fun-loving world.

Hetty's idea of a good time was playing bridge and poker with
her friends, often for rather high stakes. She ate enormous, almost
suicidal, quantities of sweets. In her fifties, when she was sick
with diabetes, she used to go into Steinway's drugstore in Hyde
Park every night and devour a huge chocolate sundae. She loved
to shop, for silver, for antiques, for jewelry. Indeed, some of the
Cohens recall that her nickname used to be "Hetty with the diamonds."

She hoped that, by involving herself in Jake's world, she would
somehow build an emotional bridge to her husband, the exotic
Eastern European. She wanted to smooth out his rough edges and
transform him into a handsome consort who would join her at the
card table, share her taste for antiques and jewelry, move easily
among her Americanized crowd. Jake did take some steps toward
assimilation. For a while, he called himself Jack, not Jake. He called
his business the Jerome Trading Company (Jerome was his middle
name), not the Cohen Trading Company. Any Jew might have done

those things for business reasons, but Jake's real concession to Hetty was to settle in the Michigan Avenue milieu, far from the rest of the Cohens, and just two blocks away from the apartment where Holly and Tillie Smitz lived.

But he could never adjust to Hetty's habits. On the contrary, he wanted her to adjust to his. When he went to shul for evening services or on the Sabbath, he often brought home down-at-the-heels cronies—*schnorrers* as Abe Cohen called them. It was an Old World trait: in Eastern Europe, relatively well-to-do Jews often brought *schnorrers* home from shul. He wanted Hetty to be kind to them, to feed them, as his mother and grandmother had. Instead, she resented them. They seemed bedraggled and uncouth to her more refined crowd. For a time, Abe Cohen said, Hetty's friends felt so uncomfortable in the Cohens' apartment that they threatened to sever all relations with her.

But Jake didn't want to lose his wife, his son, his apartment. When he paid for Hetty's jewelry, her card games, her expensive foods, he thought he was buying a place in her secular world while he remained a more traditional Jew. But those purchases were based on the deceit that was, in the end, his most self-destructive quality. For the money he spent wasn't really his own. Ever since Moses Cohen and Son went bankrupt, Jake had been living on credit.

Throughout the twenties, the Jerome Trading Company, which seemed relatively secure, was in the same fragile condition as his marriage. Though the company's fortunes rose (the capital stock was worth $1,000 in 1919, $50,000 in 1929), Jake was constantly borrowing money. Virtually every week he'd ask for cash—for thousands of dollars sometimes—from his brother Leopold, who had become a millionaire, from his Lazarus and Lieberman cousins, from his close friends. Sometimes he would borrow from one set of relatives to pay another. He rarely spent the money on himself. Instead, he used the false fortune to buy the illusions he craved. In the twenties, he used it to try to win back Hetty's waning affection. He never did.

Sometimes, late in the day, Jake would come home from the warehouse, shabbily dressed, heavy-bearded, with his customary smell of sweat and burlap. He would find Hetty in bed, reading movie magazines and eating chocolates. There was no longer any emotional connection between them. His son's friends used to hear him tease her with the words "Mrs. Cohen, Mrs. Cohen," in the angry, despairing voice of a man who fears that his wife despises his name and the entire cultural legacy it suggests.

In 1927, when the Cohens' marital conflicts were making their home life unbearable, Jake bought his son, who was eighteen, a new car. Though Louis couldn't drive, he was proud of the possession. He made a special point of taking Joe Berkenfield to the garage where it was stored so that he could show it off. Ironically, the car may have played the same role in Jake's mind as had the sarcastic remarks and gestures of dismissal that had hurt his son so much. For he was in a curiously familiar role. Jake, the nonverbal son of a brilliant father, Moses, was the nonverbal father of a brilliant son, Lou. It was as if he was in a kind of psychological prison. He could only break down the bars and communicate with his elusive, intellectual boy through muttered phrases, or abusive or lavish gestures. But the gift of a car didn't affect the relationship. Jake couldn't buy Lou's love with a present any more than he could recapture Moses' respect with his business, his unfailing piety, or his status as the husband of a German Jew.

By that time, it was clear that Lou Cohen felt a degree of affection for his uncle Holly that he would never feel for Jake. Holly's rise in the legal world had been quite rapid. By the late 1920s, he was wealthy enough and prominent enough to join one of Chicago's two fanciest Jewish country clubs, the exclusively German-Jewish Ravisloe Country Club. Friends still remember the Saturday afternoons Lou Cohen tagged along with him on the golf course. That was just one small sign of their reciprocal love. Holly, a bachelor, wanted to share all his good fortune with his nephew. Lou always knew that if he needed financial help to get through school or start a business his uncle, not his father, would help him. Indeed, many people outside the Cohen family saw the uncle and nephew as father and son. Now Jake Cohen was displaced as a father and husband, too.

Was that one of the reasons he became almost uncontrollably generous with his borrowed money? That generosity is still legendary among his nephews and nieces, who adored him. Saul Cohen describes Jake as "a Jewish Robin Hood" who gave every penny he could beg or borrow to needy members of his own family or to the poor people he met in the shuls where he *davened*. According to Saul, he loved to go into a shul and provide the herring, cakes, wine, and whiskey for the celebration of festive events that occurred after the religious services. He spent much of his spare time talking to his brother Mandel's medical patients or to the clients he met at the law office George and Abe shared. Everyone in the family remembers he would give spare cash or even an article of his own clothing to anyone who seemed needy.

How wonderful he must have felt during those moments of beneficence! What a respite those warm hours in shul must have been from the anger he felt when he was with the Smitzes, from the undercurrent of disappointment he felt when he was with the Cohens. The *schnorrers* who drove Hetty to distraction gave him the unconditional love he craved—just as his nephews and nieces would in later life. He was the mitzvah man, the bestower of good deeds. His mysterious appearances and unexpected gifts enabled him to transform the obscure, impoverished Jewish underclass into a sort of informal congregation. With them Cohen, the displaced priest, could assume the status he had lost in both his homes, the status he would have retained if his family had stayed in Lidvinova.

At the close of the twenties, everything in the secular world that had propped Jake up suddenly collapsed. In 1928, when Jake was forty-six, Moses Cohen died of cancer. He was only sixty-four. That event was the beginning of the family's dispersal. For Moses had been the force that linked the Cohens to each other and to their past. Anna, his wife, survived him by a decade and maintained the Hyde Park apartment where the children had been raised. But the family treated her like a child, fondling her, petting her, putting her on their laps as they combed her hair. Though the children were still proud of Rabbi Jacob Cohen, still proud that they came from a town called Lidvinova, their history was becoming a patchwork of half-remembered words and legends, not the coherent set of memories that gave their father such pride and stature.

Many of the Cohens remained in Hyde Park for another decade or two; some would live for years at a time in each other's apartments. But it was never the same as it had been when Moses was alive. Within a very short time, the Cohens had become a typically contentious, atomized American clan that would soon spread outward to the suburbs, then to distant regions of America. Some nieces and nephews disappeared from the family completely.

Jake couldn't prevent the gradual dissolution of the family he loved. When there were quarrels, he usually remained friendly with all parties, but he didn't have the commanding personality that would have enabled him to insist that family unity was more important than any temporary strife. Nor did he have the force of character that would have enabled him to take his father's place at the Shabbos dinners, the Passover seders—the ritual events that had helped keep the Cohens together.

Besides, he was sinking in the economic and psychological quicksand that had always threatened him. In 1929, Jake was president of the Jerome Trading Company. Hetty Cohen was the vice president. The business was earning more than it ever had before. But those were paper profits. The business went bankrupt in 1930, shortly after the stock market crashed. "After that Jake never had any money," according to Saul Cohen. "He never even had a place of business."

Jake and Hetty were formally separated in March, 1930. That year Tillie and Holly Smitz and Louis and Hetty Cohen moved to the luxurious Park Shore Hotel in Hyde Park. Lou had just graduated from the University of Chicago. No one who visited them there remembers a single mention of Jake's name. Many of Lou's friends thought that his father was dead.

In 1932, Holly Smitz was appointed Master in Chancery, a judicial job that made him well-to-do and well known. Lou Cohen, bubbling with ideas and energy, was wooing his first public relations accounts—the Aragon and Trianon ballrooms, the Methodist Church, Chicago's Christmas Seal drive, Helena Rubinstein products. Jake, broke, was borrowing and spending more compulsively than ever. Now, though, he had to fabricate stories to feed his habit.

For instance, he knew enough people in the scrap-iron business to obtain a series of part-time jobs scouting metal that would soon be discarded. But he didn't scour warehouses, used-car lots, railroad yards for machinery that really was unusable. Instead, he created another fiction. He wrote down the nonexistent numbers of nonexistent railroad cars, and then phoned the numbers in to the scrap-iron brokers—often members of the Cohen or Lazarus or Lieberman families—and told them that the fictitious trains were carrying metal that would soon be sold for scrap. According to Saul Cohen, Jake's relatives protected him for years.

Sometimes Leopold Cohen would give him a few months' work at the steel yard. Sometimes he would return to the used–cement bag business as a street vendor, not a warehouse owner. He would show up at factories or grocery stores and try to buy an allotment of bags wholesale, then resell them at retail prices. During political campaigns, he would organize rallies for his brother Abe the alderman. He was good at that job since his years in Chicago's South Side synagogues had provided him with hundreds of friends who would vote for his brother. Of course, Lou Cohen's weekly check always supplemented the rest of Jake's income.

When Jake had a little money he would devise elaborate check-kiting schemes. He would put, say, two hundred dollars in the bank. Then he would take the bank statement to four potential creditors and use it as security for the one hundred dollars he would borrow from each one. At the same time, he would go to stores and banks and cash four checks at a time, assuming it would take weeks for all those institutions to realize he had bilked them. So he would squeeze a foamy twelve hundred out of a real two hundred.

He rarely spent the money on himself. After the Jerome Trading Company folded, he tended to dress shabbily, even when he was

visiting relatives. The man who had impressed Joe Berkenfield because he bought a new Studebaker every year never purchased another car in his life. Mostly he lived with relatives, with Mandel or
his sister Jennie or his mother. When he did have a place of his
own, it was a three-room furnished apartment on a shabby street
off Drexel Boulevard. By then, his younger brother Ruby had
opened a restaurant, bar, and bookie joint called Ruby's Blue
Heaven. He ate most of his meals there or at his relatives' homes.

He used the money as he always had—to nurture his fantasy of
himself as the mitzvah man. When he dined with relatives or
friends he always brought expensive meat or fancy cake. He gave
wonderful presents to the nephews and nieces who adored him as
his son never had. He spent more time than ever supporting the
poor Jews he met in shul or in his mysterious rounds of Chicago's
hospitals and old-age homes.

Of course, Jake was an increasing source of pain and embarrassment for Lou Cohen, whose public relations business was growing
rapidly. Often, Jake's angry creditors would appear at Lou's door
and insist that the son pay off all the bad debts the father had in-
curred. What rage Lou must have felt when he thought about the
nights the indigent old man had made him sleep on the kitchen
floor, when he remembered the sarcastic, envious remarks his father had made about his scholastic achievements.

Besides, Jake Cohen's carelessness about money threatened the
thing my father cared about most—his good name. "Tell me who
you go with and I'll tell you who you are," Tillie Smitz had admonished him in the phrase that would become one of his lifelong mot-
toes. Now, his father's unpredictable conduct might damage his
good name just as it was getting established. On the most practical
level, Jake could make it hard for Lou to get the financial credit he
needed to expand his public relations business and roller rink.
What if he used his son's burgeoning reputation as a way of borrowing money from the show business celebrities, the directors of
charities, whose accounts Lou kept attracting? There was no way
Lou could possibly know what sort of people Jake had to deal with

to pay off his debts. Loan sharks? People on the fringes of the underworld? What if he were consorting with such people? What if he involved his son with them?

In 1931, when Louis Cohen was twenty-one, he changed his name to Louis G. Cowan. In part, he did it so that he would seem more American, less obviously Jewish, something that was particularly important to a public relations man named Cohen whose largest accounts included Christian organizations. But he never for a moment tried to conceal his ethnic background. Indeed, the fact that he was an extraordinarily ethical, tactful man, who never used his heritage to exclude people or to judge them, made him an excellent Jewish ambassador to the gentile world.

But he hadn't only changed his name for business reasons—something that was common in his generation. He was trying desperately to rid himself of a demon. In 1934—the year before the case of Hetty Cohen versus Jake Cohen came before the divorce court—Lou applied to Chicago's leading Jewish social club, the Standard Club, as Louis Cowan. He was sponsored by Holly Smitz. In response to the phrase "family consists of" he answered "Hetty Cowan, mother." He had already written Jacob Cohen, father, out of his personal history.

He couldn't even bear to utter his father's full name. Hetty died in 1949, long after her son had gained national renown as the producer of "The Quiz Kids" and "Stop the Music." When he testified in a Chicago court to prove his heirship to his mother's estate, the judge asked, "Was she married?"

"She was divorced," my father said.

"Who was she married to?"

"A man called Jacob."

Jake outlived Hetty by a year. It is clear, from his will, that he lived in a fantasy world until he died in July 1950. The document, written in 1947, assumed Jake would live to a successful old age. In the will, he donates three hundred dollars to each of three synagogues. He leaves one thousand dollars to each of his surviving siblings. Finally, he bequeaths his son, Louis G. Cowan, all of his jewelry, all of his watches, and all the rest of his estate.

The disposition of Jake Cohen's will is a metaphor for his life.

During the two months before he died he had been working at Leopold Cohen's steel yard. In those months, he cashed two thousand dollars' worth of bad checks at Goldblatt and Brothers, a nearby department store. Goldblatt's wanted the money back. It ordered the will to be probated.

When he died, at sixty-eight, Jake Cohen had $78.96 in cash. He had $34.52 in the bank. His watches, both in pawnshops, were worth about $50.00.

His estate was declared "hopelessly insolvent." Goldblatt's sold its claim to Leopold Cohen for three hundred dollars.

Jacob Cohen had an Orthodox funeral. Louis G. Cowan, who arrived late and left early, paid the bill of $935.

Of course, there is no way of knowing all the complex details of the relationship between my father and grandfather. Very few of the people I interviewed could give me glimpses of life behind the closed doors of the Cohen household. But by now, I feel that I've solved the mystery story of their relationship—to my own satisfaction, at least—in a way that helps me understand my own deepening interest in Judaism.

I don't believe that Jacob Cohen would have consciously done anything to hurt his son's career. Nevertheless, I'm convinced that Louis Cowan had only one emotional choice: he had to expel Jake from his life in order to preserve his own—and his family's—regard for himself. What if Geoff and Holly and Liza and I had met Jake? What if, as young children, we had learned that our grandfather was a check kiter? Would his history undermine our respect for Louis G. Cowan, whose ability to succeed in business and still remain ethical was his deepest source of pride? Lou was always telling us how much he needed our love, how his wife, Polly, and the four of us were his only close friends in the world. He saw the warm, happy home life he had helped to create as a blessed alternative to the ceaselessly quarrelsome household he had known as a boy. The specter of Jake Cohen's physical presence must have threatened to sabotage the family that gave Lou Cowan such immense pleasure.

But what if we had grown fond of Jake, as his nephews and nieces had? What if he had plied us with gifts, made the synagogues my parents didn't want to attend seem like enchanting places, prompted us to accept him as a Jewish Robin Hood? If we felt that way about our grandfather, then his hurt, angry son would have had to see him regularly. Lou would have had to relive all his old childhood wounds and get entangled with the economic mess that Jake had made of his life.

Moreover, he would have had to re-examine his own deeply divided identity. Was he a Smitz, a German Jew, who, in the 1930s, would never have gained acceptance into the Ravisloe Country Club or the Standard Club or the University of Chicago's prestigious Zeta Beta Tau fraternity if he were an Eastern European? Or was he a Cohen, the descendant of the Lidvinova rav, whose proud Eastern European origins might have forced him to violate his grandmother Tillie's advice and choose a different, less prestigious set of people to go with? Was he Louis Cohen, a Jew who knew how to *daven,* who fasted on Yom Kippur, who didn't eat pork, or Louis G. Cowan, a cosmopolitan intellectual, a Jewish WASP, who shared the disdain his wife and children felt for those customs? Those weren't questions he wanted to ask himself as a young man.

In the end, that choice—the decision about his identity—was the one he couldn't quite escape. In fact, I believe it was a choice he was increasingly eager to make. He had succeeded in isolating himself and his offspring from the Cohen family. During the years he was rising in the media, it had no outward influence on his life—or on ours. Nevertheless, he had retained some of the identity that the Cohens had tried so hard to instill in him. Was it rooted in a memory of his bar mitzvah? A pleasant image of Moses Cohen studying Talmud? A fleeting image of Jake praying in the morning? It was buried deep in the soil of his consciousness, and would only grow into an active interest during the last few years of his life.

That interest was part of my heritage, too, perhaps because of my experiences at Choate, perhaps because of my position in the family. And when my father and I discovered that we had each, independently, developed an unexpected desire to know more about Judaism, it became increasingly clear that the rift between Jake Cohen and Louis Cowan couldn't break the mysteriously strong chain that linked him and me to Moses Cohen in Chicago and Rabbi Jacob Cohen in Lidvinova—and, by extension, to the five thousand years of our people's history.

3

Most of his friends from Chicago doubted that Louis G. Cowan, the increasingly successful public relations man, would ever get married. For one thing, he inhabited a world of older people: he lived with his grandmother, until she died in 1935, his uncle, and his mother. It was hard to imagine the utterly devoted son and nephew settling down with a contemporary, let alone having children. Besides, though he was a marvelous listener, with an ebullient, radiantly self-confident approach to public relations and the mass media, he was so reticent about himself, even then, that his old friends from Michigan Avenue and the new ones he had made at the University of Chicago were wary of asking him any questions about his personal life. How could a woman enter that secret realm?

In 1939, his uncle Holly died of diabetes. He always said that loss released an untapped flow of affection in him. Months later, it began to pour out on Polly Spiegel, then a graduate student in sociology at the University of Chicago.

As a Spiegel, an undisputed member of Chicago's German-Jewish elite, Polly came from the very world that Tillie Smitz had hoped Lou would enter. He was dazzled by her sense of style and her truly free-thinking manner. More important, he had never met anyone as unpredictable, as independent, as she in his sphere of constrained, upwardly mobile strivers. But he was much too bashful to propose to her. In effect, she proposed to him. From then on, the flow of adoration never ceased.

One afternoon in the spring of 1939, Polly Spiegel drove him out to Kenilworth so that he could meet her parents for the first time.

Her father, Modie Spiegel, was a difficult, opinionated man. He had a booming voice that made most of his family cringe with fear whenever they dined with him. He was even more wary of Eastern European Jews than were most German Jews of his generation.

Of course, as the head of Spiegels, a large mail-order business, as a financier with interests throughout Chicago, he had contacts in all Jewish neighborhoods. He was well aware of his prospective son-in-law's Eastern European roots. He didn't want such a person marrying his only daughter, he told his wife Lena shortly before Polly and her suitor arrived. "I don't want that kike in my house," he said.

Lena defended Louis Cowan in terms her husband would understand. He had belonged to Zeta Beta Tau, the finest German-Jewish fraternity at the University of Chicago, she said. He was a member of the Standard Club and the Ravisloe Country Club, an impeccable credential. Many of the South Siders on Lena's carefully cultivated telephone grapevine assured her that Louis was one of the most brilliant young businessmen in Chicago.

Modie Spiegel calmed down as soon as his daughter's car arrived. My father, eager to please the older man, charmed him with his warmth, curiosity and sense of moral earnestness.

Polly and Lou Cowan were married on the Spiegels' front lawn in August, 1939 in a wedding that was performed by a judge, not a rabbi. The guest list was heavily weighted toward the Spiegels' friends. Lou invited his mother, of course, and some of his classmates, but very few of his friends from Michigan Avenue. He didn't invite any of the Cohens, or any of the Smitz and Marks relatives with whom he'd spent time as a young man.

Within months, he was accepted into Modie Spiegel's social sphere. He was enchanted by what he found there. For the next twenty years, he retained Tillie Smitz's unquestioned belief that the businessmen he met through his in-laws—and, later, in the television industry—were more refined, decent, and brighter than anyone who might possibly *daven* in the shuls Jake Cohen still frequented.

His feeling was even stronger than that. In a way, he'd been abandoned twice. He'd been unbearably disappointed by his father, and now Holly Smitz was dead. So, at the age of twenty-nine, he adopted Modie Spiegel as his surrogate father, the Spiegel family as his clan. From his point of view, as an only child who had constantly been buffeted by the conflicting demands of two very different Jewish worlds, the Spiegels and their four children seemed wonderfully committed to each other. They embodied the picture of family life which he must have developed during his lonely youth, and which he constantly sought to convey to Geoff and Holly and Liza and me. We had to be loyal to each other, he would tell us, for the rest of the world could betray us at will.

Modie Spiegel died in 1943. From then on Lou Cowan relied on his brother-in-law, Modie, Jr., ten years older than he, for personal and financial advice. My uncle was the brother my father never had. But he was also a political conservative who sometimes disapproved of the Cowans' involvement in progressive causes. He and Polly often disagreed. From her point of view, there was a gulf between his business-oriented, Chicago-based family and our intellectual, cosmopolitan one. But Modie, who cared deeply about his siblings and all their children, constantly tried to bridge it. He felt a moral obligation to be sure that the entire family was as happy and financially secure as possible, so he always kept tabs on all of us. Of course, my father appreciated that attitude. He dismissed the political conservatism that seemed to bother Polly, and described Modie as a model of the family loyalty he believed in so deeply. I think he saw his brother-in-law as the strong Jewish patriarch so conspicuously missing in his own family.

The nuances of my parents' feelings highlighted themes that kept reviving themselves in our lives. What was the role of money in our household? What was the role of politics and intellect? What was the connection—especially for a Jew—between wealth and good works?

It was difficult for Lou to discuss those issues in personal terms, by citing experiences from his own past. For he had severed himself from that past. He'd moved the family to New York in 1942, after he had been offered a prestigious job at the Office of War Information, the United States Government's propaganda arm during

World War II. Once he decided to settle there, he rarely saw any of the old bunch from the South Side of Chicago.

He presented himself to most of the world as if he had been born again in 1940, after he'd married Polly, after he'd gained acclaim as the producer of "The Quiz Kids." Outwardly, he seemed to have erased three decades from his life.

But, as he began to hint in his later years, he always carried memories of his warring family and his childhood religion just beneath the odd combination of warmth and reticence that made his personality so elusive. His childhood was both a throbbing wound and a shimmering memory, that was at once too painful and too powerful to put into words—or to forget.

4

The Spiegel family must have seemed like a model of stability to Lou. But Polly's childhood, as she described it, was even more lonely and confusing than his. She had always known she was a Jew—indeed, her social life was centered at the all-Jewish Lake Shore Country Club—but she was raised as a Christian Scientist in a particularly bigoted gentile suburb—far, far from a Reform temple, let alone an Orthodox shul. So she spent her youth with the gentiles she knew at church and at school, and with the wealthy, assimilated German Jews at the club—and felt like a stranger in both worlds. That baffling childhood must have been the source of the refracted pain that led her to dismiss her Christian Science training and to embrace her secular, post-Holocaust Judaism.

She was too much of an egalitarian to admit she subscribed to the religious idea that the Jews were a chosen people. Yet the subtext of her words carried that message. We were chosen to suffer; chosen to achieve brilliance; chosen to wage a ceaseless war for social justice. Indeed, to her, the struggle for justice was nothing less than a commandment, even though she had no interest at all in the concept of Halacha—the intricate system of laws that have bound the Jewish nation together for five thousand years. I don't think she could imagine living without fighting for the oppressed.

Outwardly, she was a very self-controlled, stoic woman. She had enormous difficulty displaying the love she felt for the four of us, although she thought about us constantly, defended us whenever her friends and relatives attacked our ideas and eccentricities, and dreamed up creative ways of reaching out to us no matter where in the psychological or physical world we wandered. She couldn't cry when her mother died, and she never forgave herself for that

dramatic proof of her inability to express her feelings. She organized her life according to the schedule she had written down in
the elaborate notebook she kept by her bed—and left herself very
little time for the impulsive activities she loved.

As I recall her now—with her dazzling smile, her well-cared for,
slender body—I think of three separate episodes which suggest
the power and the limitation of the kind of Jewishness she tried so
hard to instill in me.

In 1964, I was at Oxford, Ohio, training to do civil-rights work in
Mississippi. Early one evening we heard that three integrationists,
two whites named Michael Schwerner and Andrew Goodman and
a black named James Chaney, were missing in a rural Mississippi
town, probably killed by the Ku Klux Klan. It was headline news all
over America. We were all terrified—and so were our parents. Late
that evening I walked by a phone booth and heard a girl yell at her
mother, "Of course I'm still going to go there. If someone in Nazi
Germany had done what we're doing, your brother would still be
alive today." I realized I would never have to say anything like that
to my mother. For the earnest, eager cry I had overheard summed
up everything I had learned about Judaism since childhood.

A month later Polly and Dorothy Height, president of the National
Council of Negro Women, were on a mission to Mississippi, as part
of Wednesdays in Mississippi, an effort my mother had conceived to
bring black and white women together. Quite casually, they had decided to integrate a motel near Jackson. At about 8 P.M., Rachel and I
went over to visit them. We noticed some white teenagers drinking
beer by the motel pool, muttering racist comments. Polly and Miss
Height seemed completely unworried.

After my parents died, Dorothy Height told me that a cross had
been burned in front of their window late that night. She and Polly
doubted they would survive until the next morning. Polly, who
talked about her past, her feelings, her work, even her sexual attitudes with complete freedom, had never bothered to mention that
part of the episode. Why should she dwell on something that might
make her seem heroic? She knew that the people in whose name
she was acting—Jews in Hitler's Europe, blacks in the South—had

faced far greater dangers than she ever would. Many millions had died. In her mind, where good manners and good taste were inextricably interwoven with progressive politics, it seemed unseemly to dwell on the few minutes of fear she had faced.

Then, in 1971, when I was working for the *Voice,* I covered a story which implanted inescapable questions about my mother's brand of secular messianism—and mine. The setting was Forest Hills, Queens, a neighborhood of liberal Jews. In 1970, John Lindsay, then mayor of New York, ordered the construction of three twenty-four-story low-income housing projects that would be used mainly for blacks and Puerto Ricans. The community was enraged. Every weekend thousands of demonstrators demanded that Lindsay abandon his plan. My reaction was that the demonstrators were Jewish racists.

I spent one afternoon walking on the picket line with an elderly Jewish couple, Romanians who had fled to Russia during World War II, then migrated to Newark, Greenwich Village, and Forest Hills, where they owned a grocery store. They had been chased and harassed all their lives—first by Hitler, then by the Communists, then by blacks in Newark and Italians in the Village. They were convinced that people were better off among their own kind—an idea that sounded reactionary to me. When I mentioned that I was Jewish, the old woman asked me, "Do you think we will all be chased from New York?" What gruesome experience lingered in her mind, producing that question? Surely her desire for security wasn't merely a form of bigotry.

Soon hundreds of protesters, including the couple from Romania, began to taunt the one hundred or so counterdemonstrators who had come to Forest Hills to support the proposal for a housing project. "Good-bye, Commies; good-bye, Commies; good-bye, Commies; we're glad to see you go. Good-bye, muggers; good-bye, muggers; good-bye, muggers; we're glad to see you go."

The crowd's chant brought me back to Mississippi. Those white kids at the swimming pool had been muttering similar invectives as they drank their beer and looked at Polly's motel room. So I asked the couple from Romania if the crowd's chant about black people awakened memories of the chants that were directed at them because they were Jews?

"No," the man said.

"You see, we're trying to protect ourselves here. I wish the Jews had done the same thing in Europe."

How could I see them as any more—or any less—oppressed than the blacks and Hispanics who might move into the project they were protesting so vehemently? Talking with them, and with others in their position, I realized that my flashbacks to Mississippi were inappropriate. The issue in Forest Hills involved two competing claims, not right and wrong.

When I published my article, I was afraid that my mother would think I was too soft on the Romanians and their counterparts; that I was explaining their racism away. In fact, she agreed with my article. But the chain of thought that began during those days in Forest Hills produced new questions, new sympathies that I could never quite explain to her, though my father understood them completely. For, though she has remained my political conscience, I realized that there was a contradiction in the belief she and I had always shared, that all Jews were mandated by history to be more ethical than other people. It allowed the Cowans, with our wealth, to argue that Jews with less money, less mobility, less access to powerful people than we had were somehow immoral if they organized their lives around their own self-interest. If they were survivors, we romanticized them without understanding them—or, on the other hand, assumed that their years in the camps should have made them less bigoted. If they were American-born people, who wanted the same security for their families as we had on Park Avenue, we tended to dismiss them as selfish business people or as bigots.

I began to think that my mother's Jewish orthodoxies, which I inherited, caused me to misunderstand most Jews. If I wanted to change that, I had to examine her background. In a way, that was easier than reconstructing my father's past, since I knew all her relatives and they all had useful documents. In a way, it was harder since it forced me to confront my mother's limitations—and mine.

Virtually no novelist or social historian has sought to explore the complexities of America's German-Jewish communities, though dozens have devoted full careers to romanticizing or railing at their Eastern European counterparts. Stephen Birmingham, who is not Jewish, did try to depict that world in *Our Crowd*, and Ludwig Lewisohn, novelist and critic, plumbed some of its psychological depths in his remarkable novel *The Island Within*. But most of America's German-Jewish writers—Barbara Tuchman, Walter Lippmann, David Riesman—have focused on more far-flung, magisterial subjects, while writers with Eastern European roots like Philip Roth, Saul Bellow, Cynthia Ozick, and Chaim Potok have fashioned fiction out of the fabric of their own lives. As a result, they have created most of the enduring images of Judaism on this continent.

In fact, the milieu of Polly's forebears is well documented, through letters, diaries, wills, and pictures. But they reside in family scrapbooks or in storage cases, not in literature.

My mother's family, which migrated here from the Rhineland in the 1840s, has some of its artifacts intact. The Spiegels have an edition of the Mishna (part of the Talmud), which my great-great-grandfather Moses Spiegel acquired in his hometown of Abenheim, Germany. He must have studied it often, for he came from a family that was every bit as pious as Rabbi Jacob Cohen's. According to his obituary, in the November 20, 1857, issue of the *American Israelite*, Moses' father, Gershon Spiegel, had been a Hebrew teacher in Abenheim—a town with about twenty-five Jewish families. He had sent his oldest son Moses to study with a learned rabbi in the city of Duerkheim, so that he could expand his knowledge of Hebrew and Judaism. But a year later Moses' father died. So he had to return to Abenheim and assume Gershon Spiegel's job as a Hebrew teacher in order to support his mother and his five brothers and sisters.

In the front of his Mishna, Moses carefully recorded all the births and deaths in the family. Two generations later, my grandmother Lena Spiegel kept a scrapbook recording the triumphs, tragedies, and trivia of family life. When I read the two books I realize that, within a century, the Judaism Moses Spiegel practiced had ceased to be a religion, a source of comfort and continuity, for families like my mother's. Instead, it had become a psychological and social burden.

When I pick up the family Mishna and glance at the first and last pages, at the records of births and deaths which are written in German or Hebrew, I feel linked to people who have been pious Jews ever since the children of Israel reached Mount Sinai. Here, for instance, is what Moses Spiegel wrote in Hebrew, about my great-grandfather's birth in Abenheim:"My son Joseph, who is also to be called by his new name, Joseph Spiegel, was born in good fortune, and in the blessed and prosperous hour on the second day of the week, on the first day of the festival of Sukkoth, in the year 5600, and with God's help may he be introduced to the Torah, the marriage canopy, and a life of good deeds. Corresponding to the Common Era, September 23, 1839."

Those words assume a permanence to a way of life which turned out to be extremely perishable. The Spiegels, who had lived securely as citizens of the Rhineland for generations, came to America after the failure of the liberal revolution of 1848. Moses' oldest son Marcus, nineteen, had joined the insurrection, and was forced to go underground when the King of Prussia rallied his forces and ordered his army to occupy most of Germany. Moses and his wife feared reprisals, so they took their four younger children and fled to New York, where Marcus joined them the next year.

The Spiegels were just as pious on the S.S. *Española,* the boat that brought them to America, as they had been in Abenheim. They prayed and sang Hebrew songs every night. When they arrived in America, Moses settled on the Lower East Side where he earned his living selling tobacco and teaching Hebrew. Apparently his German background, influenced by modern ideas, made him feel more comfortable as a Reform Jew than an Orthodox Jew when he reached this country. For, though he was strict about most of Jewish law, he chose to pray at synagogues where men and women could sit together, where the liturgy and sermons contained the German language, where it was permissible to have organ music on the Sabbath. During the next few years, he introduced newer German immigrants to the secular and religious world he had found in New York—and acted as a mentor to some of them. In

1901, Leopold Mayer, a younger man from Abenheim who became Chicago's first Hebrew teacher, remembered that when he arrived in New York in 1850, "My best friend and former teacher, Moses Spiegel, took me to the first Jewish Reform Temple I ever visited, Temple Emanu-El, which was then situated on Christie Street."

In 1851 Moses' children, Joseph and Marcus, moved to Chicago, where their brother-in-law owned a hardware and tinsmith shop, and their cousins, the Greenebaums, had obtained lucrative jobs in a private bank. Moses followed his children to Chicago, but the boys left the city, too, in order to peddle needles, thread, and other light household goods from their brother-in-law's hardware store. They worked in the farming towns near Cleveland. In Millersburg, Ohio, Marcus met a Quaker woman named Caroline Hamlin, who had never seen a Jew before in her life. She teasingly called him her "Dutchman," and soon became the first convert to Judaism in the history of Chicago. In 1857, Moses went to visit the couple. He died in Cleveland, on his way home.

"He always expressed the greatest contempt for riches," Leopold Mayer wrote in the *Israelite's* obituary. "In speaking of the matter, he would say, 'I never promised to our God to be a rich man, but I promised to be an honest man, and with the Lord's help I will keep my word.'"

In the last Hebrew inscription in the family Mishna, an anonymous "I" pays Moses Spiegel a special, heartfelt tribute: "Thus I cry and my heart is pained at the passing of my teacher and scholar, Rabbi Moshe, son of the scholar Rabbi Gershon Spiegel, who passed to his eternal habitation on the second day of the week, the fifteenth day of the month of Cheshvan, and was buried with great honor in Cleveland, Ohio, on Tuesday, the sixteenth day of Cheshvan."

With Moses' death, the chain was broken—the Hebrew letters, with which he marked life's most important moments, would be meaningless squiggles to his descendants, the Spiegel family, the financial tycoons.

In the 1860s, Marcus and Joseph Spiegel both volunteered for the Civil War. Marcus, who had fought with the liberal revolutionaries in Germany, was made an officer at once. He thrilled the small

Jewish community in Chicago when he appeared in synagogue on
Yom Kippur, dressed in full military regalia. In letters to his wife,
Caroline, he sometimes cited "the God of Israel" as one of the reasons he felt so intensely about the war and the Union's cause. He
chatted with her about Jewish matters, too—in a letter from Mil-
likens Bend, Louisiana, he urged her to "return to Millersburg after
Pesach (Passover) by way of Lima and Uniontown. Enjoy yourself
and the whole *mishpoche* (family). I do not know when Pesach is,"
he added wryly, "but I expect to find out." In another letter, he
asked Caroline to mail a letter he had written in Judendeutsch—a
form of German written in Hebrew letters—to an aunt in Germany
who had written to congratulate him for being the first Spiegel
ever to be named an army officer.

Marcus, much decorated, was killed in the battle of Vicksburg,
and made a brigadier general posthumously. Joseph, a sutler, spent
a year as a prisoner of war in Fort Camp, Texas. Perhaps if he'd
stayed in Abenheim, he would have followed the wish that was inscribed in the family Mishna, and led a life that was dedicated to
the Torah. But when the Civil War was over he opened a furniture
store in Chicago. He rarely went to synagogue; he usually worked
on the Sabbath. Still, the store had a definite Jewish flavor. For
Joseph and his son, my grandfather Modie, laced their English with
Yiddish expressions like *emes* (truth), *mishpoche, ganif* (thief). It
was not just a way of fooling gentile customers as the family sometimes explains. It helped the German Jews who worked in the
store to maintain a sense of ease. They were still strangers in a
strange land—their language furnished them a small island of familiarity. Why else would they call a bookkeeper "Megillah Willie"
simply because he needed a large roll of paper to do his job? The
name bore a whisper of a secret culture. It reminded them of the
distinctiveness they had to preserve in order to survive in
Chicago—and of the superiority many still, privately, felt they possessed. Those Yiddish expressions, which my grandfather boomed
out at the dinner table long after he'd moved to Kenilworth and
adopted Christian Science, helped preserve a patina of Jewishness
long after the details of Moses Spiegel's faith were forgotten.

"These words which I teach you today shall be in your heart," says the Shema, the central creed of Judaism, which Moses Spiegel, like Jacob Cohen, recited every day. "You shall speak of them diligently to your children. . . ." Certainly Gershon Spiegel, the scholar, spoke of them diligently to his son Moses. But Joseph, the store owner, had no interest in passing on the religious traditions he barely remembered. In his old age, when he moved to the suburb of Winnetka, he did name his house "Abenheim"—and referred to it as "The home of the evening of my life." And, like his brother Marcus, who filled his letters to Caroline with quotations from Schiller and Goethe, from Milton and the Bible, he was quite a scholar, with a detailed knowledge of Shakespeare's plays. When he was in his seventies, the stern old man used to take daily walks with his grandson Modie. Instead of talking Torah, as the legendary Eastern European *zaydes,* grandfathers, did, he taught the boy how to swear. Instead of reminiscing about the old country, about the faith that sustained his family as they prayed and sang psalms during the passage out of Germany, he talked often about the rats he had eaten in the Texas prison camp.

The Spiegels didn't abandon Judaism. Like Moses Spiegel, they called themselves Reform Jews, although the meaning of that term had changed considerably during the nineteenth century.

In Germany, where it was founded, Reform Judaism had flowered as an effort to reinterpret Jewish law in the light of modern-day conditions, something that had been done repeatedly since the earliest days of Jewish history. On a liturgical level, rabbis began to ask whether there was a need to incorporate a lament for a Temple that had been destroyed two thousand years ago—or an apparently superstitious blessing to a God who revives the dead—in the daily prayer. More practically, they wondered whether it was necessary to conduct every bit of every service in Hebrew, a language that was incomprehensible to most modern-day worshipers. Perhaps the growing stream of defections from Judaism would be slowed to a trickle if prayers and sermons could be conducted in the language of the land where Jews are living.

Yet, for a while, Halacha (Jewish law) remained as stern as ever. Leopold Mayer writes that in 1858, the rabbi of Chicago's first synagogue, Kehilath Anshe Ma'ariv (Congregation of the Men of the West), where he was a Hebrew teacher, gave a sermon in German which blamed a sudden increase in mortality among young women on their failure to observe the talmudic laws of family purity—to refrain from sex when they had their menstrual period and for a week thereafter. The speech outraged many members of the congregation. Some of them founded a second synagogue, the Sinai Temple, where they renewed a strain of thought that had always been present in the Reform movement, and placed far more emphasis on the prophetic texts—on the words of men like Isaiah and Jeremiah—than on the strict code of laws recorded in the Torah and Talmud.

There had always been an accommodationist streak in Reform Judaism—an attempt to conform to the mores of a particular nation, "to be a man in the street and a Jew at home," as one famous phrase went. That became its dominant mode soon after Joseph Spiegel's generation of German Jews settled in Chicago. Some rabbis made the practical argument that fundamental talmudic strictures—like the prohibition against working on the Sabbath—had to be compromised so that the business-oriented German Jews, whose success in America was far greater than any of them had ever imagined, would retain any commitment to the faith at all. To take a practical example, Joseph Spiegel's furniture store made a large percentage of its profits on Saturdays. Would angry, punitive jeremiads from Old World rabbis encourage him to forgo those profits in the name of a religion he barely believed in? Or would he be more likely to stay in the fold if the religion was reformed to permit him to do what he would have done anyway?

In a sense, the German Reform rabbis were more farsighted than their Orthodox counterparts. For example, Yehuda Rosenthal, author of a Yiddish-language history of Chicago, complains that Eliezer Anixter, one of Chicago's early Orthodox rabbis, was addressing letters to his mentors in Lithuania which contained technical questions about metals that should be used in the mikvah—the ritual bath—or about the proper word for the body of water near Chicago—something that had to be included on a *get* (a writ of divorce)—instead of promoting Jewish education. Arguably, the changes the Reform rabbis made kept tens of thousands of Jews inside the faith. But many tried so hard to accommodate to America that they drained the religion of its distinctively Jewish qualities.

By the time Joseph was in his forties and his son Modie was a teenager, Dr. Emil G. Hirsch, the quintessential Reform rabbi (who preferred to be addressed as Doctor), had taken the pulpit at Chicago's elegant Sinai Temple, where the wealthiest German Jews now worshiped. Politically, he was far more liberal than his congregation. He supported child-labor laws and the eight-hour working day; the great libertarian lawyer Clarence Darrow was one of his best friends; Jane Addams, the head of Hull House, sometimes spoke from his pulpit. He could get away with those political views because his ideas about religion were perfectly suited to the business people in his congregation. When Dr. Hirsch died in 1925, his son-in-law, Gershon Levi, wrote that "for a community on the make, he was a prophet of Jewishness."

Dr. Hirsch was born in Luxembourg, where his father was the chief rabbi. He was fluent in seventeen languages, he was extremely learned in the Torah and Talmud, and was familiar with Christianity after years of study at the Episcopalian College in Philadelphia. A self-confident, flamboyant man, he had no doubt that his form of Judaism was the only authentic one. He was thoroughly convinced that, as a German-trained intellectual, he was far more intelligent than the Eastern European rabbis who engaged him in sustained debates. Of course, he was certain that he was brighter than any of the businessmen in his congregation.

He displayed such an angry, sarcastic dislike of Jewish rituals that he transformed even the mildest, most attractive customs into objects of scorn; he made many of his younger congregants disdain Judaism. Sometimes he displayed a random rage at his students' desire to assimilate into America—a rage that was often unprovoked. For example, my uncle Modie remembers Dr. Hirsch walking up to him once in 1908, pinching his nose, then commenting on the children in his confirmation class who had had their noses fixed with the angry maxim: "You can change your noses, but not your Moses."

He forbade people to wear yarmulkes in his synagogue, arguing
that the skullcaps were a remnant from the oriental world—an imi-
tation of the fez—that only served to emphasize Jewish particular-
ism. He appealed to higher scientific evidence to refute the belief
that there had ever been a covenant between God and Abraham.
Then, citing his own ideas of personal hygiene, he urged his congregants to ignore the sign of the covenant—he told them to refuse
to circumcise their sons. In 1885, he switched the Sabbath from Saturday to Sunday, and justified his amendment to something Jews
have always regarded as God's law by arguing that "we refuse to believe that certain times or certain seasons were chosen by God as his
reception day." He thought the tradition of fasting on Yom Kippur
was a remnant of superstitious paganism.

The adults in the congregation saw Dr. Hirsch as their Moses,
who would lead them out of bondage to the constraints of Halacha
into the promised land, free America.

They sang a hymn to Dr. Hirsch on his twenty-fifth wedding
anniversary in 1908, at a party Modie and Lena Spiegel attended.
At first, the Spiegels joined hundreds of German-Jewish congregants in "Hirsch, Hirsch, Hirsch," a song which conveyed their
gratitude at finding a rabbi who freed them from the constraints
of the Law.

> *It was 1880 when he first came to our town*
> *We weren't yet civilized, but he didn't turn us down . . .*
> *He thought we were too pious and crowding things too*
>   *much*
> *So he dropped the Shabbos and Sunday used as such.*
> *He said we needn't matzos eat on Pesach if not wished*
> *Nor fast on holy Yom Kippur*
> *And may drink milk with a meat dish.*

Then Modie Spiegel, who still lived in Hyde Park, proposed his
own toast to Dr. Hirsch:

> *With one exception, Hirsch is satisfied*
> *To remedy it, we have tried, tried, tried.*
> *He'd like to have a Temple with 100,000 pews*
> *And preach every Sunday to a million Jews.*

But I'm afraid it can't be done
For Sunday morning they have fun, fun, fun.
On this silver wedding night,
Let us do what is right
To congratulate him is not enough.
To Temple we will go,
Other pleasures we'll forgo
And he'll think we're the stuff.

Golf was one of the pleasures my grandfather mentioned in his toast to Dr. Hirsch. It wasn't just an offhand remark. It foretold a German-Jewish replacement for religion—the highly ritualized country-club life. One can see this transformation in a speech that Milton A. Strauss gave on the twenty-fifth anniversary of the all-Jewish Ravisloe golf club, the place where Holly Smitz used to take Lou Cohen on Saturday mornings. The Spiegels had belonged to Ravisloe before they helped form the even more exclusive Lake Shore Country Club. My grandmother, Lena, chose to preserve Strauss's words in her scrapbook:

The Ravisloe is the pioneer club for our people. . . . It has done more to drive our people away from synagogue than any other agency.

The Ravisloe was the first place to introduce golf and golf thought . . . now, in Chicago, there are more golf clubs than synagogues, more golf teachers than rabbis, more niblicks *in active use than Sefer Torahs.*

The speech may have been jocular. Its message summarized much of a generation's journey.

In 1910, Modie Spiegel broke his poetic promise to Dr. Hirsch. He had transformed the family business from a furniture store into a mail-order house, and the gamble, which his father and his younger brother Sidney thought was foolish, had paid off. Now that he was prospering he moved away from Sinai Temple, away from Hyde Park, to Kenilworth, where he and my grandmother became Christian Scientists.

Even before their move, my grandparents had lost their sense of ethnic nuance. In their desire to achieve status, to appear American, they did things the gentile world found ludicrous.

My uncle Modie remembers the first time he was affected by their disorientation. His parents had sent him and his brother Fred to an all-gentile boarding school. On St. Patrick's Day, 1911, he received a call on the school's only telephone—a wall phone in the dining room. A telephone call was a big event in those days, so all his classmates listened to the conversation.

"You have a younger brother," his mother told him.

"That's grand. What's his name?"

"John Patrick," she replied. He repeated the name to his brother Frederick.

"Suddenly, all the boys in the room began to laugh," my uncle recalls. "I didn't know why they were laughing. Then, they began to tease me because I was a Jewish boy with a brother named Patrick. I must have been very hurt. I still have the letter I wrote, describing my feelings."

"I hope Pat is all right," the eleven-year-old Modie wrote, five days after my uncle John was born. "If you get another son call him Mike. When you named Pat you should have let me have something to say. I could have gotten you just as good a name.

"Who suggested that name, anyhow? I guess father did. When I tell anybody his name, they laugh. I don't see anything funny about it, do you?"

My grandparents must have heeded that letter. For they changed John's middle name to Paul.

At least Frederick and Modie had spent their formative years in Hyde Park, playing with kids whose backgrounds resembled theirs, eating at their houses, attending summer camps with them, going to Sunday school at Sinai Temple. So they had a clearer sense of Jewish life than my mother or her brother John, who were both born in Kenilworth. But in Hyde Park they had never been forced to think about the fact that they were Jewish, just as I hadn't before I went to Choate. So, in a way, the ease of their early years made their reception in Kenilworth all the more shocking.

The Spiegels had bought their house there at a time when well-to-do German Jews were just moving to Chicago's northern suburbs. My grandfather liked Kenilworth's climate, but he had no idea of its sociology. It happened to be a more bigoted town than Winnetka or Highland Park, where Jews also lived. For once the Spiegels acquired their home from a renegade lawyer (who, it turned out, hated his neighbors and wanted to punish them by selling to a Jew), the town council passed a restrictive covenant saying that no more Jews could move in.

Modie, who had left boarding school, recalls his first day in Kenilworth's public school in September 1911. "When I was walking there I met two girls, twin sisters. It was raining that day. They called me a dirty Jew all the way to school. They beat me with their umbrella. I had never learned to think religiously or ethnically before. So I was very hurt.

"I got over it. Kenilworth was a small community, with maybe six hundred people. There were about fifteen kids in our graduating class. They came over to the house all the time. Mother had a wonderful cook. They liked to eat the excellent food we always served. We had a big yard, where they all played football. So I was friendly with everybody.

"But I understood we were outside the social confines they set up. I rarely went to parties at their houses, and I never went to parties at their country clubs.

"Ever since that beating by the twins, I knew that they had feelings about Jews. But I never thought they had feelings about us. We were their Jews."

Kenilworth, the town, was never a real home to Modie and Lena. It was a location—and a house—they loved, a place where Modie, a graying, distinguished-looking man, with a spreading alderman (as they called pot bellies in those days) and an orchid on the lapel of the three-piece suit he always wore, could sit in his rocking chair on the front porch and listen to his beloved radio or sing, "O Kenilworth," a song he'd written, in a voice filled with contentment. Neither he nor Lena tried to befriend their neighbors—they had learned, from the restrictive covenant, that, as

Jews, they weren't welcome in their adopted town. So their cronies were still friends from Hyde Park, who would drive to the country for a visit.

In Kenilworth, outside the comfortable home that served as their retreat, they experienced the same psychological confusion any refugee faces when he settles in a strange land. They knew very little about the town—about their children's friends, their lives in school, the social pressures they were experiencing.

As I listen to my uncle, Dr. John Spiegel, talk, I realize that his identity problem, and my mother's, was made doubly acute when their parents became Christian Scientists.

Actually, their decision to embrace that creed was not uncommon in their generation of Jews. By 1910, about sixty thousand of America's three million Jews—Eastern and Western Europeans alike—identified themselves with that sect.

They didn't have to convert—that was one of Christian Science's great attractions. In the religion, the faithful were "students," not congregants; Jesus Christ was a "healer," not a Messiah; there were no crosses on the churches; there was no clergy to exalt him. Many people, including my grandparents, argued that the act of accepting the inner discipline of Christian Science—which meant using prayer and meditation to arrive at the faith that a divine power, not doctors, could heal the sick—made them stronger people and better Jews. Of course, the rabbis disagreed. Throughout America, they denounced "the healing cult," just as fervently as rabbis denounce religious cults today. Their words had no effect on Modie and Lena's beliefs.

In 1900, their oldest son, Frederick, who was two, had fallen off their eight-foot porch and landed on his head. For several days, it seemed almost certain that he would die. After a series of operations he survived.

It is recorded in the Spiegel family Mishna that two of Moses and Regina's children died at the age of two, and that another died at the age of one. That was back in Abenheim, though, at a time when religion was so strong and infant mortality was so common, that the three tragedies didn't shatter the family's faith. By contrast, when Frederick was severely injured, my grandparents seem to have encountered a crisis—and begun a search—that must have been on their minds even as they sang their jocular odes to Dr. Hirsch. For the permissive faith they had learned at Sinai Temple provided very little sustenance, very little ballast, when they encountered a personal crisis. It contained none of the Old World wisdom that might have convinced them to see their son's fate as God's will or life's way. Instead, they seem to have wanted a religion that would help them ward off similar tragedies in the future. Christian Science, which maintains that all disease can be cured by prayer, seemed to promise that.

The elder Spiegels became Christian Scientists in 1910. Every night, they would read portions from the Bible, portions from Mary Baker Eddy's books—*Faith and Reason* and *Science and Health with Key to the Scriptures*—and seek to correlate the texts. That work was far more demanding than anything they had encountered at the Sinai Temple.

By the time their parents became Christian Scientists, Fred and Modie, Jr., were too old to be raised in the church. But Polly and John had to act as devotees. Until they were teenagers, they slept on the sunporch with their parents (it was one of the smallest rooms in their three-story house) because Mary Baker Eddy had proclaimed that fresh air brings good health. They never consulted doctors, even for themselves. They had to rely on God's love. Once, in 1916, when my grandfather was in New York on business, Polly, three, and John, five, had scarlet fever. In a letter to Lena, Modie mentions "our sorrows of yore"—by which he means Frederick's fall—and then goes on to remind his wife that "Our darlings are God's children. No harm can come to them. But we must use God's wisdom in our care of them. The next few days and weeks will be hard, but we will show our worth by going down the path of divine love, led by God's wisdom."

The religion consumed much of the children's life. "Every Sunday and Wednesday night we had to go to church and say we had thought the right thoughts," John Spiegel recalls. "Then, back home, we'd hear my parents talking to each other as they did their homework.

When someone else got sick, we used to listen to my mother and father plan ways to get them into Christian Science. My mother had terrible migraines. Polly and I used to spend our afternoons in her room, putting cold towels on her face and stroking her forehead. I rebelled against it all when I was eleven, but it had a lasting effect. I still think that if I summon up enough resistance to illness I won't get sick."

No wonder John and Polly felt even more puzzled about their Jewishness than their older brothers had! After all, they went to church, not just a highly Christianized Sinai Temple. Besides, the Hyde Park families that had given Fred and Modie some sense of identity, some context for their ethnicity, seemed very odd to John, who had always lived in Kenilworth. "They were all obsessed with food. They talked a lot and very noisily. My parents were like that, too. They loved to discuss material things. It all seemed very strange to me because that wasn't what was going on in the homes of my gentile friends in Kenilworth.

"I think it was the materialism that bothered me the most. I remember how I used to dread the days my mother would come to our school in Kenilworth. She would always appear in her chauffeur-driven car, her mink coat, her painted fingernails. The gentile kids didn't have parents like that.

"My Jewishness confused me all the time. It made me feel like a very marginal person. I knew I was different from the other kids in Kenilworth. But I had no idea of what Jews were.

"I guess that part of my identity was like the Yiddish words that would come into our dinner-table conversations—a set of fragments that didn't mean anything to me. In my mind, Jewishness was something I had to cope with. It set me apart from the kids in Kenilworth, but my complete ignorance of it set me apart from the kids in Hyde Park."

Modie and Lena's lives were filled with ambiguities. Long after they became Christian Scientists, they played a public role as benefactors of Jewish charities and the Sinai Temple. They sent Dr. Hirsch personal gifts with handwritten notes, proclaiming their love for him. ("I hope my love for you won't be deemed an evil influence by the teachings of your new creed," he wrote them after he had received a particularly handsome set of bookcases from the Spiegel's mail-order house. "With the best wishes in the old Jewish way, I am, lovingly yours, Emil G. Hirsch.") In 1915, Modie Spiegel helped found the all-Jewish Lake Shore Country Club.

In 1918, Frederick volunteered to serve as an ambulance driver for the Italian Army, in the same corps as Ernest Hemingway, whom he nicknamed Hemingstein. When he won the Cross of Honor, his father the Christian Scientist wrote, "You must know how proud and happy we are, as you are the first Jewish boy in the Chicago area who has ever won a similar award from any of our allies." When Modie, Jr., was married a few years later, the Spiegels wrote a song called "To the Mahutten." It was assumed that everyone at the reception would recognize the Yiddish word for one's children's in-laws.

Like Jacob Cohen, Modie Spiegel was named for his grandfather the rabbi. But where Jake, the used-cement-bag dealer, saw his first name as one of the few sources of pride in his troubled life, Moses Spiegel, mail-order king, altered his as soon as he could. He took an aunt's adenoidal mispronunciation of the embarrassing Hebrew name and turned it into the slangy, unforgettable American handle which he passed on to his son, Modie, Jr. My Cohen cousins remember hearing dinner-table conversations enshrining the few remaining memories of the Lidvinova rav, and concluding, from their parents' respectful voices, that their religious lineage was a great one. Modie Spiegel had a painting of his grandfather, the Hebrew teacher from Abenheim. It hung on the wall of his dining room, along with a painting of his grandmother Regina. But he always called his would-be namesake Zezmo Gelspiel (an inversion of Moses Spiegel), in the same slightly mocking tone of voice his children would often use when they pronounced the word "Jewish" as "Joosh."

So the Yiddish-speaking German-Jewish Christian Scientist, who devoted as many hours to the administrative details of his country club as religious Jews do to the inner workings of their shuls, literally couldn't bring himself to abandon his proudly religious grandfather (either his picture or his name). But he couldn't treat Moses

Spiegel with respect. How could his children understand that attitude, especially when it was accompanied by his scorn for Eastern
European Jews?

"I'll never forget how he went on about the kikes," John Spiegel
says. "He had a pet expression—'A kike is a kike in the summertime.' I never understood what it meant.

"When we talked about dating, he'd yell out an expression—I'm
not sure if it was Yiddish or German—*'Brengen me no kike in der
housen'*—'Bring me no kikes in the house.' Of course, I wasn't supposed to bring home a gentile either. Only he called them shiksas.
I wasn't even supposed to bring home a shiksa who was a Christian Scientist. So that only meant German Jews.

"For all their money, my parents didn't carve out much space for
themselves in America. I had to carve it all out for myself."

The elder Spiegels argued frequently. Since they were rich people
whose fights were usually over money, my mother could never
share my father's belief that wealth would bring quiet and harmony. Indeed, her reflex—which she passed on to us—was that,
although money could buy possessions and provide one with the
freedom to travel, create, or act on one's beliefs, it should never be
discussed directly. That was coarse. And, more important, more
paradoxical, she convinced all of us that people who dedicated
their lives to earning the wealth she so plainly enjoyed were
somehow as tainted as the father whose rages frightened her,
whose taste embarrassed her.

Sometimes Modie and Lena argued about her even wealthier
family, the Strauses. They were German Jews who had lived in the
small town of Ligonier, Indiana, until she was twelve, and then
moved to Chicago, where they established a hugely successful real
estate bond company and later a bank, which financed the
Chrysler Building in New York and three Ambassador Hotels. They
paraded their wealth before the Spiegels. Whenever Lena's sister-
in-law came to Kenilworth, she brought two personal maids, six
steamer trunks, and insisted on sleeping on her own linens. Modie

was quite jealous of his in-laws, but instead of admitting his anger, he belittled his wife.

For Polly, dinner with her father was a particularly painful time. There were the remarks about the kikes. There were the loud, boastful discussions of business. Whenever Lena mentioned a friend from Ligonier, Modie would quickly mock her by saying, "I knew a cuter one back in Hammond, Indiana." He would dismiss the Strauses as rural folk who were overwhelmed by the big buildings they saw when they first arrived in Chicago. Sometimes he would compress all his angry feelings about his in-laws into remarks about how the Strauses were "small people." The steady stream of boasts, bigotry, and invectives made my mother long to flee from the table.

Those quarrels were minor, though, compared to the loud pitched battles which often erupted between Modie and Lena. Usually, those fights were over Lena's supposed extravagance—a trait that seems to have stemmed from the situation many German-Jewish women of her class and generation found themselves in. She was a bright woman with little formal schooling, and no intellectual interests. She didn't read, she didn't care about politics, she didn't have a job. She spent her days playing mah jong or bridge, or gossiping over the phone with her friends from Hyde Park.

So she focused her leftover energy on beautifying her home. Or perhaps she was heeding an immigrant impulse that was deeper than that. After all, Lena Straus Spiegel's family had journeyed from Germany to Indiana and then to Kenilworth in less than fifty years. She had no work, no roots in her environment, no serious family chores to anchor her days. She may have needed to erect a solid physical structure, a beautiful, elaborate fortress of a home, to replace the psychological structure that had been shattered on the long march from the all-Jewish village where her parents were born to the all-gentile suburb where her younger children were raised. Maybe the huge house represented her only real security.

In any case, she would invest large sums of money in a garage, a new wing of the house, a greenhouse, without telling her husband until the workmen actually arrived. (She had the greenhouse built

while she and Modie were away on a trip.) Each new expense
would provoke her husband's rage.

Sometimes their battles became so loud that Polly and John
would sit at the top of the stairs, huddling next to each other for
protection.

Lena often developed a migraine the next day. Since she couldn't
take pills or call a doctor, she would insist that Polly or John spend the
entire afternoon massaging her forehead on the darkened sun porch.

Polly Spiegel's social life didn't furnish much of a refuge from
the problems she had at home. That was partly the result of her appearance and her nominal Judaism. Until her late teens, her friends
say, she was pudgy and shy, taller than most of the boys in her class,
a good athlete who was terrified of any social situation where she
would have to make small talk. Some of that feeling vanished when
she got to New Trier High School and became involved in student
activities and athletics.

But the allurements of the Spiegel house that made her brother
Modie feel popular in Kenilworth—the good food, the large yard,
the parties—only served to confuse her. Kids came, it was true, but
they were the children of the families who had passed Kenilworth's restrictive covenant. Polly never knew whether they came
to the house because of her personality or her possessions. They
never invited her to dances, never asked her on dates. Was that because she was shy and plump, or because she was Jewish?

Then Lena underwent a crisis that made Polly's sense of isolation even more acute.

Though Modie and Lena had both adopted Christian Science at
the same time and shared its tenets unquestioningly, the religion
seems to have been particularly important to Lena. It was a social
experience she loved. It was an intellectual challenge. And it was a
spiritual refuge.

But in 1927, she developed a severe pain in her rectum which
couldn't be cured by meditation or prayer. So, after seventeen years
of going to Christian Science Church twice a week, of testifying,
with a full heart, to the miraculous, healing power of the faith, the
terrified woman called a doctor. He said her ailment was a common

benign fissure. But soon, according to her son Dr. John Spiegel, now a psychiatrist and social scientist, Lena developed a fear of cancer. Moreover, she fell into a deep depression because she had called a doctor rather than relying on her faith. "She had flunked Christian Science," John Spiegel recalls. She could never return to the church. But without it, she felt incomplete and inadequate.

She was institutionalized in 1927, when Polly was fourteen. She stayed away for nearly two years, at a mental institution in upstate New York. During that time, her daughter, whose beloved brother John was away at boarding school, lived alone in the huge house with a staff of six servants and her intimidating father. When I think of her adolescence in that rather gothic setting, I marvel at the fact that experiences that might have left her an emotional cripple somehow reassembled themselves into a blend of moral resolve and intellectual creativity which carried her into battle with the world's ills.

Lena Spiegel's nervous ailment was anything but unique. Nowadays, when you talk with German Jews in their sixties or seventies, you often hear about a relative who had similar ailments in the 1920s and early 1930s—breakdowns, chronically tense stomachs, migraines, nameless depressions which no amount of psychoanalysis could resolve. For those people were living in a netherworld of ethnic uncertainty. How could they resolve the dilemma of remaining Jewish—and forbidding their children to bring shiksas home, as my grandfather did—in the Christian America that both threatened them and tempted them?

In Chicago, their internal torment grew especially intense in the wake of the Leopold-Loeb murder case in 1925. For that singularly grisly crime involved two brilliant, wealthy German-Jewish boys, honors students at the University of Chicago, whose parents were part of the same social set as the Spiegels and their friends. In order to prove their intellectual superiority, Nathan Leopold and Richard Loeb had decided to commit a perfect crime: to kidnap a German-Jewish child, Bobby Franks, take him from his home in Hyde Park

to a bird sanctuary at the deserted outskirts of the city, and blud-
geon him to death.

They were found out, of course, and the story, which was headline news for years, produced a shock wave among the Spiegels
and their set. What would the gentiles think? Would the crime release a wave of anti-Semitism? Thank God, they thought guiltily, that
the murderers had chosen a Jewish child—that might lessen the
gentiles' wrath. But it would still change their impression of German Jews. Would they continue to do business with the Jewish
merchants who needed their trade? What awful remarks would the
gentiles make at home, in front of the children who played with recently transplanted Jewish kids like John and Polly Spiegel, whose
families had sought refuge in the suburbs a decade before?

They did have one safe haven, the Lake Shore Country Club,
which Modie, Sr., had helped to found, which was a second home
for so many members of Polly Spiegel's generation.

Most of the adults at Lake Shore saw the club as one of the few
places in America where they could act out the fantasies with
which this land of freedom had imbued them. After all, downtown
at work they had to be the very souls of respectability. Especially
after the Leopold-Loeb murder, they had to impress the gentiles
with their sobriety, their propriety. At the same time, they had to
remain so dignified, so much like New England WASPs that they
could always be distinguished from the Eastern Europeans who,
they thought, were giving all Jews a bad name. The club was the
only place they could behave as they pleased.

Golf, the rich man's sport, became their obsession. They also
played high-stakes poker games, where a club member could lose
as much as ten thousand dollars a night. Their parties flowed with
so much liquor (even during Prohibition) and so much erotic energy that, in my grandparents' time, Lake Shore became known for
the spouse swapping that occurred among some of its members.

Most of the younger people loved the club too. It was a paradise
for the rich, a year-round camp where they could skate in the
winter, swim in the summer, play golf and tennis with kids their
age, hold dinners and dances. Furthermore, it had the social

ambiance that my grandfather and his kind wanted for their young. There were no shiksas around. There were no kikes. In those days, no one was permitted membership except the wealthiest German Jews.

"Lake Shore was like a womb for us," according to a member who is now in her fifties. "You have to remember, we were all 'the first Jews' wherever we lived—the first in a suburb or a boarding school or a summer camp. We all had experienced anti-Semitism—from gentile parents who wouldn't let us room with their kids, from friends who wouldn't invite us to their parties, from classmates who excluded us from their social clubs and hounded us with bigoted remarks. We were safe at Lake Shore. Even then most of us knew we would marry someone from there. I'll tell you, the friends I made at the club have been my friends ever since. I wish my children were lucky enough to have that sort of tight, protective social network."

These were the descendants of Hebrew scholars like Moses Spiegel, the offspring of men like Marcus Spiegel, with his taste for Goethe and Schilling, and Joseph Spiegel, with his love of Shakespeare's plays. Yet, they seldom discussed books or ideas. Their language was the broad, insulting humor of the roast. Their cultural events were elaborate efforts to forget the outside world, for a few hours at least. They were expensive extravaganzas, usually for someone's anniversary or birthday. There were always four- or five-course meals, usually with a showy foreign motif. For instance, in 1914 Lena Spiegel sponsored a banquet which included Blue Points Mignonette; Chicken Essence, *en tasse;* Filet of Salmon St. Malo with *pommes Parisienne;* Breast of Partridge d'Antoine with sweet potato soufflé; Salad Sarah Bernhardt; Nesselrode Pudding and assorted cake, and *Bar-le-Duc au Fromage.*

Often, prominent entertainers who happened to be in Chicago would sing songs set to Broadway show tunes, making fond fun of the honored guest. Usually, relatives would compose intimate, bawdy poems, like this ode to a friend on her seventieth birthday, which Lena Spiegel included in her scrapbook:

> *Waking early in the morning first I summon up Marie*
> *Then I probe at my hernia and take a little pee*

Then I levitate my ass and I pass a little gas.
I accept congratulations for my lack of palpitations,
I relieve my constipation at the can.
But if nothing is forthcoming I relax and do some
  slumming
As the scratch form and the horoscope I scan.

Outwardly, Polly Spiegel's adolescent outlook seems to have been partially shaped by that world. Back then, friends recall, she never displayed any of the interest in books or ideas, any of the taste for introspection, the capacity for character analysis, that would make her such an interesting person. Indeed, in her teens, she wanted nothing so much as to be an ordinary Betty Coed at Northwestern University.

But how she detested the Lake Shore community, the Jewish world she knew most intimately! Partly, her old friends say, her hostility stemmed from the fact that she wasn't very popular; she was a wallflower at all the dances. Certainly, when she talked about the place, it never sounded like a haven. It sounded like a prison of conformity.

Once, when I was in my twenties, my mother attended some obligatory gathering there. We were both in the civil-rights movement by then. I'll never forget the anger in her voice when she described the main event of the extravaganza, a minstrel show where whites performed in blackface. She hadn't walked out— she didn't want to insult her old friends—but the episode filled her with the same disgust she'd felt at her father's dinner table and at country club affairs all throughout her childhood.

As a child, though, she had lacked the language to express her anger. And, if it had been up to her father, who didn't really believe girls should get educations, she might have felt that way forever. She might have lived her life as the Madame Bovary of the Lake Shore Country Club, married to one of those teenaged boys with middle-aged minds she'd known as an adolescent, fantasizing about a liaison with some intellectual at the University of Chicago, a place which sounded like a hotbed of romantic radicalism from the vantage point of the suburbs.

But Lena Spiegel, entrapped by her own life, had a reserve of canny strength she rarely displayed. She wanted her daughter to acquire the independence she had craved. So she encouraged Polly to go to college—not to Northwestern, where she'd retain her old ties, but to school in the East, where she would be as far away from family and friends as possible. Polly chose Sarah Lawrence, a place where she found teachers and classmates whose radical ideas would have made her father apoplectic if he had been curious enough to ask about her education. At first, most of the sophisticated girls at the school felt a sort of protective contempt for the plump Midwesterner "who always had a smile like a Cheshire cat," as Edna Lerner, who would become her closest friend in later life, describes her. But she was changing, more rapidly than anyone realized.

It was the Depression, after all. Her brother John, who was at Dartmouth, became so upset at the disparity between the wealth the Spiegels had seen in their world and the poverty that existed in most of America, that he began a flirtation with the political left. He went on a student tour of the Soviet Union, and came back impressed.

Polly, who respected him more than anyone else, agreed with his ideas. Then both of them were stunned when their cousins, the Strauses, lost their entire fortune when their vast real estate bond business failed. They had left scores of thousands of investors penniless. One member of the family had committed suicide. So, soon, Polly became half convinced that wealth was pernicious. She became completely convinced that it was perishable. She began to define herself as a Socialist.

She fantasized about volunteering to serve as a nurse for the left-wing Loyalist forces in the Spanish Civil War. Instead, she became a graduate student in sociology at the University of Chicago. As she entered a social milieu she liked, she learned how to stay thin, how to dress well, how to carry herself with poise. Suddenly she was extremely attractive to men. She began to date artists, left-wing professors, labor organizers. She picketed with striking workers at Republic Steel in Gary, Indiana.

By the time she met Lou Cowan, she had acquired a set of friends, of social and aesthetic ideals, and a degree of self-confidence that allowed her to articulate the values which separated her from Modie Spiegel and his world.

She saw Lou through the lens of her fantasies, just as he saw her through the lens of his. She loved the easy way he moved through places like the Aragon and Trianon ballrooms—places that seemed charmingly low-life from her suburban point of view. In those days, he radiated enormous self-confidence—and that, combined with his obvious adoration of her, gave her an extra shot of the self-esteem she needed so desperately. Besides, he was idealistic about his business—something that made him seem like a contrast to the money-minded merchants she had known at the club. He was convinced that radio would make America a better nation. Her cause-oriented nature responded to his idealism.

He was a half-German-Jewish businessman who hung out in raffish places; different enough from her parents to feed her rebellious fantasies, similar enough to them to let her feel secure. From her point of view, he was a safe risk.

But he also had Eastern European roots—and, in spite of her fondly disparaging remarks about his overprotective "Jewish mother's" instincts, in spite of her inability to comprehend traits like his aversion to pork, she was secretly proud that she'd married someone with that background. But the subtle difference between my parents complicated their relationship in ways that neither of them quite defined. For Lou was fleeing from the shul, not the country club; from Jake Cohen's brand of Orthodoxy, not from the Jewish world. When he met Polly he still fasted every Yom Kippur. Until they married, he had always assumed that he would live his private life in a predominantly Jewish environment and conduct his business in an assimilated one.

That reveals something about my parents' disagreement about Modie Spiegel—a disagreement whose themes would echo through their marriage. Polly saw her father as a sort of Jewish Babbit; she saw Lake Shore Country Club as Gopher Falls. But Lou, who was usually more tolerant than she was about human nature, saw him from the vantage point of his own experiences, his own needs. For the loud, coarse man might rail against kikes, belittle his wife, extol the virtues of his new universalist creed, the Unity religion, which he and Lena both adopted after they left the Christian Science Church. ("He loved Jesus Christ, but he saw him as the greatest Jew who ever lived," says his son, Modie, Jr.) But then he'd reveal the vulnerable core of his true, conflicted self by making out a huge check to Jewish charities or taking a highly visible role as the Anti-Defamation League's main fighter against corporate anti-Semitism. There was a frightened love behind those Yiddish words he used at the dinner table, behind his decision to leave Zezmo Gelspiel's picture hanging in the dining room. Inside that corporate magnate, there was a lonely little Yid struggling vainly to get free. Didn't Lou harbor some of those same feelings? He accepted Modie Spiegel as an easily recognizable businessman, whose wealth was inviting, whose outrageous personality was gloriously familiar.

In 1942, three years after their wedding, Lou became Director of Domestic Affairs for the Office of War Information (OWI), and moved the entire family to New York. Now he was even farther away from Michigan Avenue than he'd seemed to be after he married Polly. His new OWI world consisted of famous playwrights like Robert Sherwood, famous newscasters like Elmer Davis. He hob-nobbed easily with media executives who were serving the government as dollar-a-year men during the war. Once or twice he ate at the White House and rode with President Roosevelt in his private limousine.

After the war, he decided to stay in New York, the media capital of America. So, suddenly, Polly's dispute with the Spiegels and his dispute with the Cohens were half a continent away. Half a continent and a new, exciting set of friends; an immense distance between my parents and their strange, unhappy childhoods.

Now they were able to choose their social milieu, their home, their work, their children's schools, even their own version of their life histories without the encumbrances of parents, relatives, or old friends. They were New York-based Cowans now, not a Cohen and a Spiegel from two separate strata of Chicago's Jewish milieu. To all

outward appearances they had transcended their pasts. And, for
years, these two very different people portrayed themselves as an
indissoluble, interchangeable unit. Certainly, growing up, I saw
them as Polly and Lou Cowan, an almost ideally harmonious couple whose backgrounds, ideas, and values complemented each
other perfectly.

Still, their differences did crop up in small ways—often over
issues that related to wealth or Jewishness. For example, the Century
Country Club is New York's more cosmopolitan version of the Lake
Shore Country Club. Lou joined it as soon as he moved to the city.
The place filled him with the same pleasant sense of professional
achievement and cultural comfort that he felt at the Spiegels' house.
Besides, it represented the level of Jewish life that Tillie Smitz had always wanted him to reach. *His* children would certainly make useful contacts there. The club, of course, reminded Polly of the life she
was fleeing. But she was very nervous about settling in New York.
Her husband had found his interesting world at work. How would
she become friends with the sophisticated intellectuals who lived in
the city—especially since she was determined to remain herself, not
become Lou's appendage? That question, with its undercurrent of
the self-doubt that had been such a strong reflex when she was a
child, haunted her so much that she did spend some time at Century,
the one culture whose cues she knew by heart.

But within a few years she overcame her shyness and began to
spend time with people she met through her liberal political work,
through Lou's television business, through the parents of our
friends at the Dalton School. At last, her living room was filled with
writers, politicians, actors, not the merchants she had known at
Century. She refused to spend time at the club. Instead, she organized our weekends around concerts, the ballet, visits to museums.
Those activities seemed to bore her as much as they bored us, but
she was convinced that when we were older we'd need the culture
they furnished more than we'd need the friends we made at Century. Lou acquiesced to her wishes. I assumed he agreed with them.

But Geoff reflected Lou's instincts far more clearly than I could.
Geoff liked the club; in grade school he enjoyed the weekends he

spent with classmates who belonged. Once, as a teenager, he drove there to visit a friend who was a tennis pro. He mentioned the visit to Polly. Although she didn't forbid him to return, she questioned his taste in friends. She made him feel that by associating with the bankers and businessmen who belonged, he would absorb their mercantile taste and indifference to books.

In his mid-teens Geoff decided to satisfy her desire that he be part of the intelligentsia by severing those old ties. He never went back to Century. Nor did anyone else in our family.

It was only after my father died that I discovered he had retained a lifetime membership in the club.

5

My parents' disagreement over the Century Country Club was a minor one, but it augured conflicts which reverberated through their marriage, influencing all of us. The conflict burst forth during my father's season of triumph and torment—during the years when he produced "The $64,000 Question"; then, when as president of CBS-TV he became one of the most powerful, respected people in the media; and finally, when he was forced to resign once the quiz-show scandals broke.

"The $64,000 Question" and the quiz-show scandals that followed represented a watershed in my family's life. Before it, we were a corporate American family. Afterward, we were an increasingly Jewish one.

It is necessary to see the program in the context of its time. For the seed of "The $64,000 Question" began to sprout in the mid-fifties, at the height of Senator Joseph McCarthy's powers, when America's entire cerebral cortex was clogged with intolerance and fear. Of course, my parents and their friends hated McCarthy. Our dinner table was always a forum where we'd play unusual games—sometimes games my father was thinking of putting on TV—or discuss political or cultural ideas. In those years, my parents and their friends talked about the red scare almost every night. Polly usually focused on the climate of repression that had sent so many people she knew to exile or jail. She did so with her usual infectious bravado, since she always professed to be insulted that her activities in the thirties (the petitions she signed, the picket lines she had marched on) hadn't placed her on any black-list. From my point of view, she made the blacklist sound like a scroll of honor.

Lou, who had been a Republican until long after he met Polly Spiegel, talked about the repression too, though he had no reason to be personally worried. He was acutely aware of the anti-Communist publication *Red Channels,* with its power to blacklist actors and producers by innuendo alone, and saddened by his inability to fight it effectively. But he was also troubled and angered by America's growing contempt for the intelligentsia, by the attitude that prompted magazines like *Time* to dismiss thoughtful people as "eggheads."

McCarthyism was a family obsession. I remember the Sunday afternoons when we would all gather in the study, close the door tightly, turn on the phonograph, and listen gleefully to a bootlegged Canadian parody of the junior senator from Wisconsin, a record called *The Investigator.* In eighth grade, I would usually skip the baseball game or poker game my classmates had organized, to come home and watch the Army vs. McCarthy hearings with my mother. Each time Henry Jackson or Stuart Symington spoke out against McCarthy, I felt as if I were watching the cavalry rescuing the good guys.

For years, Lou wondered how to combat the atmosphere of repression in a practical way; how to invent a TV show that would make knowledge respectable again. His Chicago childhood—in which his grandfather, the scrap-iron dealer, was the most learned person he knew—had shown him that ordinary people everywhere possessed great storehouses of knowledge. By the 1950s, Americans were no longer satisfied with the intense competition over information which had made "The Quiz Kids"—and its adult equivalent, "Information, Please!"—seem like the World Series of facts. They wanted to witness battles for lavish prizes, like those that had been offered to people who could name the mystery melody on "Stop the Music," another of Lou's hit shows.

Once he had put the old radio show, "The $64 Question," in the workshop of his mind, he had the formula: a program where marines, housewives, school kids, cops would display their expertise in such subjects as cooking or Shakespeare or spelling. Their appetite for knowledge would have far more impact on the people Lou Cohen had seen at those vaudeville shows he'd attended with Jake, on the people who had danced at the Aragon Ballroom or skated at the Riverside Roller Rink, than would a college professor's or a movie star's. Besides, nothing could be quite so suspenseful as watching Gino Prato, an Italian-born shoemaker, the first contestant who became famous on the show, standing in an isolation booth week after week, trying to decide whether to answer increasingly difficult questions about opera for increasingly large sums of money. It was information made dramatic.

From the start, Polly hated the premise of the program. In dinner-table conversations, she would remind Lou that there was a difference between ideas and information. She didn't think that people should be awarded huge sums of money because they were mental gymnasts. Could they conceptualize? she always asked. That was the real issue. She was convinced that the show would commercialize—and therefore debase—the very intellectual life he wanted to rescue.

In those days, Lou had his own independent production company, packaging and selling his programs to whichever network was the highest bidder. Polly worked there, too, producing her own shows, and she had some very close friends at his office. But she distrusted some of his colleagues in a way that Lou could never mistrust anyone in the corporate world. She felt a profound suspicion for some of the sponsors with whom he would have to deal. She had seen enough of big money in her childhood to be sure that, at some point, her husband's faith in people would prove naïve, that people would corrupt a show like "The $64,000 Question" in order to enrich themselves.

My parents' disagreement was reflected in their work. In those years, Polly was producing an elegantly witty television show called "Down You Go," and a radio program called "Conversation," an award-winning attempt to get writers, show-business people, college professors, to discuss lively subjects. "Conversation" was a salon of the air; an attempt to bring good talk to an audience that was starved for it.

I remember going to the studio with her and watching her absorption with every last detail of her job. She became very excited when she talked with her co-producers; she loved conceptualizing topics, deciding which famous people would be interesting enough, witty enough, compatible enough, to converse with a verve that would engage listeners. She got as much satisfaction from a good mix of guests as Lou did from choosing the first contestants for "The $64,000 Question." And she loved the actual process of editing tape: of taking notes on each segment of the show, of working with technicians to cut the tape into small plastic strips, and splicing the strips into tape again so that the words that emerged on the radio would be more intelligent, less jumbled, than those she heard in the studio.

So, when she argued with her husband, it was as one professional to another: it was a practical discussion about work they shared, not an ideological debate over cultural abstractions.

Plainly, they both were right. "Conversation" was a marvelous show for a small audience. "The $64,000 Question" was a national sensation. "Conversation" stimulated good talk. "The $64,000 Question" helped reawaken a nation's appetite to learn.

Until "The $64,000 Question" went on the air, Polly and Lou could work in the same office, venting their disagreements through programs that were, in fact, complementary. But by 1955 Lou was becoming emotionally exhausted with his job as president of an independent production company. It was a precarious way of life—more precarious than working for a network. For example, right after World War II, he took the money he had made from "The Quiz Kids," raised more from his friends, and dedicated himself to producing quality shows like "The Fighting Senator," where a principled populist politician, a state senator, battled corruption in episode after episode. But those programs didn't make any money. He wished he owned the business outright, since he worried constantly about protecting his stockholders' investments. Indeed, he used to convey that concern to Geoff and me by repeating the advice Tillie Smitz had implanted in his consciousness. "Own your own business," she had said, "even if it's an apple stand. Always be independent."

Lou was about a month away from bankruptcy when a producer named Mark Goodson brought him the idea for "Stop the Music." The program made him a great deal of money, but it was a far cry from "The Fighting Senator," the kind of quality show he'd hoped to produce. Secretly, he felt it was much too gimmicky. And he always felt somewhat guilty because the astronomical ratings of "Stop the Music" had knocked its competitor, Fred Allen, Lou's favorite comedian, off the air. What's more, Lou hated being typecast as a quizmaster, a man with a knack for devising games and gimmicks, rather than a communicator, a purveyor of ideas. Sometimes he toyed with the notion of indulging his limitless appetite for books and ideas by becoming a college professor or a book publisher. But that was only a fantasy. In reality, his business was becoming successful. That satisfied his ambition and his intense desire to provide his four children with the economic stability, the business connections, that he had missed so much as Jake Cohen's child.

"The $64,000 Question" was a synthesis of his intellectual tastes and his show-business talents. And, once he had created it, it promised to become his pathway to freedom. It would let him pay off his stockholders to whom he had always felt obliged, and make his business permanently solvent. When he realized that, he approached CBS and asked for a job where he could do creative programming for the network. He thought that, as one of the most successful, imaginative producers in the business, he could develop his own ideas without always having to peddle programs from network to network. He thought he could live a freelance life within a corporate structure.

Even before "The $64,000 Question" went on the air, CBS-TV offered Louis G. Cowan the job he wanted—vice president in charge of Creative Services.

Polly and most of his closest associates begged him to turn the offer down. They reminded him that the network was full of ambitious, backbiting corporate climbers. Lou Cowan, with his dislike of confrontation, with the compulsive integrity that made him feel like a sinner if he talked behind someone's back, would never survive in that atmosphere, they warned. But he refused to listen to them—or to the inner voice Tillie Smitz had drilled into his consciousness. He refused to recognize that CBS-TV could never be his own apple stand.

Six weeks after "The $64,000 Question" went on the air—just as it was beginning to achieve its spectacular success—he left his company to join CBS.

At the time he went there, the network was the most respected, tasteful place in the business—the *New York Times* of TV. Its symbol was its president, William Paley, a Jew from Maxwell Street in Chicago who now lived at the pinnacle of society and seemed to combine business genius with exquisite taste in art and fashion. I think the chance to enter Paley's rarefied world must have represented the final step of Louis Cohen's effort to leave his father's house, to become Louis G. Cowan—a quest he couldn't describe to anyone, even to his wife, even to himself.

The job promised complete, unquestioned admission into the world of the corporate elite, where company-hired chauffeurs drove you to and from work; where headwaiters treated you as if you were American royalty; where you could get tickets to any show, any ball game, spend a day at any country club you pleased; where you were identified with sober crusading journalists like Edward R. Murrow; where you commanded the respect of superstars like Red Skelton and Lucille Ball, and had immense power over their careers.

Besides, for Louis G. Cowan, the exemplary citizen, CBS's offer sounded like an idealist's dream come true: vice president in charge of Creative Services. In the end, that often meant he had to get up at six or seven every morning to work on "Captain Kangaroo." Still, in theory, it sounded as if he could continue to whet America's appetite for knowledge by dreaming up shows like "The

$64,000 Question." He could use the propaganda skills he had honed during World War II to awaken America from its McCarthy-induced lethargy by turning public-affairs programs into spectacles that would reach millions.

Lou must have done the job remarkably well. For, two years later, he was made president of CBS-TV. His only superiors were Frank Stanton, president of the corporation, and William Paley, chairman of the board.

Polly admired him, but she was more depressed than ever. She wondered whether he was changing—certainly sometimes her perception of him seemed to be changing. Nearly twenty years earlier she had fallen in love with a resolutely independent, glowingly self-confident Jewish intellectual, who seemed able to help her escape the merchants and bankers she'd known at Lake Shore, the people who had seemed so stuffy, so bigoted, so decadent, when she was growing up. Now, the intellectual had become an executive of a giant corporation—much bigger than Spiegel's—whose owners were getting rich in very much the same way her father had! They were peddling carefully packaged American products and dreams over the TV screen, just as Modie Spiegel had peddled clothes and household appliances through the mail-order catalogue that reached millions of homes across America.

Of course, Polly benefited from her husband's job. She liked some of the glamorous parties, the exciting trips, the instant recognition that came with the vast territory her husband had conquered. And she was proud of him, especially when her respect for his decency and creativity was reinforced by admiring feature stories in magazines like *Esquire*—stories which asserted that he was one of a kind—a cultivated, generous, honest man in a cutthroat profession.

She continued to produce "Conversation" when Lou went to CBS, but the company she worked for had undergone a transformation. Lou had sold all his stock in it when he went to the network. He had insisted that its name be changed from Louis G. Cowan Inc. to Entertainment Productions Inc. (EPI). He never talked to his old associates, since he feared there was a conflict of interest involved in even discussing details about the office. He was less attentive to his wife's work than usual.

Meanwhile, Polly felt somewhat violated by his job. Much as she liked the perquisites, she hated being his adjunct. Even more than that, she hated spending her evenings trying to charm sponsors' wives: those women who had no interests outside their homes and their husband's careers. Why wasn't she mingling with the intellectuals whose sparkling company she loved? She felt she had lost something precious.

That feeling intensified when NBC canceled "Conversation," and my parents decided that Polly should stay away from EPI completely, in order to avoid any appearance of impropriety. After a sad year, she combined her social activism and her knowledge of broadcasting by co-producing with Ellen Strauss a radio show named "Call for Action," during which citizens phoned WMCA with complaints about slum housing or bad heating. She worked hard at that show, but it didn't satisfy her as much as producing "Conversation" and "Down You Go" had. She felt that she had no career of her own—no niche from which she could exercise her talents. During these years, she told me, she felt terribly tense and lonely. She was cooped up in the mercantile world she hated, very much as she had been as a child.

At work, Lou was accomplishing some of what he had set out to do—taking calculated gambles with his career in order to help enlighten viewers. He protected public-affairs programming as no network official ever had. Once he convinced CBS to cancel a full Saturday afternoon's worth of commercial shows (with all the revenue from the sponsors) in order to televise a complete United Nations debate over a civil war in Lebanon. It was poor show business judgment. The debate was uneventful. The ratings were microscopic. In the end, his bosses never forgave him for that decision. He remained proud of it all of his life.

As part of his job, Lou had to put programs like "Rawhide" and "The Beverly Hillbillies" on the air. Not only that: he had to be their pitchman. In person or on kinescopes, he had to describe their great qualities to the sponsors who, in effect, ran the entire business. My mother used to tell him that he was promoting escapist trash—and I would echo her charge. A little defensively, he would remind us that working people are tired at the end of the day, that many of them need to escape. He could have reminded us that he was often tired after his twelve hour day, but he would never mention that.

He could never get over his fear that if a quarrel resulted in an intense confrontation, we would reject him. Nor could he overcome the awe he felt at our Jewish WASP social ease, our ability to speak our minds. Sometimes our principles pained him—as they did when we applied them to his work—and sometimes they frightened him—as they did when we went South. But he always insisted that the ability to act on our beliefs was the quality he admired most in his wife and in his children.

He regretted the guarded, acquiescent streak in his personality. But it was a reflex—a way of surviving as a child and succeeding as an adult. He couldn't change it. So he maintained a martyred silence in those arguments over television instead of defending himself with an obvious, logical angry remark—the kind of remark Polly would have relished if their roles had been reversed. For as he knew, the truth was that none of us had ever been forced to work day after day. We didn't know anything about the physical exhaustion, the work pressures, that made people need some form of escape.

Still, there was an undercurrent of truth to Polly's argument—or, at least, it defined a problem her husband was reluctant to face. Unlike Modie Spiegel, Lou Cowan wasn't his own boss—and Polly could see the difference. He was always telling us how cultured and brilliant Paley and Stanton were; she thought that the deferential tone in his voice reflected his position as an underling, not his considered judgment. After all, her father and her brother admired people too, but they usually appraised them—as she did—instead of describing them with a note of awe. She wasn't very fond of Paley or Stanton; they seemed very much like the people at Lake Shore. So her face would grow taut when Lou, once so very commanding, came home with stories about executive meetings where he had watched Paley make a decision. How impressed he was that his boss had followed his suggestion to televise the sensational kitchen debate between Richard Nixon and Nikita Khrushchev which took place in the Soviet Union! That night he praised Paley's minimally decent, highly commercial judgment as the work of a great American.

Polly was angry that the husband she'd once been so proud of idolized the corporate executives who awakened all of her childhood pain and disdain. What's more, she had a practical reason to worry about his attitude. For she had an unflinching awareness of how powerful people behaved. She knew, as her husband never would, that from the vantage point of the boardroom everyone is expendable, even those with fancy titles and immaculate public reputations. She tried to tell him he might get hurt. Maybe he was too flush with success and ambition to hear her. Maybe she was too angry at him for taking the job in the first place to express herself with the kind of compassion that would have allowed him to listen. Anyway, he disregarded her warnings.

Louis G. Cowan's success was most visible to us at Christmastime.

Most of the year, the front-hall closet in our apartment was filled with coats. But after Thanksgiving it would suddenly empty. By the beginning of December the presents began to pour in. Within a few weeks we would have a four-foot tall heap of boxes—candy, liquor, cigarettes, expensive perfume, even suitcases and toilet kits. They came from the independent producers, the advertising agencies, the talent agents, the lower-level CBS executives who figured that a twenty- or thirty-dollar investment in a Christmas gift would buy a few hours of Lou Cowan's time later in the year. I remember that, however much I might criticize my father in our arguments about television, however often my mother might speculate about the impermanence of power, I used to feel pride in the evidence of his importance and popularity.

Then, in 1958, NBC developed a quiz program called "Twenty-One," a replica of "The $64,000 Question" that imitated his format to the last dramatic detail of the isolation booth. "Twenty-One" captured the public's attention when a Columbia professor named Charles Van Doren—the sort of contestant my father would have deemed inappropriate—earned $129,000, until he was defeated by Vivian Nearing. While Van Doren was still on the air, a contestant who had lost began to tell reporters that "Twenty-One" was rigged.

The information was accurate. Van Doren had been told the answer to each question. He had been given acting lessons so that he could appear uncertain enough to keep the tension alive. That way, audiences came to identify with Van Doren's personality and with his unfailingly dramatic attempt to win ever-increasing prizes. The program's ratings swelled. More important, the sponsor's product sold. It was a caricature of everything Lou had dreamed of when he conceived "The $64,000 Question." It was worse than anything Polly had feared.

By autumn 1959, Van Doren's improprieties had swelled into the quiz-show scandals, which were headline news for months. As the story unraveled, it turned out that long after my father had left his company and sold his stock, long after it had become Entertainment Productions Inc., two employees had rigged a show called "The $64,000 Challenge," which was patterned after "The $64,000 Question."

There was no legitimate reason Lou should have been implicated. He had gone to work for CBS years earlier and divested himself of all his stock in his former business. When he began to hear rumors about "Twenty-One," he called up one of his former partners and said that he hoped to God nothing like that was going on with Entertainment Productions Inc.'s shows. Lou, who could be quite moralistic, told the man that all the company's employees had to conduct themselves as if they were living in a goldfish bowl. "You have nothing to worry about, Lou," his former associate said. "Your name is like a diamond in the industry and we would never do anything to tarnish it."

Still, once the scandals broke, the facts of Lou's conduct didn't matter much. So far as the industry and much of the public was concerned, Louis G. Cowan was the legendary quizmaster, not Jack Barry or Dan Enright, producers of "Twenty-One."

CBS's response was to protect its corporate image, not its network president, not the truth. They asked Lou Cowan to resign. There was no investigation. There were no allegations of impropriety. The company's officials simply asserted that he was a poor administrator. But the code was clear. Most people assumed that Lou had been fired because his role as the creator of the biggest quiz show of them all made him an embarrassment to the network.

He was asked to resign in November 1959. No one in the industry sent him a Christmas gift that year. Our front hall closet remained a clothes closet through the winter.

The episode had wounded him where he was most vulnerable. It had impugned the integrity that was so precious to him. It threatened to tarnish his good name.

He had become Louis G. Cowan, partly to Americanize himself, partly to disassociate himself from Jacob Cohen's cruelty and his compulsively irresponsible financial behavior. He had risen from Jake's Orthodox background, from his own childhood milieu on Michigan Avenue, to heights that his ambitious grandmother Tillie Smitz couldn't even imagine. But he felt that the name he had chosen, Louis G. Cowan, was inextricably linked with a moral and financial scandal over which he had as little control as he'd had over Jake Cohen's check kiting.

He might have rescued his name from his father's, but he could never, even in the obituary columns, rescue it from Charles Van Doren. After his death, *Newsweek* wrote that he had produced "Twenty-One."

In later years, my father would occasionally make an angry remark about Jake Cohen. But his real wrath was directed at corporate television. He retained many friends in the media, in politics, in business, but still the tycoons who had flattered him and then discarded him replaced his father as his real villains. Those men, who had sculpted the myths that governed his life for so long, had once been his idols. But, in the wake of the quiz-show scandals, they seemed more frightened, less loyal, more personally corrupt, than the *schnorrers* in Jake Cohen's shul.

In retrospect, it is clear that Lou's departure from CBS represented a release from a corporate prison, not an exile from a magnate's kingdom. At last, he and Polly were able to enjoy their work, their friendships, their relationships with their children—they were free to write the scripts of their own lives, not perform roles in a corporate drama that someone else had composed. That freedom never filled Polly with the same contentment that Lou seemed to feel toward the end of his life. In fact, the differences between those two people—whom I'd always seen as an inextricable unit: my parents—proved very important to me when they died and I began to reflect on the very different psychological legacies they had left me.

If Louis G. Cowan had possessed a driven, thick-skinned magnate's personality he would have made a comeback in the media in a very few years. After all, at some point in their careers many business people are tainted with a serious malfeasance—price-rigging or bribery or putting an unsafe product on the market. They usually ride out the storm of controversy. Even if my father had been involved, rigging a TV show is a relatively minor matter in comparison with those things.

But he was much too hurt by the innuendos about him to return to the industry that seemed to treat gossip as gospel. He could have returned. By the mid-1970s, most of the producers who had actually rigged programs had made comebacks. Many had game shows back on the air. By then Lou could no longer imagine himself working with them or pursuing their way of life.

The painful realization that his name had been tarnished by events beyond his control forced Lou to face himself for the first time in his adult life. He had plenty of time to do that. Until November 1959, he had worked twelve hours a day, six days a week. Now he had vast blank spaces on his calendar. He didn't like to go out. Most of the public knew the outlines of the scandal, not the details, and many people thought "The $64,000 Question" was involved. He hated to keep explaining himself. He hated the thought that there were people who thought he had been involved in wrongdoing. But during the winter and spring of 1960, Geoff and I were away at school, Polly was traveling in Asia with her college friend Edna Lerner; Holly and Liza were involved with their social lives and their school work. So, at the age of fifty, Lou was alone and idle in his huge apartment. He'd sit up past midnight, in the small study where we all used to listen to *The Investigator,* sipping scotch, musing about his life.

Ever since he produced "Stop the Music," he had toyed with the idea of leaving the media. And he took breaks whenever he could. For example, in 1952, he had served as adviser to Adlai Stevenson, the Democratic Party's candidate for President, and he loved the job as he'd never loved his work in TV. In the late 1950s he was very active on the boards of National Library Week and National Book Week, and he talked about those activities with more enthusiasm than he did CBS. Before the quiz-show scandals broke, he had agreed to give a six-week course on American television at an annual seminar in Salzburg, Austria, and he saw that attractive task as a time when he and Polly would pause to think about the rest of their lives.

Now, of course, CBS had forced him to pause—and inadvertently allowed him to heed his deepest impulses and leave the entertainment world altogether. His decisions about his career suggest that Lou Cohen the rav's descendant, Moses Cohen's grandson, always inhabited a large part of Louis G. Cowan's mind. Once he emerged from the cocoon of silence he had woven around himself, he involved himself with ideas and learning, as a teacher and a book publisher; and, through volunteer work, he became prominent in the Jewish world he had abandoned for nearly thirty years.

In 1962 he took a job as professor of communications at Brandeis—one of the few specifically Jewish colleges in America. He stayed there, teaching classes and raising funds, until the mid-1960s, when a cancer operation restricted his travel. Then he accepted a post at the Columbia University School of Journalism where he taught a course in Media Management.

In both places, he revealed a great teacher's passion for his students. He used to spend hours in his study, scanning the seven or eight newspapers and magazines he read every day, making notes to himself on small scraps of paper, in preparation for each week's seminar on media management. Usually he'd invite some prominent media executive as a guest, so that his class could see how news is really gathered, how decisions are really made in the corporate world he had once inhabited. He'd spend hours talking with his students, at school and at home, showing them passages from books, citing episodes from his career, listening to their questions, their dreams. When his students were about to graduate, he would spend a great deal of time phoning media executives throughout America to find them jobs. They would write him, phone him, visit him long after they left school, asking for the advice that he was eager to give. In the classroom, he was the mitzvah man Jake Cohen had always wanted to become. Most of his students trace their media lineage back to him.

During those years he set up a small book-publishing company, the Chilmark Press, and published books that were so difficult, so specialized, that even his intellectual friends rarely read them. Indeed, I always thought of Chilmark as his way of atoning for the emphasis on money which, he now believed, was the corruption at the core of the quiz-show scandals.

And, he became increasingly involved with the American Jewish Committee. Back in Chicago, his high school and college classmates felt a wry sense of surprise that the friend who had left them so long ago, who had assimilated with such apparent ease, was now so publicly identified as a Jew.

He was passionate about his work. He helped establish an oral history of Jews in America. When he raised money for it, he usually gave an intensely earnest, enthusiastic speech about the importance of preserving every scrap of Jewish life in this country. He'd cajole prominent friends into being subjects. He drew up the question- naires for the study and worked hard to find the right interviewer for each interviewee. He spent a day or two each week at the Commit- tee, and kept phoning his co-workers with new suggestions when- ever he couldn't see them face to face.

Once, when he was helping to raise money for an oral history of the Holocaust, he convened a meeting with a sentence I can barely imagine his uttering: "In a sense, we are all survivors," he said. He met with Israeli officials to suggest ways of explaining their policies to the American public. Sometimes he would be among the most hard-line, uncompromising American Jews in the room, insisting that Israel emphasize its own self-interest, its own point of view, in- stead of concocting the bland, half-true justifications for controver- sial policies that Americans might want to hear. When he took positions like that, he'd go back to the oral-history office, describe the arguments to his friend Selma Hirsch, Associate Director of the American Jewish Committee, and laughingly ascribe his rather hawkish positions to the fact that most of his colleagues were Ger- man Jews, afraid of offending America's sensibilities. That was not the kind of remark he was likely to make at home.

Clearly, the Committee helped him feel a link to his childhood. It was a place where he could recover the Judaism he had left be- hind without re-examining the specific details that had caused him such pain. And it was a place where he could share his joy at his children's turn toward Judaism in a way he never quite dared do with my mother, or even with us.

When I was writing my *Voice* article "Jews Without Money, Re- visited," Ann Wolf, a social-welfare consultant for the Committee, had just published a report which provided the statistical basis for my journalistic impressions. Somehow my father had the idea that Ann had inspired me to write the article.

After he died, she told me that one day he saw her in an eleva- tor at the Committee and said, simply, "Thank you for making a Jew of my son."

Soon after that article was published, I visited the Munkaczer tallis factory on the Lower East Side and told my father about the conversation there. That was when he began to lay the ground-work for the article on Orthodox craftsmen that would eventually take me into the world of 5743.

After my father died, Selma Hirsch told me he had discussed the prospective article with her. He told her—as he had never told me—that he hoped it would deepen my knowledge of Jewish life and secure my bonds to the Jewish community.

The oral history project would take Jewish lives and let them reverberate back and forth through time. My father's interest in Judaism would reverberate through the Cowan family, intertwin-ing with Holly's active involvement in the religion, fortifying the impulse that had taken Geoff to Israel before any of the rest of us thought of going, strengthening the instinct that had prompted Liza to study Hebrew when she was a senior in high school in 1966 and for most of the next year. So there must have been to-tally unexpected moments when my father was filled with the proud, startling feeling that he had been true to his past. Some-how he and my mother had fulfilled an important commandment: they had kept their offspring within the mysterious, unbroken chain of Jewish history.

Polly became more openly Jewish in those years, too. Though she never cared much for ceremony, in 1970 she encouraged Rachel and Holly and me to have our first seder—Arthur Waskow's very secular Freedom Seder—and she followed our intensifying re-ligious involvement with a detached, bemused fascination. Always a philanthropist, she was giving her largest donation to the United Jewish Appeal by the 1970s. In fact, her feelings about Israel as a vital, precarious symbol of Jewish survival were deeper than I imagined, even when I thought about her lifelong obsession with the Holocaust. After she died, Liza found a letter from her former psychoanalyst, her closest confidante, that was written after the 1973 Yom Kippur War. The analyst quotes some phrases from my mother's letter. "They will kill all the Jews," Polly had written. "Israel will be abandoned." Polly never mentioned those apocalyptic sentiments to any of us. The connection between Israel's survival and her own must have been an utterly reflexive emotion that she was embarrassed to discuss. Did it stretch back past the Yom Kippur War, past the Holocaust, to the loneliness and the fear she felt as the only Jew in Kenilworth? She taught us to be proud of our Jewishness. But was Jewishness secretly a source of terror for her?

Certainly, she could not act out her feelings in a specifically Jewish arena, as my father could. Her past had made her feel that the religion contained proud, prophetic ideals, but that people who identified with it directly were somewhat alien. Of course, she didn't like the merchants she had known as a child. What's more, despite herself she had inherited some of her father's bias against Eastern European Jews, "Jewish Jews," unless she knew them well or they had acquired the kind of cosmopolitanism and intellectual status she loved. So she felt far more comfortable with her friends in the civil-rights movement than with the people Lou was meeting as he got involved in organized Jewish life; more at home in Jackson, Mississippi, than in Forest Hills, Queens.

But she remained true to her own version of Judaism. It was the vision that had first inspired her children: the visceral sense of justice that had prompted her to risk her life during those Wednesdays in Mississippi.

She stayed in the civil-rights movement until she died—for more than a decade after I, like many of the self-proclaimed radicals I knew, had left it for other causes. She was the only white woman on the board of the National Council of Negro Women. She interested herself in detailed work, as she had when she produced "Conversation"—she helped establish a day care center in Mississippi; she worked for a drug rehabilitation program in New York; she spent almost as much time preparing questions for an oral history of Dorothy Height as my father did preparing his notes for his classes; she became the National Council of Negro Women's delegate to the United Nations, where she campaigned constantly on behalf of blacks in southern Africa.

Of course she felt uneasy with the polarization that had beset the movement—with slogans like "black power," which often communicated strong anti-white feelings; indeed, the polarization was more painful to her than to most people, since it affected her daily, as the only white official of a black organization. But her loyalty to black allies like Dorothy Height remained unshakable.

She spent a lot of time chatting about the movement, gossiping about the people she was working with, chuckling proudly over incongruous experiences like her induction into a sorority that had always been all black.

Once in a while she mentioned the fact that in Germany, during the tough times, many Christians, including liberals, had abandoned the Jews. In her stoic way, I think that she retained a deep commitment—almost a spiritual commitment—to the importance of bearing witness to the fact that that needn't happen between blacks and whites in the United States.

One Thursday morning in mid-November 1976, I telephoned my parents to chat. Polly answered the phone. I told her about a reunion of black and white civil-rights workers that Rachel and I had attended in Atlanta, Georgia, the previous weekend. It had been an exuberant, emotional gathering, untainted by the name-calling and guilt-tripping that had begun to divide blacks and whites a decade earlier. My mother was glad to hear about it, particularly because in those first deceptively optimistic weeks of the new Democratic administration it seemed as if the black vote we had helped to register would shape Jimmy Carter's refreshingly liberal, humane social programs. "You know," she said, in a voice that was full of pride in herself and Geoff and Rachel and me, "the movement was really our war. I think we're going to win it." Then she handed the phone over to my father.

That week the *New York Times* had been carrying articles about the protest movement in French-speaking Canada. Lou, fascinated, discussed the problem at length. Maybe, one day, Canada would dissolve as a nation. What would that mean for the United States?

Then I got to the reason for my call. For months, Lou had been asking me if he could attend the Havurah School—the weekly Jewish school which Rachel and I had helped establish, which Lisa, then eight, and Matt, six, both attended. But I had been procrastinating.

In order to conserve gas, my parents had bought a green Volkswagen. But, in keeping with twenty years of habit, they had hired a black chauffeur to drive it. I didn't want my friends on the Upper West Side to see such embarrassing, conspicuous signs of my parents' wealth.

During the past five years, my father had suffered three heart attacks. Two years earlier the doctors had given him six months to live. Rachel, who had spent almost as much time with him in intensive care as I had, began to chide me. "He's a dying man who wants to see his grandchildren get a Jewish education. How can you deny him that?"

That morning I had talked with one of the teachers in the school. We had arranged for him to visit it the next week. He sounded very pleased when I told him the news.

He never did visit the school. He died in the fire that night. Ever since then, those last conversations have echoed in my mind with a particular intensity.

The Havurah School was another link in the historic chain my father had grown so proud of ever since he left CBS-TV. I'm sure his feeling about Judaism intertwined with mine, helping to transform my lifelong obsession about the rift between him and Jake Cohen into a decision to explore the religion that fascinated us both.

The civil-rights movement was a symbol of my mother's dilemma—and mine. It had been a magnificent moment in American history—she and Geoff and Rachel and I spent some of the best years of our lives working in the South. But we were there as the allies of black people. It wasn't our war—not really. Besides, it was over. It had left a void in all of our lives. For me, I think, that void left room for the unexpected feelings about Jews and Judaism that I'd tried to explain to my mother ever since I covered the fight over the low-income housing project in Forest Hills.

I realize now, that in many ways I was her child, more than my father's. I identified with her pain as much as I did with her principles. My years at Choate helped shape my view of her—and me—as quintessential outsiders. She was the only girl in a male-dominated family—the only Jewish family in a gentile town; the daughter of a wealthy merchant, whose possessions may have been the principal reason her friends consented to play with her; the wallflower at the country club; the frightened Midwesterner in New York. She felt no desire to go home again, as my father must have when he became so active at the American Jewish Committee. She had never really had a home in the first place.

Of course, she had moments of great joy. She savored the periods she and Lou spent by themselves. She loved producing "Conversation" and "Down You Go," and organizing Wednesdays in Mississippi. When I was a child, my family had a summer home in Redding, Connecticut, and I remember moments that were almost electric with shared pleasure. She liked teaching her children how to swim and play tennis. I think she must have enjoyed driving us around the back roads of rural Connecticut by day, and watching TV with us by night. For I have happy childhood memories of sitting in the back seat of our Buick while she taught us George M. Cohan's songs and the tunes she and Lou used to dance to when they were courting at the Aragon Ballroom; memories of sitting in our living room with her and Geoff and Holly, watching Milton Berle or Jimmy Durante or one of those television mysteries whose endings she invariably guessed.

But Lou was usually in the city during the summer days we were there. She didn't have much of an independent life, and she talked freely about the sense of isolation she felt there.

In 1960, soon after my father resigned from CBS, my parents sold the house in Redding and bought a much smaller one on Martha's Vineyard, in Chilmark, Massachusetts, which, my mother always told us, was the Jewish part of the island. (She made it clear to me that I'd be unwelcome in Edgartown or West Chop, where the WASPs lived.) Most of our neighbors were writers, academics, Kennedy era government employees; indeed, the few outsiders who had heard of Martha's Vineyard in the early 1960s regarded it as a summertime headquarters for the eastern intelligentsia. My mother experienced it as the first friendly, cohesive community she had ever lived in, the first place where people cared more about her ideas than her income.

In a way, it was her dream world. Her friends were intellectuals who shared her taste for frivolous activities like clamming and antiquing, and for rugged outdoor sports like sailing and surfing. The Vineyard was the only place I ever saw her relax for more than a day or two, the only place she was ever genuinely content. It was the only place that she seemed to feel part of a community that wanted to protect her, that cared about *her,* about her flawed, unfolding life, not about each microscopic detail of her character or her conduct.

But, for most of her life, she seemed to think that even her closest friends were always inspecting each individual frame from the movie of her existence, instead of relaxing with her and enjoying the movie itself.

Through the extraordinary power of her personality, she was able to infuse her children with her bravery and her commitment to underdogs everywhere—and to convince us to see those traits as Judaism. But the more I thought about them the surer I was that they were also rooted in a ceaseless despair. Beneath her dazzling exterior, one could almost always see the frightened little girl who had to sit at the top of the stairs at the Spiegels' house in Kenilworth, Illinois, huddling close to her brother John to get protection from her father's booming voice, knowing that the next day she would have to spend hours in her mother's darkened room, massaging away the inevitable migraine headache.

Her secular messianism—the kind of Judaism that shaped her beliefs—was a lonely faith. It demanded immense courage, for she had to overcome her own fears, her own innate sense of inadequacy, as well as take risks in the world. But, in her case at least, it was also intertwined with the isolation she seemed to feel among the scores of people who loved her.

As I thought about that creed, which had shaped me too, I became convinced that my own need to understand my past, to cease feeling like an orphan in history, to overcome my own recurrent feeling that I was an outsider wherever I went, was so deep that I had to find some version of the cohesive, communal Judaism that my father was beginning to rediscover.

I think now, that in his uncannily sensitive, nurturing way, my father sensed that I needed what my mother had never had and what he'd missed for so much of his life—and he thought that I'd see it if I would heed his advice and risk embarking on a voyage into the Jewish tradition.

———◆———

PART TWO

6

I was not the kind of son who accepted his parents' advice readily. And I was particularly stubborn when it came to my father's wishes. So far, I have described his career as a busy, powerful television executive without emphasizing the complexities of being his son. I often felt overshadowed by him, and worried that I would never achieve a similar success on my own. Since he could be such a loving parent, I often felt quite hurt when he became so involved with his work that he seemed to vanish from the family for months at a time. Indeed, my response to the quiz-show scandal was much more ambivalent than I dared recognize back then. My father's pain was a terrible thing to see. But it made him depend on his family in a way he had never had to before. At last, when I was in college, the intimacy I had always wanted was necessary for him, too. As he recreated himself into a person who felt free to explore all his broad interests—and his children's interests, too—our relationship kept enriching itself. We became increasingly close during the last fifteen years of his life.

Nevertheless, I almost always felt I had to resist his suggestions in order to remain my own person. For example, he was very careful about protecting the money he earned. He thought I had a responsibility to adopt his attitude—and learn to earn more—by taking college courses in business and economics. I refused to do that. With his reverence for education, he felt deeply that I should get a Ph.D.—a "doctorate," as he'd say with a touch of awe in his voice—but I balked at that, too: I insisted that I could learn more in the world than in academia. When I traveled, he always urged me to mingle with his powerful friends. Though I occasionally did, I usually avoided telephoning those friends in order to keep some distance from him. A fastidious dresser, he was very uncomfortable with my inexpensive clothes and my sloppy way of wearing them. He had what I thought were conventional ideas about my career. When I decided to become a journalist, he urged me to go to work for the *New York Times.* He was puzzled and a little saddened when I took a job with the *Voice,* which he regarded as a left-wing counter-cultural newspaper that would be a professional dead end.

When he had his first heart attack in 1971, I began to visit him or phone him nearly every day I was in New York, and to rent a house that was near my parents' home on Martha's Vineyard. I paid more attention to my father than to my mother, since I always feared he was about to die and figured that, with her excellent health, she'd be vigorous until she was eighty. So the bond between us grew very deep. But I still resisted most of his professional ideas. For instance, in 1973 he saw, prophetically, that oil would become a central issue in world politics and he wanted me to learn as much as possible about it. But the information was too technical for my tastes. And, of course, I was so reluctant to write about Orthodox Jewish craftsmen that the subject became a slightly painful joke between us.

Nevertheless, after he died, that was the request that meant the most to me. By contrast, Geoff, my closest childhood friend, had few of my disagreements with my father. Geoff went to law school, and became a highly respected public-interest communications lawyer and an academician, teaching law at UCLA. Geoff built my father a very different kind of memorial by reviving "The Quiz Kids" on TV. Holly, who shares my involvement with Judaism, transformed her interest in my father's role at the Office of War Information into a Ph.D. thesis about the OWI's overseas propaganda in the period of World War II. Liza, as rebellious as I, has been in publishing and broadcasting for most of her adult life. Now Liza is president of the Chamber of Commerce of her adopted home of Woodstock, New York—how Lou would have loved that!

When I reflect on those paradoxes, I realize that I have to re-examine my own past to understand why I instinctively regarded my father's Judaism as his most important legacy, and why the religion literally reshaped my life.

Of course, at Choate most of my life was defined by the fact that I was a Jew. If I'd gone to a private school in the city, I'd have remained within the protective, tolerant environment that might have allowed me to feel comfortable with my ethnic identity. I'm sure that the intensity of the anti-Semitism I encountered at prep school made me a more driven, introspective, lonely person than I would have been if I'd stayed at home. Certainly, it furnished me with an intense desire to study as hard as possible so that I could get into Harvard, the college I equated with freedom from bigotry.

I never encountered any prejudice there. In some ways I loved the college. But there was no way it could help me resolve the questions that had become so urgent at Choate.

I could forget them for long periods of time. At the *Crimson,* the college newspaper which I joined as a freshman, one's ethnic background didn't seem to matter at all. For four years, that building seemed to be my real home. I loved the sensation of walking through Harvard Yard during Cambridge's soft, sweet spring, then turning down the narrow, shady Plympton Street, which always reminded me of the thinkers I idolized, men like William James and George Santayana, and entering the *Crimson* building, with its acrid smell of newsprint, so alien to the academic world. Often I would stay in the building, talking with anyone who happened to be around, until two or three in the morning, when the paper went to press. I felt as if midnight America was alive with great ideas, wonderful possibilities.

But I could never find the same excitement in the classroom. I had decided to major in American history and literature. I chose that subject, I suppose, because I thought it would enable me to read past the confines of my protected background and discover the pulsating America I'd imagined as a boy when I sat in my room, daydreaming over writers like John Dos Passos or John Steinbeck.

And, of course, I wanted to learn as much as possible about immigrants in America so that I could understand myself as the grandson of a wealthy Jewish mail-order magnate and an impoverished Jewish used-cement-bag dealer.

But Harvard's History and Literature Department was dominated by brilliant professors like Perry Miller, Bernard Bailyn, and Alan Heimert, whose passion was for Puritan New England. So I spent a great deal of time reading theologians like Jonathan Edwards and Cotton Mather, whose ideas were too dense for me. Those studies didn't quite satisfy me. Where, I'd sometimes wonder, were the Cohens and the Spiegels when the New England divines were writing their books? Then I'd forget those questions and begin to muse lovingly, almost reverently, about the New England towns that produced those puzzling thinkers. I would blame myself for my inability to grasp the essence of the world whose promise seemed to shimmer so beautifully through my courses.

In the spring of 1961, I flunked an exam that would have enabled me to write an honors thesis. In reality, it was a minor failure—I was spending most of my time at the *Crimson* building, where I was the editor of a weekly magazine—but I felt as if I'd been ex-communicated from Harvard, my secular church. But I also had the strangely exhilarated feeling that I'd received a summons to leave the world I had always known, and roam as freely as possible. So I decided to drop out of college until I'd found a way of acquiring the courage and the wisdom to use books and experiences in a way that would let me find myself, my history, my country.

I remember, in my junior year at Harvard, during the same month I was studying for the exam I flunked, I read Norman Mailer's work of fiction, "The Time of Her Time," in which a twenty-seven-year-old blond Irish-Catholic bullfighting teacher gives a nineteen-year-old Jewish undergraduate at NYU a degree of sexual pleasure that her twenty-one-year-old boyfriend, Arthur, can't provide. Arthur, a Jew, is "too passive," according to the story. In those days, Mailer's prose had an enormous influence on me. I identified with Arthur in a very frightened way. For the vignette from "The

Time of Her Time" gave a specific emotional cast to the memories of Choate that still tormented me. Passive Jews. Jews who don't fight back. Womanly men who can't make love as well as manly gentiles. Who are paralyzed with self-doubt and fear. Who go to the gas chambers passively. Passive. That was the word that defined me. I had to change somehow.

I realized that year that I could only change myself—and my image of myself—among the bravest of my own people: the Jews who lived in Israel.

Within weeks of my arrival there, an explosion had taken place in my consciousness. I could never have imagined the new ways, woven into details that most Israelis take for granted, that I learned to obtain the sense of identity, the sense of pride, that I had sought throughout my adolescence. My name, for example. Maagan Michael, the kibbutz to which I'd been assigned, was a completely secular place. But Paul Cowan wasn't a fit name for a Jewish worker. Within an hour of arriving I was told that I'd be called Saul Cohen on the work sheets that were posted every morning, on my laundry, on the envelopes that contained my subsistance allowance. I kept the name until I returned to America.

I arrived on the kibbutz December 23. I spent all of December 25 working in a chicken yard, next to a middle-aged Polish refugee who had the blue numbers of a concentration camp on his arm, who sang the Yiddish song "Tum Balalaika" all day. "Tum Balalaika" was my *Christmas Carol* in 1961. Back home my father was reading Dickens' book, my family was decorating the tree and opening presents. That juxtaposition was the most abrupt possible reminder that I was a Jew working in a Jewish land.

On one side, kibbutz Maagan Michael was bounded by the Mediterranean Sea. If you walked a few miles down the beach you arrived at Caesarea, where Pontius Pilate once presided. Mount Carmel was just across the highway. It was easy to climb up to a cave that contained the bones of a being who had lived there ten thousand years before. Sometimes when I explored those ruins, I was accompanied by people who had been on the kibbutz for years. Our conversations covered millennia. Standing on the jetty at Caesarea, where the first Crusaders had landed their vessels, we would talk about guns that had been smuggled in on the Mediter- ranean coast during World War II, about the prospect for establish- ing a fishing industry in those waters now.

Those Israelis were comfortable with their identities. They pos- sessed a past they could use, a present they had created, a future they were building. They felt a degree of emotional security as Jews that I had never imagined possible.

One day I took a vacation from the kibbutz and hitchhiked to Tiberias. The man who picked me up had spent all of World War II working with the Haganah, the clandestine Jewish army, to smug- gle immigrants into Palestine. He described his adventures for hours. Then, after nightfall, we arrived in the Galilee and began to drive through its hills. The man, whose young daughter was in the front seat next to him, stopped the car. He took the girl by the hand and, with a flashlight to show the way beneath the Galilean sky, began to wander through a huge meadow. "I have studied the flow- ers of Israel for many years," he said. "Now I know every plant that grows in this country. I came here from Poland, a young boy who knew nothing about crops and cultivation. Now I want to share with my children what I have done, what my country has done."

I longed to feel that emotion, too. Certainly I could never imag- ine my parents speaking to me like that. How could they, when they were so ambivalent about their personal pasts, when they were try- ing to create a richly textured world out of the thin fabric of the present? More to the point, I couldn't imagine myself possessing a sense of place, a deep feeling for a specific culture that I would be so eager to pass on to my children.

Two months later, I drifted down to Beersheba, an immigrant town, Israel's Wild West, where I used my rusty French to teach English to children from North Africa. This wasn't just leaving Christmas behind; it was freeing myself from the all-pervasive stare of Western eyes. Of course, I continued my internal dialogue with America—continued it almost obsessively—but I let it mingle with the completely alien, completely Jewish experiences that were the substance of my daily life.

I loved to watch my students' grandparents, old bearded patriarchs who had spent most of their lives in Tunisia or Morocco, who dressed in long robes, with turbans wrapped around their heads, as they grazed their goats along the shallow valley that set their poor, dry community off from the rest of Beersheba. Near there, it was said, Abraham's tribesmen had dug their first underground homes and lived in the caves for decades. Now, after centuries, their descendants were home from the Diaspora. Israelis called them the desert generation and the meaning of that biblical term was clear. Their bodies had reached the promised land, but in their minds they were forever sealed off from the modern world. While they grazed their sheep, their grandchildren, my students, yearned to possess the motorcycles, television sets, Kodak cameras they saw whenever they walked down Beersheba's streets.

The cultural conflict was devastating. For the Orthodox Judaism that had sustained the North African families for centuries had been battered to bits by Israel's modern, surprisingly secular, society. I could see that conflict in my classroom. The kids, whose grandparents carried holy books along with their shepherd staffs and prayed three times a day, were taught in school by agnostic sabras (native-born Israelis), usually from European families, who had very little respect for the pious faith and patriarchal family structure the North Africans had always known. They regarded the immigrants as backward people, and wanted to turn them into carbon copies of themselves. In turn, older North Africans saw them as paternalistic infidels who were stealing their young.

The older people, whose Zion was the land they had read about in the Torah, had no means of dealing with their children's experiences in the frontier town. What if a kid saw a film like *Pillow Talk*, starring Rock Hudson and Doris Day: something that seemed foolishly cute and tame to sophisticated Westerners, but outrageously licentious to North African immigrants? The visual images—the sleek, suggestive way of dressing, the wealth, the offhand kisses and caresses—took them to the threshold of a world that social class and ancestral conscience deemed off limits. How could they possibly discuss their intimate feelings with their tradition bound parents? Every day, the kids heard records by Elvis Presley and Paul Anka blasting out of Beersheba's storefronts. They were so fascinated by the music—which, of course, had no cultural resonance for them—that I decided to teach them English by translating the lyrics to songs like "Wake Up Little Susie." Still, it was clear that they were utterly bewildered by the culture those songs represented. One of my students told me he would never go to New York City because of the big gorilla that lived on the Empire State Building. I could never convince him that King Kong was an imaginary character.

I spent my nights in Beersheba at a bar called The Last Chance, drinking cognac, listening to Odetta's latest album of spirituals, listening to Nina Simone sing songs from *Porgy and Bess,* chatting with the cocaine addict from France, the wealthy disbarred boxer from South Africa, who were part of the regular clientele.

Betty, lithe and petite, The Last Chance's owner, had written for Albert Camus' newspaper *Combat* during World War II, and had then come to Israel in 1945 to join the anti-British terrorist underground organization, the Stern group. Once, in the early days of Israel's war of independence, she had been arrested in Belgium for hurling a bomb at England's Foreign Minister, Ernest Bevin, who was thought to support the Arabs. She said she was in the room when her tiny faction decided to murder the Swedish UN mediator, Count Folke Bernadotte, but that she had quit the organization because she had ceased to believe in violence. She could outdrink, outtalk, outlaugh us all.

I had an enemy in Beersheba, a man named Itzhak, the city's leading stud. He'd been a gigolo on the French Riviera, had run drugs from Israel to Syria, and now owned his own bar, a place called the Barsheba, where you could often find the sort of brawls that seemed so exciting in American Westerns. He was always stealing women. I had a particular grudge against him because he had seduced Pam, an Englishwoman I was dating, made her a hostess at his bar, and had then become her part-time pimp.

One night after the Barsheba closed, Itzhak wandered into The Last Chance with a Hungarian woman named Cynthia. She had fled after the revolution of 1956, arrived in Israel with no money, and had been a prostitute ever since. Now she was said to be in love with Itzhak.

As soon as they walked through the door Itzhak ordered her to strip. She refused. "But everyone wants to see your big tits," he said. There were about twenty customers at The Last Chance that night. Most of them were regulars. None of them said a word.

To my astonishment, I heard myself talking. "I don't want her to strip, Itzhak," I said.

"Who doesn't want to see her strip?" he asked.

"I don't, Itzhak."

He seemed to decide the fight wasn't worth the trouble—he could have beaten me easily, I'm sure—for he said simply, "All right," took Cynthia by the hand, and left. Afterward, everyone who had witnessed the confrontation congratulated me. Betty gave me a kiss. The next day she asked me to stand next to the mural outside the bar, the pantheon of her closest friends, and drew a sketch of my face.

I had never felt so proud of myself. In a way, it was the moment I had come to Israel to experience.

In December, on the day my ship landed in Haifa, a tough, gnarled old Russian Jew—a lifetime Socialist who was an executive in a left-wing kibbutz movement—had told me, "This is the only country in the world where a Jew can walk down the streets of any city without worrying that somebody will make an anti-Semitic remark to him." Something in his manner attracted me. He was the first person with whom I ever discussed my difficulties at Choate. I guess he saw me as a potential immigrant to the homeland. For a while, I entertained that fantasy, too.

But late in the spring, a few days after my confrontation with Itzhak at The Last Chance, a friend of mine from Harvard sent me a copy of the *Crimson* which included an article about the Student Non-Violent Coordinating Committee (SNCC), a group that was working for civil rights in the South. Evidently, they were constantly harassed for helping Mississippi blacks get the right to vote.

I read the article as I walked down Beersheba's most pleasant street, Rehov Negba, a block full of comfortable stucco homes. Many of my good friends lived there—bright, idealistic men and women who had fled Hitler's Europe and settled in Israel. In 1962, a time of relative peace for the country, they seemed safe and happy, building their land. The school where I taught was behind Rehov Negba, on the other side of the shallow valley where the old patriarchs grazed their goats. At that hour of the morning, many of my students' fathers, middle-aged North African men, who earned their living cleaning Beersheba's streets, were just returning home from work. Of course, there was some tension between the generations of North Africans and even more between the Europeans who had settled the country and the North Africans who would form the majority of its population. But when I thought about the *Crimson* article, the tension seemed almost incidental. Most of the North Africans' sons and daughters would have better jobs and live in better homes than the millions of black people whom SNCC was trying to help.

Now, as I walked in Beersheba, I thought about my Russian friend again. He'd been right, of course, though he wouldn't like the conclusion I drew from his proselytizer's remark. In Beersheba, no one—not Wade Pearson or Lester the Lout or Ned the Gimp— would ever call me a kike. But in the country where I was raised, their counterparts still jailed some people and murdered others simply because they wanted the rights my North African students had been guaranteed as soon as they arrived in Israel. It was clear to me that their fight—SNCC's fight—was mine.

Back then, I thought I had conquered the demons that had raged inside me since Choate. Now, though, I realize that I'd overcome my fears but not my ambivalences. They manifested themselves most clearly in a bias against Jewish women that I was unaware of then, which disturbs me very deeply now.

My brother Geoff still remembers that when we were at Choate I often initiated conversations—tirades, really, he says—about a shallow, self-deluded girl in Herman Wouk's novel *Marjorie Morningstar,* a composite of well-to-do Jewish girls whom the book's most interesting character, Noel Airman (born Saul Ehrman) calls by the generic name Shirley. Now, I had no firsthand knowledge of these girls. They lived on the West Side, in a mercantile Jewish milieu that was very different from our assimilated, intellectual world on the East Side. In effect, then, Shirley was a symbol of the ideas about Judaism I'd inherited from my mother.

In their teens and early twenties, these Shirleys wanted some career on the fringe of bohemia—they wanted to be writers or singers or, in Marjorie's case, an actress. But when they were married they turned out to be as cautious and matronly as their mothers.

When Wouk's novel begins, Marjorie Morningstar (born Morgenstern), who is astonishingly beautiful, lives with her parents, who were Orthodox as long as they remained in the Bronx, and kept kosher and observed Shabbos after they prospered and moved to the Upper West Side. Marjorie defies her parents in many ways, although she never exactly rebels against them.

Noel Airman is a brilliant young songwriter and stage director with a long history as a roué. Infatuated with him, Marjorie gets a job at the summer camp where he directs plays, despite her mother's feeling that the place is Sodom. The clash of wills never results in a breach of the relationship.

Marjorie is indifferent to her parents' religious practices. For example, though she can't bring herself to eat shellfish or pork, the reader sees that scruple as a habit, not as an affirmation of her family's faith.

I know that when I read the book—in 1955, just after I entered Choate—I identified completely with Noel Airman's bohemian point of view. I cared greatly that Marjorie transcend her past, that she escape becoming a Shirley, that she and Noel enter a Jewish world as exciting as the gentile milieu my favorite writers, Hemingway and Fitzgerald, were always describing.

That didn't happen. It is interesting that Herman Wouk, who did so much to popularize religious Judaism in *This Is My God,* makes the act of adopting religious ritual seem almost like a form of defeat in *Marjorie Morningstar.*

The book's epilogue—set a decade after its main drama—contains its covert message. It is in the form of a diary entry by Wally Wronken, a 1950s Neil Simon, who once felt a completely unrequited love for Marjorie when he was a young gofer and she was smitten with Noel Airman. (Noel winds up as a third-rate radio writer in Hollywood.)

By chance, Wally visits Marjorie when she is the contented forty-year-old wife of a lawyer named Milton Schwartz. She has four kids and owns a large home in Mamaroneck, New York. As Wally approaches Marjorie's house, he sees "a gray-haired lady who was sitting on a flagstone terrace out front . . . one of the grandmothers out for a Sunday visit, I figured. It was a complete shock when the gray-haired woman turned out to be Marjorie. The fact is that she looks very much like Mrs. Milton Schwartz."

It turns out that the woman Wally once loved has experienced considerable tragedy—a brother, Seth, was killed in World War II, a child died in infancy. Still, he writes, "she is dull, dull as can be. You couldn't write a play about her that would last a week, or a novel that would sell one thousand copies."

They drink highballs and the talk turns to religion. "She's a regular synagogue goer," Wally writes, "active in all the Jewish organizations in town." She and her husband "seem to be rather strictly observant; Majorie has separate milk and meat dishes in the kitchen and all that. I tried to pin her down on what she believed. She was curiously evasive. She said her parents would never have survived her brother's death without religion and she didn't know if she and her husband would have stayed in one piece after their baby died without it."

Clearly, in Wally's eyes, Marjorie has become a "Shirley"—and Wally is too credible and decent a witness for the reader to dismiss his judgment as that of a jaded man. His tone is a wistful one. Once spurned, he is now saddened. When he was a gawky young gag writer and Marjorie was the poised, unattainably beautiful consort of Noel Airman, he had dreamed that, one day, he would present himself as a highly successful playwright and "humiliate Marjorie, just another suburban housewife gone to seed."

But, "The person I wanted to triumph over is gone, that's the catch. And what use is there crowing over the sweet, placid gray-haired mama she turned out to be.

"The only remarkable thing about Mrs. Schwartz is that she ever hoped to be remarkable, that she ever dreamed of becoming Marjorie Morningstar. She couldn't be a more run-of-the-mill wife and mother."

I know now that the experience of reading *Marjorie Morningstar* reinforced the ambivalences I was raised with. For who was she, who was Shirley, in my life? Except for the fact that she was an Eastern European Jew, she was the prototype of the dull, housebound woman whose lifeless conversation, business-oriented husband, boring materialistic children, had caused my mother to flee the Lake Shore Country Club.

In a curious way, I look at *Marjorie Morningstar* as a symbolic turning point in my romantic life. Before I read it, I'd only dated Jewish girls. Afterward, I usually dated non-Jewish ones. Now, I'm sure that Choate and Harvard had something to do with that. In boarding school, I wanted to use my romance with a blond woman who played the harp beautifully, sang American folk songs, and had a father who was in the State Department, as a way of proving that I could gain the approval of the society that had spurned me. At Harvard, I know, blond women, particularly WASPs from New England, blended in perfectly with the America that seemed so alluring and unobtainable when I studied it in my history courses.

But I also think that the book intertwined with my mother's descriptions of her childhood to make me fear that Jewish women would imprison me. It left me feeling scared that my idealized version of my adult self—as a latter-day James Agee or John Dos Passos—would be stifled by some Shirley (or her Century Country Club equivalent) who outwardly encouraged me to adventure, but who privately planned to trap me in a stifling suburban home, where I would have to deny the spontaneity I was trying to develop in myself because of some strange, meaningless religious rules.

By contrast, the blondes to whom I was attracted were golden girls who would help me act out my journalist's version of the frontiersman's dream. They would provide me—or, at least, the passive Arthur, the Mr. Kitzel in me—with protective coloration. They were my passport to the America I wanted to discover.

Once I had lived in Israel, though, there was a clear limitation on that fantasy. For I wanted to retain the Jewish self I had found—to investigate religious traditions that attracted me—to fight for Israel if need be. In other words, at the hidden level of the mind where the search for a mate has less to do with romance than with a carefully unconsciously calculated plan for one's future, I was looking for a woman who would help me achieve my American dream and explore my Judaism. I tested everyone I dated to see if she'd be able to share those very different fantasies and, perhaps, help me reconcile them. I see that clearly when I juxtapose two episodes that seemed completely unrelated back then.

A few weeks after I got back from Israel, I invited my girlfriend, Beth, a Smith undergraduate, an Episcopalian-born poet from suburban Connecticut, whose literary ideas had influenced me, to spend time at my family's house on Martha's Vineyard. Ever since I had returned to America, I'd been toying with the idea of retaining the name Saul Cohen, since I thought that act would allow me to feel the same clear sense of my own identity as I had in Israel. It was a whimsical notion, of course, since it would plainly wound my father far more deeply than it would satisfy me. In fact, Beth was the only person to whom I ever mentioned the fantasy. Was I testing her? Probing for her innermost feelings about Jews? Probably.

They came, in a rush, when she rubbed her hands in a Shylock-like gesture and said, "Saul Cohen. That's not you. You don't want to go back to the ghetto." It seemed like a flash of bigotry, and it bothered me so much that I never dated her again.

When we discussed the episode, years later, she remembered it as vividly as I did. She had been sure that I was abandoning my identity as an American for a romantic illusion. The illusion might not have been so threatening if it had included her. But that night at supper my sister Holly had glanced toward Beth, then turned toward me and said, "I feel proud to be a Jew. Don't you?" I nodded, Beth recalls. Then, later, when I told Beth I was thinking of changing my name, she began to feel so excluded from my family's—and my—inner core that she went outside and wept. For years I remembered her as a latent anti-Semite. She remembered me as one of the chosen people, who secretly believed that everyone else was inferior.

I thought it was the day before Yom Kippur 1963, when Rachel Brown and I found ourselves driving to the University of Chicago together. She was entering social work school, and I was avoiding the draft in graduate school, though I never had any hope of getting a degree. Actually, I'd never expected to go on any sort of journey with her. When we had first met, in the civil-rights movement in Cambridge, Maryland, I had thought of her as the kind of preppy I'd been avoiding since I broke up with Beth: an earnest blond social worker who felt enough guilt about racism to try to combat it for a single summer of a life that was destined to be safe and untroubled.

That week, though, I was visiting a friend at Swarthmore, and Rachel's sister, who went to that college, suggested that we drive West in tandem. We stopped at every Howard Johnson's on the turnpike: we felt an immediate, totally unexpected attraction, and wanted to bathe in each other's words. By the time we had driven past the huge Pennsylvania Dutch barns, over the mountain called Snowshoe that terrifies so many truck drivers, through Indiana, with its flat land, its farmers who were harvesting the autumn wheat, we knew that we were in love.

At twilight, we ate at a hamburger joint in Benton Harbor, Michigan. That was when I told Rachel I was going to fast so that I could observe the Day of Atonement. The fast was like my proposed name change—a way of affirming my Jewish identity, not an expression of faith. It impressed Rachel. She had never met a Jew who fasted on Yom Kippur. She didn't tease me about it, as my mother might have done, or make a major theoretical point of it, as Beth would have. She simply accepted it.

Toward midnight, we drove past Gary, Indiana, past the clattering, smoking steel mills. The sights and sounds of that city seemed like an awesomely beautiful symbol of the industrial America I loved. Then, almost an hour later, we arrived in Hyde Park, where the Spiegel and Cohen families had lived, where the University of Chicago was located.

My sister Holly was an undergraduate there. When Rachel and I got to her apartment Holly suggested we go to a delicatessen for a bite. I was astonished. Holly: the only religiously knowledgeable member of the Cowan family. Holly: who had been disappointed as a teenager because our parents wouldn't let her do anything as parochial as joining a synagogue. Why, I asked her, wasn't she fasting on Yom Kippur?

She looked at me with an almost maternal wryness. "Paul, Yom Kippur isn't until next week." I was chagrined. Rachel, who formed an instant, warm friendship with my sister, was amused. But she didn't mock me because I had misread the calendar. From then on, Rachel, the blond descendant of early New England Protestants, never had any doubts about my ethnic loyalties or my strange search for a heritage that was so different from my American upbringing. Indeed, in time, that search began to touch something very deep inside her.

7

When I think about Rachel and me in the mid-sixties I view us, quite fondly, as a pair of spiritual seekers who believed, with much of our generation, that we could find most of our answers through politics.

We had a great deal in common. Each of us was the oldest of four children. We had both been yanked out of pleasant, accepting environments—in my case, Dalton; in Rachel's, Tauxmont, Virginia, a very liberal community near Washington, D.C.—and set down, as teenagers, in very bigoted environments. Wellesley, Massachusetts, where Rachel went to high school, was every bit as prejudiced as Choate. We were both Adlai Stevenson Democrats amid Dwight Eisenhower Republicans, dismayed by our classmates' political conservatism because our parents were such outspoken liberals.

Rachel even had a religious conflict that was similar to mine. Her grandmother, after whom she was named, was a devout Episcopalian, but her parents, atheists, had refused to have her baptized. But, unlike me, she had never been denied access to her history. Her grandmother possessed family letters and a family tree dating back to seventeenth-century New England, and she displayed the documents proudly whenever Rachel visited. Rachel felt no need to learn more about her roots.

As a child, she had read *The Diary of Anne Frank* and had developed a silent, lifelong conviction that she possessed some sort of spiritual kinship to Holocaust victims. So, though she knew very few Jews, she fought the anti-Semites who dominated her school with much more self-confidence than I was able to muster at Choate.

As soon as I settled in Chicago, I began my meandering search for information about Jake Cohen, and Rachel took almost as much pleasure in that as in the fact that our personal lives were increasingly intertwined with those of black people.

I had rented a shabby apartment in a black community near the university. My neighbors and Rachel and I used to bowl together, or play cards, or sit on the stoop and drink beer and "signify" as they called their special, supple, and witty form of conversation. After a few months, our friendships blended into a form of politics based on neighborhood problems. We began to pressure academic bureaucrats to give us some vacant land so that we could build a playground where black kids would be safe from the cars that roared up and down the street. We succeeded, and, as we built the playground, many of the janitors, bricklayers, truck drivers, and welfare recipients who lived in my building became Rachel's and my friends. Often, though, Rachel and I would walk two blocks farther into the ghetto and chat with the old Jewish merchants on Sixty-third Street, the main commercial area. That was part of my search for Jake Cohen. None of them had ever heard of my grandfather, but they intrigued me anyway. Many were concentration-camp survivors. Most were said to overcharge my black neighbors, but I couldn't bring myself to engage them in ethical or political arguments. They displayed such interest in me, a Jewish college boy, that I felt immense warmth toward them. Of course, it would have been possible for Rachel to challenge my dual loyalties: to ask what a self-styled radical like me was doing, consorting with exploiters, often accepting bargains from them simply because I was Jewish. Instead of asking that question, though, she seemed to share my two conflicting intertwined feelings: my belief in social justice and my visceral loyalty to the generation whose lives had been disfigured by the Holocaust.

If anything, she felt a faint, flickering regret that my Judaism only involved an occasional very private act, like fasting on Yom Kippur, and an ill-defined search for a will-o'-the-wisp grandfather. From the beginning of our relationship she was attracted to the ceremonial aspects of the faith I knew so little about. Her first gift to me was a copy of Ben Shahn's edition of the Passover Haggadah. She didn't buy the volume as an ornament or a keepsake, but in the hope that I knew how to use it. She was disappointed when I said I'd never used a Haggadah in my life. But it never occurred to me, back then, that there was any reason to learn. And it never occurred to Rachel to question my indifference to the event that commemorated my people's freedom. For even if she regretted my ignorance of Judaism, she took it for granted. In our intellectually cosmopolitan, politically liberal world, anything that contained the slightest hint of religion seemed so remote that one could barely imagine discussing it seriously.

Anyway, in those years, the civil-rights movement provided each of us with an entirely satisfying secular creed. I had joined it in the summer of 1962, just after I returned from Israel, just after I broke up with Beth, when I volunteered for a tutorial project in Chestertown, Maryland. Rachel had become involved a year later, when she and her sister Connie had decided to do similar work in the nearby town of Cambridge.

I am not using the term secular creed in any kind of metaphorical sense. I know that when I was working in the South I was acting out an American morality that was as deep as faith itself. My mother's obsession with the Holocaust had played a large role in my decision to become an integrationist; but so had my own reverence for democracy, for the idea that it was worth risking death to help a black child learn to read in Maryland or a black sharecropper register to vote in Mississippi. That feeling, refracted through the movement, transformed my interior life. For the first time I believed that my friends and I mattered to America in the same way as the Israeli I met in Tiberias mattered to his country.

Nowadays, the sixties as a word is a kind of Rorschach test—a halcyon time to some who lived through it, a time of brutal disillusionment to others, an era of violence and insane permissiveness to its critics. Since many of us carry all three of those conflicting attitudes in our minds, it is almost impossible to get a fixed perspective on those years which reshaped America. But several things are clear to me. Whatever its flaws, the movement achieved some astonishing successes: it stopped segregation in the South and it stopped the war in Vietnam. Its own ending was terribly sour, because so many of us were so young, because our cultural diversity was so vast, because the forces we were facing were so great—and because of the paradoxical fact that we wanted to form a spiritual community out of something as evanescent and changeable as politics. But the movement's early years—which are rarely described anymore—represented some of the happiest days of our lives.

There were just four of us tutoring black children in the summer of 1962, two black men, a white woman, and myself. In order to raise money from black and white moderates our project director had pledged not to organize any demonstrations that might cause disturbances in town. So Chestertown's white people, who had attacked a busload of freedom riders the summer before, never harassed us. We didn't threaten them enough. A few people even seemed proud that the town could tolerate our integrated group. One day, when I was walking toward the church that served as our headquarters, I saw an elderly white woman turn to a friend and boast, "There goes our outside agitator."

It was a glimpse of the America I had been looking for in my college courses. A distinct nation seemed to be preserved in the slow-paced black community. I loved discovering how it worked; I loved sharing its pleasures, learning its language. It was far more satisfying, for example, to hear Mrs. Albert Deacy, who had spent thirty years "working private" in Philadelphia, recount kitchen gossip about the rich people who had sunk on the Titanic than to take notes on the sociological generalizations about America's millionaires with which Harvard professors like Arthur Schlesinger, Jr., and Oscar Handlin filled their lectures. In college classrooms, it had been difficult for me to comprehend the meaning of concepts like "the impact of technological innovation on poor societies." Now, when I watched the sixty-five-year-old woman at whose house I was living try to understand the workings of a dial telephone that had just been installed in her house, I understood that concept in a human way. Her look of confusion reflected the same sense of displacement as the lost expressions on the faces of the old North African men in Israel who listened to Patti Page songs on their transistor radios as they grazed their sheep near Abraham's caves.

Sometimes I'd hear my black friends turn white folks' stereotypes into jokes on themselves. Once, a mother gave her teenage son instructions about how to act at a picnic which Campbell's Soup, the town's leading employer, had organized for its workers. "Take care, boy. Mind you, don't eat the watermelons, hear. You don't want the white man to catch you doing that. But bring me home one. Because, you know, they're right. Us niggers do love watermelons." Then I'd realize that the culture segregation had produced was far more resilient and complicated than my austere abolitionist's view of the South had allowed me to believe.

Of course ugly things happened that summer, too, and each injustice we encountered exposed the tremendous psychological difference between my black co-workers and me. But I was so eager to understand the new world I had entered that I regarded their angry comments as lessons, not as rebukes.

One of our main jobs in Chestertown was to tutor a black girl who would integrate the white high school the next fall. She was entering her senior year, and the gaps in her education astonished me. She was supposed to take a second-year French class, for example, but it was impossible to review the rudiments of the language with her because she had never learned English grammar, not even the difference between an adjective and an adverb. We were talking about books one day and she told me that her sophomore English class had spent nearly a month on a single text, "Oh, Susannah." I was outraged. I told the two black men on the project that we should complain. "Complain to whom?" the project director asked, with a slightly bitter laugh. "You're in the South now, not at Choate or Harvard. Do you think the white people who run the schools here are going to care what happens to a bunch of little nigger kids? The worse they're taught, the less trouble they make. That's the way the white folks see it."

There was an integrated group of labor organizers in Chester-town, trying to unionize the Campbell's Soup plant. One day a white woman who was working with them fell ill and was rushed to the town's only hospital by a black friend. For hours the doctors ignored her. When they finally decided she had suffered a heart at-tack they refused to put her in an oxygen tent, until a union exec-utive from Baltimore telephoned an angry protest.

That kind of callousness horrified me, and I described it at a church meeting the next night. The audience didn't seem to re-spond at all. "You really don't understand us, do you?" the project director said afterward. "You know, there's not a day when one of our people doesn't experience segregation at the same hospital. When they're admitted they're sent to the Negro ward in the base-ment. It's a damp, dirty place. What makes you think they're going to get angry now because some white lady experiences the same treatment as they do?"

One afternoon I was playing outside our office with some kids from town, trying to teach them to make a loud, clicking sound I had learned from a Miriam Makeba album. I knew them all by name, and felt flattered that they seemed to know me. I loved the fact that, whenever I walked through the streets of the community, kids would holler out friendly greetings from houses and apart-ments everywhere.

But that afternoon Bill, the black I worked with most closely, began to denounce me. "What kind of game did you come down here to play, anyway? What do you think you are, some modern Jesus who is going to lead all the poor darky urchins away from the hovels they live in and into the promised land? Don't you realize that they flock to you because your skin is white, not because of anything you do? I wish you'd learn what's happening. I don't want our black children to model themselves after you."

But, in our personal relations, Bill's anger at me, his contempt for my naïveté about black people was tempered by a desire—which, in retrospect seems almost desperate—to show me what America was like for him. We would talk for hours about the gradations of prejudice inside the black community; about the anger he felt at his parents because they didn't want him to date any girl whose skin was darker than his own. Or he would tell me about the conflicts he had experienced when he attended integrated schools. He always felt a temptation to be whiter than the white man, he said: to talk a more precise English, to dress more carefully, to rise to the top of the professions we dominated. Sometimes he imposed disciplines on himself that were so severe he drove himself mad. He used to smoke three packs of cigarettes a day but now had given them up altogether. He would study in his room for days at a time, never sleeping, cooking all his meals on a one-burner hot plate. As a teenager he had weighed almost three hundred pounds. In college he had fasted down to 180. Now he did exercises every day, to keep himself in shape for the violent future he feared and desired.

Such confessions seemed to provide a perspective into which I could fit Bill's angry outbursts. By the summer's end, I was convinced that I understood him well enough to transform myself and win his trust. I was convinced that the effort to understand people with backgrounds different from my own would equip my reflexes for democracy.

Back at Harvard, my work in the movement brought me unexpected benefits. I wrote about Chestertown in the *Crimson,* and my articles made me something of a campus celebrity. In those years, the Kennedy years, a Harvard undergraduate with ideas about social policy had some chance of influencing scholar activists like McGeorge Bundy and Arthur Schlesinger, Jr., who worked at the White House and spent much of their spare time in Cambridge. In Beersheba and in Cambridge, the discomfort I'd felt in their classroom had been transformed, in my mind, into a debate over acquiring information. They had once given their lectures as they now made decisions on issues like civil rights; I thought they were more influenced by ideas they'd accumulated in libraries and by discussions among their peers, than by their experiences in the world. So, at the age of twenty-two, I resolved to give myself a better preparation than my elders had. I decided to keep viewing

America from its ghettos and its slums so that, when my time came, I could write about the country more accurately and help govern it more sensibly. In retrospect, I believe that feeling pervaded much of the early New Left. Most of us who sought community and a spiritual home in those early days of sixties' political activism were also functioning from a visceral sense of our professional and class interests.

If I had ever revealed that thought to the blacks who led the civil-rights movement they would have condemned me, quite correctly, for my paternalism. They wouldn't have been very interested in my feeling that, by coming to understand my partner, Bill, I'd begun to transform myself, to equip myself to live in a democracy. For their goal was to end segregation, not to educate white liberals from elite colleges. From their standpoint, the movement was in a difficult, dangerous war, not a protracted Brotherhood Week.

Most of the SNCC workers I'd read about on Rehov Negba were waging the war in Mississippi, which we all perceived as hatred's capital. For years, they had only let blacks work there, not because they were separatists but because they thought the presence of northern whites might make an extremely tense situation even tenser. Still, they were often beaten or jailed for things as innocent as citizenship classes. They received very little publicity and even less support—none, certainly, from state or even federal officials.

Their outstanding strategist was a brilliant, New York-born black man named Bob Moses, my own idol during the sixties, an almost compulsively modest Harvard M.A. who had taught math at New York City's prestigious Horace Mann School until a film clip of some Freedom Riders who were beaten in Alabama convinced him to give up a certain future in America's elite and set out alone for the South. Within a year, he was SNCC's chief organizer in Mississippi, working with local blacks on tactics that might help them win the vote. He was a completely unlikely revolutionary. He had an almost religious belief in the value of anonymity, which caused him to shun most media interviews and to sit in the back of the room during almost every heated movement debate, lest his presence intimidate less well-educated, less articulate people who might want to talk. He hated the thought that, as an organizer, he might imperil other people. Once, for example, in the tiny town of Liberty, Mississippi, he'd led a group of sharecroppers down to the registrar's office at the courthouse. He had been clubbed by the sheriff. As soon as he felt blood oozing from his head he put on a hat. He made sure that everyone was safely home, then got into his car and drove off, alone, to see a black doctor in the distant city of Greenwood so that he could be sure no rumor of his beating would reach Liberty and provoke a riot. He needed ten stitches.

But, after two years of watching friends risk their lives—and sometimes die—for the United States' most fundamental right, Bob reached a personally heart-rending conclusion. The only thing America responds to is violence, he decided—and not violence against blacks, but against sons and daughters of the white elite.

That was the rationale for the 1964 Freedom Summer. It was a brilliant, if desperate, public relations stunt; an attempt to use people like Rachel and my brother Geoff and me as human magnets to attract the news media to the dangerous Mississippi towns where we'd be stationed. It was perfectly straightforward, since we all knew that SNCC's leaders regarded us, at once, as human beings and as chess pieces to be moved around in a crucial national political game. And it was a tragically sound strategy, since it took the deaths of Andy Goodman, Michael Schwerner, and James Chaney to show the rest of the country the dangers that had always faced blacks who wanted to be treated as citizens in the segregated South. It laid the groundwork for the 1965 Voting Rights Act. But, for me, it ended the emotionally satisfying adventure that had taken me from Chestertown and Cambridge, Maryland, to the ghettos of Chicago. For, as a civil-rights worker in Vicksburg, Mississippi, I found myself caught in a web of disastrous relations between blacks and whites, where normal fears and misunderstandings—like Bill's and mine—were almost always defined as signs of racism, not human frailties. Instead of transcending ourselves, we began to turn on ourselves. So the movement began to tear itself apart at the moment of its greatest triumph.

In many towns, the project directors were ebullient, witty sophisticated northern blacks like Stokely Carmichael or Ivanhoe Donaldson, who might not have the time or inclination to befriend white volunteers, but who could certainly match their verbal skills. But in Vicksburg, our tense, quiet, Mississippi-educated black project director was unable to cope with the ideas and demands of twenty highly aggressive northern whites.

Every day, the Vicksburg Freedom House was full of students from Harvard, Yale, Stanford, and Columbia who wanted to use their skills as well as their skin color to transform the state. We couldn't move freely around the white part of town. Klansmen chased our cars every several days; bomb threats were part of our daily routine. So we were confined to the black ghetto, with very little practical work to do.

Most of us had befriended local blacks—a barber, a beautician, a doctor, a retired Pullman porter—and they worked with us to devise programs. For example, after a dozen meetings we figured out the format and contents for the first civil-rights-oriented black community newspaper in the South, and we raised the money for a sample issue. But an idea like that would remain a fantasy unless the project director approved it. He was a SNCC staffer and we were volunteers. It was an article of faith with all of us that a black person who had been active in the movement should make all the decisions.

But instead of dealing with us directly, he'd vanish for days at a time. At meetings, he only communicated his feelings through moody silences and brusque commands. He refused to encourage our work or to make any decisions of his own.

Finally, frustrated and impatient, I began to call the project director Papa Doc, after the Haitian dictator, because he was unwilling to consult with people who were his subordinates. Since he was abandoning Vicksburg's blacks, our friends, as well as us, the nickname didn't seem particularly racist to me. But later I realized that his stomach must have knotted with resentment and fear each time he entered the Freedom House and heard us discuss his life, his town, as if it were material for an Ivy League seminar. He stayed away from us for the same reasons that my more articulate partner, Bill, had raged at me in Chestertown.

I now think that my use of the code name Papa Doc bore a disturbing resemblance to Ned the Gimp's Mr. Kitzel jokes. But, in retrospect, I am more convinced than ever that the discussions between black and white contemporaries, which seemed so promising in Chestertown, were impossible in Mississippi. For our quarrel in Vicksburg was replicated in dozens of project sites across the state. From the point of view of many blacks in SNCC, the whites seemed to be plotting to take over the movement for which the blacks had risked their lives day after day, year after year. From our point of view, their flashes of anger, their seeming contempt for our ideas were a rejection of the selves we so desperately wanted them to use.

There were blacks who saw the disastrous implications of these tensions. A few, like Bob Moses, withdrew from the struggle. Others, like John Lewis, SNCC's president in 1964 and 1965, were religious southern-born college graduates, veterans of the early sit-ins who had started the movement and who still believed deeply in integration. Had they retained control of SNCC, they might have found some way of bringing blacks and whites back together.

But by 1964, civil rights was a glamour stock on the American left. Whoever controlled SNCC controlled a great deal of money and a great deal of publicity. In 1966, there was a power struggle in the organization. In its wake, very brave, very savvy northern-born blacks like Stokely Carmichael assumed leadership roles. Most of them had roots in the West Indies, not the American South; most had been part of the small minority of black students at big-city schools that served the intelligentsia, like the Bronx High School of Science. Even though they'd been personally successful (Stokely was a charismatic leader wherever he went), they still felt like outsiders, in much the same way as Joel Cassel and I had at Choate. So they possessed a degree of empathy for people like my project director, which arose out of their own very different sense of marginality. And that empathy blended in quite nicely with their calculated desire to gain power in what seemed like the growing kingdom of the freedom movement.

Soon, they became spokesmen for "black power," an attitude that was born of tensions like those that existed in Vicksburg. They argued that since most whites didn't know—or care—about the rudiments of black culture—they should give blacks the power to develop their own organization, their own strategies, their own technical skills. Indeed, whites should leave the South and do political work in their own communities. Their underlying assumption—that political movements had to develop autonomously, from within the framework of their own cultures—was an important one. Indeed, if one took it seriously, one had to question the whole idea that America was a melting pot and see the country as a pressure cooker of distinct ethnic groups, as a nation of tribes; one had to rethink the fundamental premises of our history.

But "black power" was never an idea that was open for debate or for modification. It released a fusillade of rage, which defined every white person as a "honky," everyone with power as a "pig."

Suddenly, insults, not sermons, had become the new form of movement rhetoric. In just a few months, the most effective leaders like Stokely learned that they could turn on the red lights of the TV cameras by transforming the style of political confrontation developed by Bob Moses with such gentleness, such pain in Mississippi, into a self-conscious decision to create flamboyant personal confrontations. For America, it turned out, didn't respond only to violence—it responded to dramatic statements that threatened violence. In 1966, Stokely Carmichael became a national celebrity, commanding immense publicity and huge lecture fees. That year, under his leadership, SNCC all but abandoned the organizing work it had begun in the South.

But in 1964 and 1965 one didn't have to face those problems. In those years, whites like Rachel and me were pouring all our political energy into the movement against the war in Vietnam. Dozens of us organized teach-ins that were living testimony to our creed that reasoned argument would end irrational violence. We loved that work, and the friends who shared it. We were a fraternity with a purpose. We'd finish our studies and our leafleting, then spend an afternoon playing softball, our evenings drinking beer, reveling in our decency.

Besides, in 1965, the civil-rights movement was still open enough that thousands of whites could march with Martin Luther King, Jr., and John Lewis in Selma, Alabama. For that brief period, it was possible to believe that the civil-rights movement and the peace movement were still intertwined, and that any ethical political action—from organizing a picket line to tutoring a black child—was an act of devotion to our secular creed.

But what a brief, transitional phase it was! For our secular creed reflected our faith in our country. In 1965, we called ourselves radicals, but the truth was that in those days—when even Eugene McCarthy and Bobby Kennedy still favored the war in Vietnam—we were almost the only loyal opposition in America.

After all, most of us who had gone South to fight segregation and returned to the campuses to oppose the war were still part of our generation's elite. We wanted to be different from our elders: to create loving communities; to make the people we'd met in places like Mississippi living, active presences in our minds. We dreamed of making America a gentler country. The motto SDS had chosen to oppose the war—"build, don't burn"—was indicative of our cast of mind. Most of us wanted to preserve the nation, to help guide it some day, not to become revolutionaries and destroy it. In that last hopeful phase of American history, we were trying to convince our government not to act like reckless, free-spending parents who squandered their most precious resources, their young. We were trying to evolve into a prophetic generation which embodied optimism for a more humane future.

In June 1965, Rachel and I were married under a butternut tree at her uncle's farm in Williamsburg, Massachusetts. Unlike most interfaith couples, we never focused on the issue of who would officiate.

The chaplain of Smith College, a black minister, a civil-rights advocate, and a poker-playing buddy of Rachel's uncle agreed to perform the ceremony. I think it was Rachel, not I, who insisted that Jesus' name be excised from the service. In the end, we devised our own secular litany which consisted of readings from James Agee and Albert Camus, and of personal statements about what we meant to each other, what marriage meant to each of us. After that, the Reverend Anderson pronounced us husband and wife. I put a glass on the ground and broke it with my heel—that was the only Jewish wedding custom I knew—and the minister said "shalom." Then Rachel, in her wedding dress, I, in my suit pants, and all our friends went off to play softball.

We had planned to live in New York. I had a job as a reporter for *The Village Voice,* and Rachel had been hired as a social worker for the Hudson Guild Settlement House. But, before we could get settled, I received a letter telling me I was about to be drafted.

No decision had ever troubled me so much. Of course, I refused to fight in Vietnam, but I wasn't a pacifist. I knew I would have fought in Israel's War of Independence. I wasn't imbued with the kind of idealism that would let me leave Rachel and go to jail. Neither Rachel nor I had any desire to resettle in Canada or Israel. Besides, for the most part, America had been good to my ancestors. I still had the old-fashioned belief that I owed my country a debt. So, finally, after months of discussion, Rachel and I decided we should serve as Peace Corps Volunteers in Ecuador.

We lived in the port city of Guayaquil. We were part of a project designed to recruit young American leftists and technicians into something that was a social engineer's fantasy. In theory, the twenty-five of us, college graduates in our early twenties, with few technical skills and no command of Spanish, were supposed to work in Guayaquil's city hall as social workers, architects, transportation experts, and live in the city slums. That way, we could organize our neighbors into militant community organizations—like those Saul Alinsky organized in the United States. These organizations could march on city hall demanding that its officials, our bosses, provide the social services they so desperately needed. Frank Mankiewicz, then the Peace Corps director of Latin affairs, later Robert Kennedy's press secretary and George McGovern's campaign manager in 1972, borrowed a phrase from the civil-rights movement and created a metaphor for the scheme. It was supposed to be part of a "worldwide sit-in movement." The notion sounded somewhat plausible at home. It had no relationship to anything we saw in Ecuador.

There were tens of thousands of unemployed people in Guayaquil, many of whom lived in rickety cane shacks, in communities that used garbage for landfill, where children would drown in the swamp during the four-month rainy season, where malaria and dysentery were endemic. The country was governed by a tiny inbred oligarchy, which had no interest in surrendering any part of its wealth. These aristocrats were business people, for the most part, who made their decisions at the very exclusive country clubs and weekend resorts where they spent their time.

City hall, where we were supposed to work, was in debt to Ecuador's major bankers—the most powerful figures in the oligarchy. The mayors and department heads, our bosses, were deposed every few months. None of them possessed the power to help the poor, even if they had the will. Of course the slum dwellers, our neighbors, knew that; to them, *la oligarchia* (the oligarchy), was an immutable fact of life, not an arcane radical idea. They saw us as intriguing curiosities; they'd watch out for our personal welfare; they'd invite us to their homes or organize huge parties for us where they'd acknowledge our good intentions by plying us with beer or puro, a dreadful drink made out of distilled sugar cane juice. But they didn't see any point in joining a "worldwide sit-in movement"—or even attending meetings of the community organizations we were supposed to create. They saw us as a source of used clothes or, if they were lucky, of scholarships to the United States. In the eyes of the Peace Corps, we were agents of social change. The Ecuadorians, far more realistic, viewed us as potential personal benefactors.

Soon after Rachel and I arrived in Guayaquil, we left our jobs in city hall and began to work with two Ecuadorians, teaching a course in community development. We became quite friendly with students and university graduates with relatively good jobs. In a more progressive country, they would have been part of a bureaucratic infrastructure. In Ecuador, they saw no more future for themselves than did the slum dwellers. Most of them were more anxious to settle in the United States, than to bring American ideas into Ecuador.

Some of the other volunteers found work that was equally satisfying—and, as a rule, equally irrelevant to Ecuador's society. But many, who believed their mere presence would transform the country completely, became quite embittered when we weren't greeted as an American army of spiritual and political liberation.

In Peace Corps training, we had been told that everything we had absorbed from living in the United States—from high schools and colleges, Boy Scout troops and summer camps—would enable us to help modernize the Latins. And we had been told that our willingness to live among poor people—to eat rice with them—would enhance America's image and enhance the slum dwellers' self-esteem. There was very little truth to those assertions.

Far from influencing Ecuadorians, most volunteers I knew—in our group and every other—had experienced an enervating sense of uselessness in every job they tried. That uselessness destroyed their self-esteem. But instead of questioning the American attitudes that lay at the root of their despair—that astonishing arrogance that assumed we could lead an "international sit-in movement," or influence South American bureaucrats with mannerisms we'd picked up in the Boy Scouts—they blamed Ecuador—or at least Ecuadorians—for their relentless sense of failure. Among themselves, they called the country's people "Ekkies" or even "spics." As a result, they wound up hurting themselves and the people they had set out to help.

I remember the first week we were in the country, meeting a volunteer who was just finishing his two-year tour of duty. After about a year of living in a rural town, he said, he had finally persuaded his Ecuadorian neighbors to build a playground. "That really felt good," he told Rachel and me. "At least I'd have something to show for those years of my life." But the project was aborted when some members of the local *comité* stole the money. "Now, I can't wait until I get in the Army," he said in a mild, serious voice. "I want to go over there to Vietnam and shoot some of those Vietcong. It sure will feel good to pretend they're the Ecuadorian *campesinos* I've been working with."

One day at lunch, Rachel and I talked with a volunteer who had quit his job in a rural school. After traveling all over Ecuador in search of work, he had decided to become a community developer in Guayaquil. But he couldn't find a satisfying job in the urban slums. Soon he began to stay in his house for days at a stretch. One day a neighbor of his, a student in the class we were teaching, grew worried that he was lonely and tried to visit him. She wanted to show him he had friends. "He ordered me to get away from his house and tell everyone else in the neighborhood that he didn't want to be bothered again," she told us. Then, with pain in her voice, she added, "I guess he doesn't like us."

When we first got to Ecuador, I thought we were meeting a group of displaced, disturbed Americans whose problems had as much to do with culture shock and youth as they did with bad programming. To some extent, I suppose, that was true. But, as I came to know older people—Peace Corps staffers and officials from other United States government agencies—I realized that their shared premise that Americans were superior to Ecuadorians had produced an epidemic of bigotry.

Once, when an American naval band came to Guayaquil, the man in charge of the United States Information Office told us that the group couldn't play in the slum communities we were supposed to be helping. "Those people aren't able to appreciate the things we do for them," he said. "They're like animals. They never should have been allowed to come to the city. The government should have a policy making it illegal for them to migrate from their villages."

Several months after we arrived in Ecuador, the Peace Corps staff members gathered in the capital city of Quito to devise a five-year plan. Just two Ecuadorians were there—both Peace Corps employees. It was the mirror image of the decision-making process in the civil-rights movement, which recognized the wisdom of local people and encouraged them to think for themselves. Several days later, the Country Director came to Guayaquil for one of his periodic meetings. Influenced, of course, by my years in the movement, I told him that the session sounded like colonialism at its worst.

"Call it colonialism if you want," he said, "but all I know is that if Ecuadorians were involved in Peace Corps programming decisions, ninety percent of our projects would be failures. It will take two generations until they can make wise decisions for themselves. Until then, we have to show them what to do."

In October 1967—the same month that our movement friends in America were organizing the highly controversial march on the Pentagon—Rachel and I accompanied the Ecuadorian teachers and students in our class to Bogotá, Colombia to study community development.

One day, everyone on our trip had lunch at Bogotá's National University. As we were all standing in line, I heard a great deal of whistling and stamping, but I assumed it was just some students impatient to eat. Then, in the dining room I was conscious of people staring at me, but I figured that, like many South Americans, they were amused by my height and the sweat that frequently pours off my face in hot weather.

I had a headache so I went back to the lunch counter to buy an aspirin. As I walked back to the table I began to hear a great clatter. People were banging their cups, their plates, their chairs—any hard object they could find. And yelling in English and Spanish, "*Yanqui,* go home. *Afuera. Cuerpo de Paz. Abajo, imperialismo.*" I saw one of the Ecuadorian students restraining a Colombian who was about to throw a bottle at me.

I returned to my table, trying to look as calm as possible. Then we all got up, and the noise resumed, louder than ever. Fortunately, we had been eating near an exit so we didn't have to pass many people on the way to the door. Soon the bus we had rented came to take our group to its next visit.

As we were leaving the university, a Colombian student tried to console us. "Don't take it personally," she said. "To them, you are not Paul and Rachel Cowan, two special people who are doing a special job. You are symbols of a government that is exploiting this country. If I hadn't known you, I would have been yelling, too." Everyone who had been listening to the conversation, Ecuadorian and Colombian, agreed.

I agreed, too. In my own mind I was always yelling, "Yanqui, go home" at my government; at people who treated their hosts as "Ekkies," as "spics." Were they so different from the Americans in Vietnam who called their allies "gooks"? Some must have been innocents abroad who felt genuinely insulted because the Asians for whom they were risking their lives didn't particularly want to fight in the war. Conversely, I could imagine United States government officials in Ecuador who felt such contempt for the slum dwellers who behaved like "animals"—or for their middle-class counterparts who needed two generations until they could make wise decisions for themselves—that they could honestly convince themselves that they had to destroy a culture in order to save it. Like the students at the University of Bogotá, I felt that I had to fight such people.

Until the episode in Colombia, I'd always kept my criticisms of the Peace Corps within the organization's framework. Now, the realization that I was on the Colombians' side, not the North Americans', made me feel emotionally torn. For my own sake, I had better wage an open battle against the American attitudes I loathed. So, as soon as Rachel and I returned to Guayaquil, I wrote an article for the *Voice* describing the incident in the cafeteria and the emotions it released in me. The week it was published, Rachel and I worked with eight other volunteers to write a statement which charged that "The Peace Corps is as arrogant and colonialistic as the government of which it is a part." About twenty newspapers printed the broadside.

Rachel and I left for the United States as soon as the course we were teaching had ended. So we were in New York during the 1967 Tet offensive—the turning point in the Vietnam War. I remember reading that the Vietcong had taken over the American Embassy in Saigon, and feeling an enormous surge of sympathy for my country's enemy.

That emotion forced me to realize that I was no longer part of the loyal opposition, trying to change the government so that I could help run it one day. Reluctantly, I had become a political rebel, though I had no clear idea of what those words meant. For now that I had seen the America I loved from the vantage point of Maryland and Mississippi, from the slums of Guayaquil, from the nightly television images of the anguish in Vietnam, I began to think of my country as the God that failed.

During the spring of 1968, Rachel and I were living in Washington, working at the Institute for Policy Studies, a haven for political thinkers and activists. I was writing for the Voice and trying to communicate the experiences behind my growing radicalism through my book, *The Making of an Un-American.* We were both preparing to become parents. That July, our daughter Lisa Pilar was born on Martha's Vineyard.

It was an exhilarating, confusing roller coaster of a time; a time of hope that swelled as the antiwar candidates, Robert Kennedy and Eugene McCarthy, won primary after primary; of shattering grief when Martin Luther King was assassinated; of unmitigated defiance that propelled the campus takeovers like the one at Columbia University in April. Then, after Robert Kennedy was assassinated, all the movement people I knew, from the most optimistic liberals to the most confrontational radicals, were consumed by a mood of angry despair.

What could one do? What did it mean to be a radical, a rebel, a revolutionary? Should one write defiant articles or detailed studies of American imperialism? Work for Eugene McCarthy? Organize militant demonstrations? Every day one felt an almost obsessive anger about the war in Vietnam, about racial injustice in America, and a personal, ethical obligation to change those things. Sometimes, one felt obliged to change them "by any means necessary," as one of the period's most popular slogans went. But what if some means threatened to fragment the movement or antagonize our liberal friends? What if others seemed downright immoral?

How should one act if one felt that some tactics were becoming increasingly ugly? It wasn't an atmosphere in which one could raise those questions.

I felt those conflicting emotions in myself on the August night in 1968, when I arrived in Chicago to take part in the antiwar protest at the Democratic Party convention. This was Sunday, before the convention began, before the police began to beat the demonstrators so savagely, so indiscriminately that a whole nation was stunned. In the lazy hours of the late summer afternoon, I wandered around Lincoln Park, watching the long-haired kids who had drifted in from all over the country as they lit up joints, or made dinners of wine and cheese, or hugged and kissed uninhibitedly, or improvised flute and guitar arrangements to Bob Dylan and Beatles songs, even to classical music. It seemed like a pastoral glimpse of the new culture.

At dusk about five hundred of us began to walk toward Chicago's gentrified Old Town neighborhood. The police, who were still watchful, still peaceful, stared at us as we carried our antiwar signs and gazed into store windows. Then, suddenly, a skirmish began—I have no idea how. I remember seeing a few demonstrators jam helmets over their shaggy hair and grab every available heavy object—rocks they carried in their knapsacks, chunks of cement, a few golf balls with nails in them. They hurled the missiles at the police, and then ran away. It wasn't the kind of tableau I'd expected—fresh-faced kids and evil cops—but an episode of urban guerrilla warfare, an American version of *The Battle of Algiers,* a popular movie that year. It taught me my own limits as a rebel. I was happy to tell hostile onlookers why I opposed the war, even if they cursed at me or threatened to hit me, but I didn't want to throw a rock at anyone or anything. Indeed, when I saw some demonstrators surround a police

car, then tip it back and forth, I felt enough sympathy for those be-
leaguered cops that I flashed my *Voice* press card and distracted the
radicals by telling them that I wanted to interview them.

I wrote a *Voice* article describing that complex Sunday night
scene. But by midweek, before the piece would have been typeset,
the demonstrators' provocations seemed tiny in comparison to the
police's brutality. I'd seen scores of genuinely innocent people—
passersby, demonstrators, and convention delegates—sent to jail
simply for walking on Chicago's streets; I'd watched nightsticks
pound the faces of a dozen long-haired kids until mouths that had
perhaps hollered a few obscenities were bathed in blood; I'd been
on carefully planned, non-violent marches that were dispersed by
a brand of tear gas that made me fall to the ground, feeling as if I
would never breathe again, as if I'd be crushed by one of the bull-
dozer-tanks that cruised up and down Chicago's streets during the
week of the convention. So I asked the *Voice* to kill my first article.
I wrote two other pieces dwelling on the cruelty of the Chicago
police, and focusing on the thousands of protesters who were
overwhelmed by the relentless quality of the cops' rage, who still
wanted to bring out their decency so that they would quit fighting
us, and "join us." In doing so, I minimized the role of the militants
who were so intent on creating a conflict. Those articles reflected
the situation in Chicago accurately. But they failed to confront a
problem within the movement that would continue to grow.

I know many reporters and activists made similar decisions—to
ignore the existence of a cadre of activists who desired some kind
of violence. We were doing a cosmetic job on an increasingly scarred
New Left so that we could emphasize what seemed to be the threat
of American fascism—of police forces that would use nightsticks
on any black, any long-haired kid, any dissenter—and so that we
could help to hasten the end of the war that was destroying us all.

These things might have been possible if Eugene McCarthy or
even Hubert Humphrey had been elected President. But they
seemed out of the question once Richard Nixon took office. In 1969
John Mitchell handed down the conspiracy indictments that led to

the long, raucous trial of the Chicago Seven, antiwar activists who had helped plan the convention demonstration. That seemed to augur a replay of McCarthyism, a new era of domestic repression. In Vietnam, the napalming was relentless. The war was beginning to widen into Cambodia. There was talk of mining Haiphong Harbor. Maybe specific actions like teach-ins, leafleting, draft resistance, speaking at Chambers of Commerce or Lions Clubs would begin to influence public opinion, but that slow process was dwarfed by the evil of a military policy we had begun to define as genocidal.

The only way to fight back, we thought, was to create an increasingly unruly domestic resistance movement to run wild in the streets, as the phrase went at the time. But that brought out the worst in ourselves as well as in our enemies. For tens of thousands of Americans in their teens, twenties, and thirties experienced a degree of frustration and rage that encouraged them, half-consciously, to embrace the terms and the tactics of the warfare state they despised: to become the Green Berets of the left. Our objective—ending the war—remained impossibly elusive. So it often seemed that we—the movement—were imprisoned within the walls of our collective anger: as if we were making ourselves the victims of our collective wrath.

I remember a particularly dreadful week in November 1969, when Rachel and I were living with Rachel's mother in Cambridge. I was finishing *The Making of an Un-American* and we were both active in the Committee of Returned Volunteers (CRV), an organization of people who had shared the kinds of experiences we'd had in the Peace Corps, and who wanted to keep opposing the war in Vietnam.

In Cambridge, CRV joined a panoply of radical organizations to stage a demonstration at the Massachusetts Institute of Technology's Instrumentation Labs (I-Labs), which made some of the weapons America was using in Vietnam. By then, extreme bravado and derisive personal remarks had become the normal form of movement speech. If someone slipped and talked about police, an angry chorus would shout him down, reminding him to use the word "pig." Blacks

denounced whites, women denounced men, activists who believed
in street fighting denounced those who preferred orderly protest.

It was increasingly clear that anyone who could claim oppression possessed a perverse kind of power. As we discussed the
demonstration at the I-Labs, we frequently dissolved from a single
unit into smaller caucuses, after which organizations of the victim-
ized would issue specific demands—for a guaranteed number of
people who would speak to the media, say, or who would deliver
speeches at a rally—and insist that, if those demands weren't met,
they would withdraw from the coalition that had been designed to
oppose the war.

It was clear, that week, that once you conferred the status of "oppressed" on yourself and your caste, you could make all outsiders
feel paralyzed with guilt. You could make your ethnic background,
your age, your color, your gender, your sexual preference into a private preserve by insisting, as Stokely Carmichael had, that people
can only organize within their own communities. Sometimes, during those meetings, it seemed as if the movement had been transformed into a topsy-turvy version of a very American state fair,
where the blue ribbon went to the person or group who could display its anguish most dramatically.

It had also turned into a tactical game of chicken, where verbal
machismo was far more important than strategic resourcefulness.

So, when we focused on the demonstrations at the I-Labs, we
usually discussed the degree of violence demonstrators should em-
ploy. Should we carry rocks and, if so, should we aim them at buildings, at windows, or hurl them in volleys to drive back the pigs? A
friend of mine, who had become active in the New Left when I did,
said, with a disgusted laugh, that we were witnessing the last gasp
of parliamentary militarism. In a way, she was right. During the
next few months, the people who were most committed to violence would join the Weatherman faction of SDS. Some would
learn to make bombs. In a ghastly episode, three died while they
were assembling explosives at a town house in Greenwich Village.

One morning after the protesters had occupied the administration building for several days, after they had hurled rocks at the I-Labs and the cops in demonstration after demonstration for nearly a week, Rachel and I and two friends from CRV went to a large chemistry class at MIT to distribute some leaflets that described the reasons behind our protests.

Just before the lecture began the professor saw us at the door and rushed over, looking furious. "Get out of here," he said. I knew I should, but the journalist in me wanted to see what effect the week's actions had—indeed, what effect the movement had—on what must have been a fairly representative group of MIT students. So I smiled as casually as possible and asked them, "Do you want to hear us?"

"No," they chorused.

The professor moved a step closer to us as we were beginning to leave. Perhaps it looked as if he was escorting us from the room. When I looked over my shoulder I saw that most students were applauding him. I heard most of them telling us to go home.

It reminded me of that moment in the National University in Bogotá, when the Colombian students had yelled, *"Yanqui,* go home." I described the episode in just those terms in a *Voice* article about the MIT demonstrations—and urged radicals to help create organizations that offered people the kind of hope America was denying us.

I felt as if I had come full circle in a very few years. Just as I'd wanted to leave the Peace Corps that antagonized the Latins it was supposed to help, now I wanted to leave the part of the New Left that antagonized a substantial number of the Americans it was trying to reach. I wanted to keep opposing the war and fighting for social justice, of course, but from within a cohesive community, a spiritual home that offered the qualities of humanity and compassion—and the concrete ways to be useful—that had attracted me to the movement in the first place.

In May 1968, two priests, Daniel and Philip Berrigan, joined seven other clergymen in a dramatic, non-violent protest against the war. They journeyed to the town of Catonsville, Maryland, went to the draft board, and asked the clerk for selective service files. Then they went outside and poured their own blood over the draft cards. They explained the moral logic behind their civil disobedience in a trial near Baltimore, and were sentenced to five years in jail. But in April 1970, both Berrigans decided to evade arrest and continue to resist the war as fugitive priests. Phil Berrigan was caught in a matter of days. Dan Berrigan remained underground for more than a year.

One weekend in April 1970, Rachel took our son, Matthew, just a month old, on a journalistic assignment in Pennsylvania. Early that Saturday afternoon, I was sitting in our apartment, taking care of Lisa, when a movement person I knew very slightly called and said he had to see me at once. "But I'm at home alone with my baby daughter," I said, reveling in the fact that the exchange was letting me prove that I was a nonsexist parent. "You don't understand," the caller said, angry that he had to disclose dangerous evidence over a phone that was probably tapped. "Daniel Berrigan is here, and he wants you to interview him underground."

I had barely heard of Berrigan until that moment, or, rather, I kept confusing him with a secular poet named Ted Berrigan—but my journalistic and political instincts told me to do the story. But I was very worried about exposing my twenty-month-old baby to the dangers of the underground. Finally, I decided to put her in her back pack, strap it onto me, and take a subway to the neighborhood where Berrigan was staying.

He was very nervous when we got to his temporary headquarters. Philip had been arrested two days earlier, and Dan was trying to prepare himself for a visit from the FBI—and for a long stint in jail. Lisa was fussy with midday fatigue, and I was afraid that her crying would jar his nerves. But the priest helped me soothe her. He made a point of calming a jumpy cat who threatened to interrupt her nap. It was immeasurably important to me that this religious radical was tender with my daughter—more tender, I thought, than many people on the New Left, whose reaction to feminism often was to negotiate over kids, not to nurture them.

The substance of our conversation doesn't matter much anymore. But I remember that when I heard this religious man, whose name I barely knew, whom I'd never expected to meet, attribute his resistance to the war and to the Left's internal cruelty to his own unabashed belief in God, I felt more inspired than I had since the early days of the civil-rights movement. And now, when I reread the last paragraphs of my *Voice* article, I'm amazed at the tone of my prose. For it sounds like an endorsement of his Catholicism and a clear acknowledgment that, despite my public definition of myself as a political radical (a definition that attracted some attention because *The Making of an Un-American* had been published three weeks earlier), I was getting ready to resume my spiritual journey.

"Berrigan became most emotional when we talked about the possible meaning of his act for other Catholics," I wrote. "'There might be something to this faith, if not this religion. Jesus still means something to young people.' Here his voice soared and he chuckled happily. 'It's clear that He means something to young people.'"

Then Berrigan began to talk about Jesus' belief in non-violence—and, I realized, about the hope that undergirded his own act.

"Jesus decided in his own life that it was more important to undergo violence than to inflict it," the fugitive priest told his rootless Jewish interviewer. "He wasn't just offering one man's opinion. The Sermon on the Mount was a blueprint. It helps show how to look for the points of resistance that have to do with vindicating the dignity of man."

When Lisa and I were back on the street, I realized that the two-hour conversation had made me question the atheism I'd taken for granted ever since I left Choate.

The *Voice* has a policy of letting its reporters follow their own obsessions, in the very wise, very commercial realization that our passions, our odysseys, will carry thousands of readers along with us. So I decided to pursue the feelings that swept over me the day I met Father Berrigan and make the Catholic left one of my beats.

I wrote profiles of two nuns, Sister Jogues Egan and Sister Elizabeth McAlister, and began to spend a great deal of time in their convent, a brownstone house on West Eighty-fifth Street. Often, toward the end of the evening, they sang the Irish freedom songs that still brought tears to their eyes. I loved their community. It was a place where people celebrated at weddings, grieved at funerals, remembered bourgeois details like thank-you notes and punctuality, maintained bourgeois ideas like faith in God, and understood that all those things were cornerstones of a stability that contributed to their strength to oppose the war.

It was the one phase of my spiritual search that never interested Rachel. She was as disappointed in the New Left as I was, but she chose to create a community where we lived, instead of experiencing one vicariously through religious Christians. Her own childhood, as the daughter of militant atheists, as a gentile in an anti-Semitic WASP suburb, had left her with a lasting distrust for anything that had to do with the church. So, instead of hanging around with its latter-day apostles, she and some friends started a day-care center in the neighborhood—an act which turned out to be the cornerstone of our family's involvement with Judaism.

My involvement with the Catholic left had a completely unexpected journalistic payoff. In January 1971, a federal grand jury convened in Harrisburg, Pennsylvania, near the town where Philip Berrigan had been in prison. It indicted Father Phil, Sister Elizabeth McAlister, and four other priests and nuns for conspiring to raid draft boards, blow up federal heating systems, and kidnap Henry Kissinger in an effort to end the war. That year, the trial of the Harrisburg Seven (Eqbal Ahmad, a Pakistani intellectual and friend of the Berrigans', was indicted too) was a nationally important news story, and, since it involved my friends, I had considerable access to information.

I spent most weekdays in Harrisburg throughout the three-month-long trial, and I found myself talking more personally than ever with the priests and nuns who came there to testify or show their solidarity. Sometimes I'd pray with them or take communion with them, and I found my admiration for the qualities that had drawn me to Dan Berrigan growing even deeper: they were able to be calm and brave because they were sure of their roots, sure of their faith.

Furthermore, I felt a keen appreciation for their tactical skill, particularly when I compared their actions to demonstrations like the one at the I-Labs. I was convinced that the draft-board raids, which kept thousands of kids home from Vietnam, were the most important acts of resistance to the war. They grew out of a sustained sense of humanity, not a willed effort to become a full-time street fighter.

Ironically, though, the closer I got to the Catholic radicals, the greater the cultural distance between us seemed. My friendships with them made me think about my Judaism more intensely than I had since I returned from Israel.

As far as I could tell, most members of the Catholic left were from working-class and middle-class families, and had been raised to feel that they were Americans in a way that I never quite could. Many of their parents had supported Senator Joseph McCarthy. Quite a few had graduated from colleges like Holy Cross and Fordham, where the FBI recruited many of its agents. So they had parents, roommates, relatives in the law-enforcement establishment I had come to dread. They came from the same culture as their foes.

They felt that they were protecting their country by burning draft cards. But whenever I thought of asking if I could join them on a raid—as I did quite often—I remembered my mother's childhood warnings that, for people like us, outward prosperity had nothing to do with real security. I remembered her admonition that I should learn a trade in case I had to flee to some foreign land, where my survival would be insured by a skill that didn't depend on language; I remembered my father urging Geoff and me to write letters to the FBI telling them that our motives for going South were patriotic. I never did ask to go on a draft-board raid. For I knew that I'd feel unbearably frightened—and unaccountably subversive—if I ever joined my Catholic friends in an action that represented such a flagrant violation of the law. From their viewpoint,

I realized, they thought they'd be saved. From mine, I was sure I'd be punished.

Then, one night, I realized the difference in our backgrounds made concepts that usually seemed like routine formulas echo entirely differently in our psyches.

I was covering a rally when one of the defendants, a witty, outgoing former priest, said that his decision to spend his life helping blacks in Baltimore's slums, and to oppose the war in Vietnam, stemmed from his belief in Jesus Christ. I'd heard dozens of similar speeches, of course, including the one that moved me so much when I interviewed Daniel Berrigan underground. But suddenly, while I was taking notes, I did a double-take. My political activities had resembled his. I'd helped poor blacks in the South and in Chicago; worked with poor people in South America; taken some risks to resist the war. But if any religious ideology had instructed me to do those things, it was my mother's post-Holocaust world view. It certainly wasn't any belief in Jesus. Suddenly, I felt excluded from my friends' inviting culture.

Then a Mennonite minister whose son was an unindicted co-conspirator got up to describe his antiwar views. It was a sermon that depended on a repeated refrain. So, to describe his commitment to pacifism and justice, he kept repeating the litany "Jesus Christ is my problem"—meaning, I knew, that Jesus was the reason he couldn't remain indifferent to the world's woes. But, in my mood of sudden loneliness, I heard the sentence differently. I began to muse about the fact that Jesus Christ had been my problem, too: during the Crusades, during the Inquisition, even, for that matter, at Choate. I liked the minister and his son almost as much as I liked the former priest. I knew there was nothing malicious in their remarks. Yet, they haunted me for days.

The New Left—the movement that had been Rachel's and my secular creed—was over forever. There was no doubt about that. The Catholic left was no substitute. Rachel was right about that. I could be a journalist, a sympathizer, a fellow traveler. I could never be one of them. But I wanted to be something—to live on the ground, with people, not in the air with theories and resentments and an unfulfilled longing for community.

I wanted to understand my roots, Jewish roots—to pursue the feelings that had awakened when I was in Israel, that slumbered during the years when the movement seemed like my spiritual home.

But I still had to justify that feeling on political terms. So, on a conscious level, I responded to the ex-priest's insistence that he worked in the ghetto because of Jesus—and, I think, to Stokely Carmichael's argument that white people should work in their own communities—by deciding to explore the Lower East Side of New York: to find the forces in my culture that had spawned generation after generation of socialist thinkers and organizers.

I never did learn very much about that. Instead, very slowly, I began to recover my buried past—and to find something in the present that I could affirm.

8

It was a very hot July morning when I first went down to the Lower East Side. As soon as I got off the subway on East Broadway I noticed some teenagers on bikes, sitting outside a kosher pizza parlor, talking so heatedly that their yarmulkes kept bobbing up and down on their long hair. I decided to introduce myself to them. One, Elliot Jaeger, a *Voice* reader, greeted me warmly and asked what sort of article I was researching in the neighborhood. An article about socialism on the Lower East Side, I said.

He laughed a little bitterly, and said that most Socialists had abandoned the neighborhood long ago—most had become businessmen and moved to the suburbs. Now, the Jewish Lower East Side was an economically depressed area. There were some middle-class people who lived in attractive cooperative apartments on Grand Street. But most of the ten thousand Jews in the neighborhood were impoverished elderly people, mostly Orthodox, often estranged from their children. Like Elliot himself, they lived in tiny apartments in low-income projects. Many were either housebound or afraid to go out on streets filled with traffic and muggers. (Indeed, there was a hidden epidemic of Jewish poverty in New York. According to a study compiled by Ann Wolf of the American Jewish Committee, about 250,000 people had incomes that were below the 1972 poverty level of three thousand dollars a year; 150,000 more earned less than forty-five hundred dollars a year.)

When I asked Elliot Jaeger how I could meet these Jews without money, he suggested I talk to a young Orthodox rabbi named Joel Price, a warm, friendly person who spent his time working with poor Jews.

I felt as if I had stepped through a looking glass. For one thing, I'd always assumed that most Jews had prospered in America, and that in Jewish culture, with its legendary emphasis on family, most successful young people took care of their parents. Now, it seemed, I had set out to find a heritage I never really possessed—Jewish socialism—and stumbled on a metaphorical version of the past that obsessed me—a neighborhood of Jake Cohens.

It was easy to fantasize about meeting religious Jews, particularly after I'd read Chaim Potok's novel *The Chosen.* By making the Orthodox Jewish world seem like a compellingly attractive, secure place, Potok reversed the stereotypes Norman Mailer and Herman Wouk had created in my mind. I also identified with the novel because Reuven Malter, the adolescent narrator, and David Malter, his father, have a wonderfully intimate relationship rooted in their commitment to Jewish life and their love of Jewish texts. As I read the book, I found myself thinking about my own adolescence, and wishing that I had enjoyed a similarly close relationship to my father back then.

Once I was actually on the Lower East Side, though, it seemed somewhat threatening to realize that the best way to learn about the neighborhood was to befriend an Orthodox rabbi—a person whose life was governed by laws my family had abandoned decades ago, laws that seemed completely alien to me.

I'd known how to relate to North Africans in Beersheba, to blacks in Mississippi, to Ecuadorians, to the priests and nuns on the Catholic left. I had no idea of how to relate to Rabbi Joel Price.

At least I wanted to hear a voice from my world before I became entangled in this new, strange one. There was a yeshiva across the street from the kosher pizza parlor, so I went in there to call Rachel. As I was dialing, I noticed students and black-garbed men who seemed to be teachers gathering outside the phone booth. They were staring at me, as if I was some peculiar form of human species. Then I noticed they were all wearing yarmulkes. It had never occurred to me that you were supposed to wear a yarmulke in a yeshiva. As soon as I hung up, I fled in embarrassment.

Elliot Jaeger, who was still standing outside the pizza parlor, told me I could buy a yarmulke for about two dollars at any of the stores on Essex Street that sold Judaica—a word I didn't quite understand. So I purchased a dark blue one, fastened it on my head with a bobby pin—a technique I remembered from Israel—and ate a very tasty corned beef sandwich at Sam's Delicatessen. I remember going to the bathroom after I ate, and seeing an old man praying on the stairwell. Now, I assume he was saying the mandatory Grace After Meals, though I still don't know why he was standing on the stairs instead of sitting at his table. Back then, I didn't even know the prayer existed.

After lunch I summoned up the courage to meet Rabbi Price. In those days, he was the youth director for Young Israel, an Orthodox synagogue on East Broadway. I found him in the synagogue's ill-lit basement, where religious kids were playing Ping-Pong or pool or registering for summer jobs. At one point they began to discuss a weekend they had spent taking rifle practice at a Jewish Defense League camp with the same flip bravado black militants had been using.

Luckily, I had found a man who loved to talk. So, within a few minutes, Joel and I were engaged in a heated version of the long conversation about politics and religion we've conducted for nearly a decade now. That day, though, I spent most of my time listening to him. I suppose, in retrospect, that I was an available symbol for his pent-up feelings about assimilated Jews. With as much frustration as anger in his voice, he told me that my decisions to work in the civil-rights movement and the Peace Corps, my job with *The Village Voice,* were signs that I'd betrayed Judaism and the Jewish people. Often he used the teenagers to underscore his point. Although his instincts were more cautious than theirs, he would ask political questions in his rigorous, talmudic way and then flick me a knowing smile when someone made an angry reference to a welfare recipient, or to a mugger, or extolled the virtues of the JDL. That was his way of making me understand the relationship between liberal, relatively off-beat cosmopolitan Jews like

me and the poorer, more rooted people who lived in his neighborhood. Why, he wondered, had we focused on oppressed blacks or on
peasants in South America or Vietnam and dismissed the oppression
of poor Jews—their fear of crime, for example—as fantasies or
forms of racism? We estranged ourselves completely from the Jews
without money. Some of his older friends and some of the kids in the
synagogues perceived those of us who had been in the movement
in the sixties as a privileged caste that had betrayed the rest of the
community, as class enemies. As a result, we had intensified their
sense of isolation and fueled their desperate anger.

Joel was so vehement in his opinions that I didn't dare risk rup-
turing our very delicate relationship by mentioning that I had committed what he might consider the ultimate act of abandonment
by marrying a gentile.

Our conversation was constantly interrupted by Joel's shouting
telephone arguments with elderly Jews who wanted to find themselves new apartments at once, or with housing officials who had
no room in their projects for the people Joel thought were genuinely
needy. I had spent most of a decade working with clergymen who
helped poor people: with ministers in the South, missionaries in
Ecuador, the priests and nuns I knew in the Catholic left. Mostly,
they had a gentle, orderly way of talking. They exuded compassion.
They seemed to live lives that were ten decibels lower than Joel's.
His words tumbled out so randomly, so noisily, in such an unpredictable pattern of jokes and personalized arguments, that I was
completely off-balance when I was with him. Besides, I didn't
know how to respond to his opinions, which, from my universalist
perspective, contained an odd blend of parochialism and compassion. For example, he'd mention a single unpleasant experience
with a black or Puerto Rican and use it to generalize about the entire
group. Then he would cite several pleasant experiences which
showed that, in his mind the generalization didn't really apply.

Over time, our Jewishness connected us in a way that was quite
different from the connections I felt with my movement friends. I'm
sure I was the first assimilated Jew who had ever remained in Joel's

life long enough to develop any rapport with him. He wanted to know about my world, especially when I described my father's work and my own travels. His questions were often eager, and certainly not hostile. And, at some level, I think, he saw himself as my *melamed* (teacher). He insisted that I wear a yarmulke whenever I entered the Young Israel. One night he invited me to eat dinner in the three-room apartment in the Gompers housing project that he and his brother, Martin, a law student at NYU, shared with their parents. Before we ate the tasty fried steak his mother had prepared, Joel insisted that I rinse each hand three times, according to Orthodox ritual, and join him in reciting the traditional Hebrew blessings over the food. I was perfectly willing but a little embarrassed, since I'd never heard those blessings in my life. During my four years at Choate I used to say a Christian grace before every meal. The previous winter I'd occasionally prayed with the Berrigans and their friends when they ate. But this was the first time in my thirty-one years that I had ever thanked the Lord for my food as my ancestors Jacob Cohen and Moses Spiegel had done. Joel was very patient about showing me the rituals and explaining their history. The next time I ate at his house I performed them flawlessly. He and his mother joked about how I'd become religious before I knew it. I laughed off their remark.

That summer, Joel and Martin were candidates for the Lower East Side's poverty board. The composition of their insurgent slate reminded me that it was dangerous to judge new acquaintances from unfamiliar backgrounds by words alone. For, during a time of accelerating ethnic separatism, they were part of a rainbow coalition that included Orthodox and assimilated Jews, Puerto Ricans, blacks, and Italians. Their ticket was accusing the mostly Puerto Rican incumbents of siphoning off city poverty funds. They won easily.

One Saturday, the Price brothers planned to campaign among the older Jews who sat on the Lower East Side's park benches every Shabbos afternoon. I said I'd come downtown to watch them. At first, they were receptive to the idea, but after a few minutes Martin realized that the trip would force me to violate Orthodox law by riding the bus or subway on Shabbos. I laughed and told him I doubted there was a Saturday in my life when I hadn't violated the prohibition against traveling. "Yes, but this is different," Martin said. "You'll be doing it because of us. It will be our responsibility."

The exchange troubled me. It reminded me of the difference between me and the Jews I wanted to write about—differences rooted in ancient laws, which seemed like atavisms to me but were vital, living realities to them. Sometimes I feared that I had strayed so far from my heritage that I'd never understand its most rudimentary ways. I was never sure whether something I took for granted—like traveling on Saturdays or walking bareheaded on the street or ordering a cheeseburger for lunch—would offend my new friends. In that sense, it was as difficult to learn the Lower East Side's culture as it had been to learn the culture I'd encountered when I went to Chestertown.

I wanted to meet the Jews without money, and I learned that the best way of doing that was to hang around the courtyard of the low-income Vladeck housing project and to eat at the daily lunch program that took place there. For a month, those were my haunts.

One morning I struck up a conversation with Moishe Kimmel, eighty-seven—"Moishe the Cleanly," as he called himself proudly. He had come to the United States from Poland sixty years earlier, after a series of episodes in which Polish soldiers beat him up because he happened to be out after the curfew.

He found a job in a Lower East Side jewelry store, and learned English quickly enough to rush through the "greenhorn" phase every immigrant dreaded. Now he spoke with only a trace of an accent. During the Depression his wife died and the small store he was working in went bankrupt. He had a nervous breakdown and was hospitalized for several years. When he got out, the Henry Street Settlement House gave him a job greeting visitors. He kept a very careful guest book and told everyone that celebrities like Herbert Lehman and Mrs. Roosevelt, who met him on a brief visit, were his close friends.

He was too old to stray far from his three-room apartment. But he was very eager for company. He urged me to visit him moments after we met in the Vladeck courtyard. When I appeared at his door, several days later, he kissed me with joy. He had to stand on tiptoes to reach my cheeks.

Proudly, he showed me his immaculate apartment. He had fashioned a tiny brown frame house, with windows and green shutters, out of Popsicle sticks and cellophane. He had framed a routine letter from Herbert Lehman, thanking him for some shred of political advice. He'd kept a police whistle and toy badge a friendly cop at the Seventh Precinct Station had given him. Clean ties and freshly pressed suits filled about one third of his small closet. His refrigerator was spotless—and empty. He had polished his galoshes in March to make sure they'd stay in shape all the next winter. "This is the cleanest of all the 3,071 apartments here," Moishe told me joyfully.

Until recently he would go out at night to sit in a small park on Water Street where his gregariousness found an outlet in conversations with old friends. Then, about eighteen months before we met, he was mugged in the lobby of his building. The muggers got eighty cents. It happened again, a few weeks before my visit, when he was walking to Gouverneur Clinic for a checkup. Two black men darted out of a cluster of bushes, shoved him hard enough to push him to the ground, and ripped the pocket from his shirt. They found a dollar. Moishe rarely went out anymore.

After the first mugging, Moishe's daughter, the wife of a doctor, offered to rent a small apartment for him a few blocks away from her house in Yonkers. But she never repeated the invitation. "It's all right," he said. "I never wanted to go there anyway. I ask her all the time how come she doesn't keep kosher, and she always argues back. And her house. It's such a mess."

She visited him occasionally. She was coming later that afternoon, to leave a cat with Moishe while she and her husband and kids went off on a short vacation. "Moishe the Cleanly" was very excited about the prospect of a weekend companion. Before I left he showed me the tiny corner of his living room, where he had placed a pillow of his bed for his cat to sleep on. He asked if a smart fellow like me had any ideas about how he could make the cat's home cozier.

Sometimes, I'd travel to the Lower East Side on Shabbos, taking care not to let the Price family see me. Even though it was mid-summer, the large shuls on East Broadway filled up with men and boys wearing their prayer shawls, chanting Hebrew psalms, prayers, and songs like "Adon Olam," which echoed up and down the block. Later in the morning, small groups clustered around wooden tables, savoring long discussions of complex passages of the Talmud, disputes that have endured for centuries. Strolling home, people paused to wish each other "Good Shabbos," as their ancestors had done for centuries, or to exchange the latest gossip, talking in Yiddish or in English. Many of the old people in the projects were too frail to go to shul. So they made a point of cooking lunch for each other, spending afternoons together, letting the rich tide of memory wash away the present's loneliness and fear.

Many weekday evenings, to my surprise, I found myself lingering on the Lower East Side until it was time to go to synagogue for evening services. There were about fifty shuls in the neighborhood. If you looked carefully enough, you found a microcosm of Eastern Europe, for each had been founded decades earlier by men from a particular village in Lithuania, Poland, or Russia. The old-timers insisted on the correctness of their villages' own traditions of worship. Those shuls were more than houses of worship; they were homes for the lonely, where people got together to recapture the life they had left behind.

The shuls fascinated me, but they made me uncomfortable. It had been much easier to worship with the Catholic left. Their ceremonies were in English. Their sedate, clearly stated rituals were much more comprehensible to me than the strange, mumbled services that made these old men stand up and sit down in no order that I could understand. But I was afraid to ask for an explanation of the religion I was observing. What if someone wheeled at me in the midst of prayer and denounced me as an impostor? Certainly I felt like one. I'd rock back and forth a little, faking a *daven*. I tried to remember to turn the pages of the prayer books backwards, pretended to follow the Hebrew text I couldn't understand. Sometimes

I'd moan a little, hoping that whoever heard me would regard my barely audible sounds as the appropriate psalm.

I was working on the Lower East Side during the weeks preceding Tisha B'Av, the anniversary of the destruction of the first and second Temples in Jerusalem, a day of fasting and mourning for all traditional Jews. I'd never heard of Tisha B'Av before that summer.

On Tisha B'Av, the *bimah* was shrouded with black curtains, and only a few candles lit the murky room. The congregants, sitting on the floor in the traditional position of mourning, chanted dirges from the Book of Lamentations, recalling the destruction of Jerusalem. *How doth the city sit solitary, that was full of people. How she is become as a widow. She that was great among the nations, and princess among the provinces, how she is become a tributary.*

Of course, I was still a stranger to religious Judaism, peering into it through the peephole of collateral reading and discreet questioning. Still that Tisha B'Av, I felt an unexpected sense of pride as I sat in a shul where I was completely anonymous, watching the old men, my kinsmen, keeping our imperiled history alive.

I suppose I felt a certain envy, too, since the history Rachel and I had helped to make seemed so very perishable. Just seven years earlier, three men, Andy Goodman, Michael Schwerner, and James Chaney had been martyred because they were willing to die for freedom. The invasion of Cambodia, the murders at Kent State, had occurred only two years before. The left had not created ceremonies to commemorate those tragedies, which shook a generation. Would my grandchildren know anything about them?

There is no liberation without the memory of liberation, or the memory of oppression. The old men in their murky downtown shuls were remembering. That precious feature of their religion— my religion—was entirely absent from the politics that had been my faith for nearly a decade.

By 1972, I had begun to evolve my own journalistic method. I loved to immerse myself in the lives of the people I wrote about. So, outwardly, my research on the Lower East Side didn't differ substantially from the research I'd done on Italians who lived in the Northeast Bronx or coal miners in western Pennsylvania or the Catholic left.

But I had never felt the depths of personal connection to those communities that I did to the people I met in the Vladeck courtyards or in shul during the days before Tisha B'Av.

In shul, I was beginning to glimpse my people's religious past, and hoping to find words that would convey some of my puzzling attraction to it. On the street, I was a crusader, listening to tales that, I hoped, would make the existence of Jewish poverty seem as shameful to my readers as it did to me.

On that political level, I know I was reacting to Joel Price's arguments and to the books I was reading which all bore out his point. For it was clear that ever since the Eastern European immigration began, wealthy German Jews, "uptowners" like me, *had* acted as a privileged caste. At the turn of the century, they sought to Americanize the newcomers whose crude manner of speech and worship threatened their position here. They funded settlement houses, cultivated intimate relationships with community leaders like Abraham Cahan, editor of the influential, socialist *Jewish Daily Forward,* sent out stump speakers and social workers to spread the message that it was unpatriotic to adhere to Jewish traditions in this promised land.

Their generation had sought to integrate the kinds of people I was meeting. My generation barely knew that there were still poor Jews on the Lower East Side. After talking with Joel and meeting people like Moishe, I became convinced that that situation had to be remedied. I came to believe that the New Left and its slightly more moderate electoral counterparts—George McGovern's presidential campaign of 1972, Mayor John Lindsay's liberal administration, Ramsey Clark's senatorial campaign of 1974—should fight for the rights of poor Jews with as much passion as we fought for the rights of women and blacks and Hispanics. It wasn't a question of changing our beliefs. It was a question of expanding our horizons.

Clearly, though, my feelings were more intense than any political argument can suggest. For days at a time, I'd find myself acting as a social worker, not a journalist. I'd try to get an old man a new set of false teeth. I'd spend hours talking to an old lady who had been mugged and who didn't know whether to help the community by reporting the episode to the police or remain silent so that she would be safe from any reprisals by the muggers. I sought some way to help a frightened old woman who lived with an unmarried daughter— and a brother and sister-in-law who both had Parkinson's disease—in her small apartment in the Vladeck. She was harboring more tenants than the city law allowed. She was scared she would be evicted.

Sometimes those encounters depressed and exhausted me. Many of the people I was meeting required professional help. They were so needy, so demanding that, when I wasn't waiting to *daven,* I often fled them and their neighborhood much earlier than I'd planned. Rachel and the kids were visiting friends in Vermont, so I would go back to the *Voice* and banter about politics or movies, or involve myself in some office intrigue, and pretend that those safe, familiar forms of human contact really represented work. But I'd always return to the Vladeck the next morning, notebook and tape recorder in hand. This went on for a month, far more time than I needed for the piece I planned to write. It took me that long to understand the feelings behind my obsession.

They became clear to me one evening when I met a pudgy, soft-spoken woman named Rebecca Schwartz in the Vladeck courtyard, and she invited me to her ground-floor apartment for a cup of tea. I said I'd come, even though I knew she was about to describe some problem I couldn't possibly solve.

She moved very slowly, using a walker. As she entered by her triple-locked door, she kissed her fingers and ran them lightly over the mezuzah. That ancient tribute to faith and stability at home filled me with a searing, almost tribal grief for all those old people lost here in America.

In the shtetl, their age would have been taken as a mark of wisdom, or at least as an acceptable stage of human development, not as a burden too great for most of their offspring to bear. They would have lived with their children and grandchildren, quarreling, of course, but accepting generational battles as a natural part of human existence. They wouldn't have aged in terrified isolation, but would have remained part of a cohesive community, with familiar institutions and ceremonies to comfort even those with the worst luck, the most debilitating mental and physical ailments. Beggars and rich men, cripples, fools, and sages all shared the joys of Shabbos, the awe of Yom Kippur, the crazy, rollicking abandon of Purim. On Shabbos, some of the old men who looked so lonely on the Vladeck benches would have known the serene pleasure of hearing their grandsons recite a week's lessons from the Torah or the Talmud. Some of the women would have confidently supervised the preparations for the day of rest. And, day after day, their special talents, like Moishe Kimmel's gift for crafting things, would have remained skills useful to the whole community, not just private, isolated hobbies that seemed a little sad and quirky. Now, though, like their contemporary, Jake Cohen, they were part of a generation that was still lost in the desert.

Mrs. Schwartz offered me some tea and a piece of crumbling cake. It looked completely unappetizing to me. But I knew that buying it had probably involved a painful, scary journey across Henry Street to the nearest food store. So I accepted the cake because I knew she'd take the refusal of her food as a sign that I was refusing her as a person. And I listened to her story.

Her family had left their shtetl during a Russian pogrom in 1906, and she spent most of her childhood working in her father's tiny grocery store on the Lower East Side. She married at twenty, but her husband, a sickly man, never found a steady job. Sometimes, when business was good, he got part-time work at a small neighborhood newsstand. He died when Mrs. Schwartz was thirty-five. The couple never had any children.

For thirty years, Mrs. Schwartz had been a ticket-taker in a Loew's movie theater. She had lived in the Vladeck since the project first opened, in the early 1940s.

In June 1964, she had had a stroke. Two nephews, both doctors, paid her medical bills. But they didn't send her money or visit her anymore. "What do they want with an old lady like me?" she asked. "I have enough money in the bank to pay for my rent and my food and buy my tombstone. What else do I need?"

It was hard for her to sleep at night. She went to bed at seven or eight, but usually woke up at midnight. Then her aches, her fear that each pain would bring a lonely death, kept her up for hours. She wished she could watch the late movie, but she never turned the television on for fear of bothering her neighbors. She couldn't read English very well. But she spent a few hours every day looking through the Yiddish-language *Daily Forward*. It reminded her of the time when, as a teenager, she used to read the paper's popular advice column, "A Bintel Brief" to her illiterate mother.

She got the paper from an old Jewish war veteran she had known for years. He bought it every morning and gave it to her every night. "He isn't all there," she told me. "I think he was shell-shocked in World War I." He repeated himself constantly, and sometimes those repetitions made her so irritable that she feared she would have another stroke. She never complained, though. She didn't want to hurt the old man's feelings or make him so angry he would quit giving her his *Daily Forward*.

She used several kinds of medication each day—heart pills, painkillers, pills for high blood pressure. But the previous April her Medicaid had run out. She had enough pills to get her through the summer. But what would happen the next fall? That was what she had wanted to ask me about.

Whenever she went to the local health clinic for an application form, they told her to make an appointment at the new office on Thirty-fourth Street. But how could she get there? "Do they think I can climb up and down the subway stairs on this walker? That I can afford to pay for a taxi? I telephone the office on Thirty-fourth Street. But they always give me one of those recordings that says that so-and-so is too busy to talk right now. They must be very busy up there. I've called six times and I've always been cut off before I can talk to anyone. I can't afford to waste all the dimes.

"Anyway, what good will it do me to reach them? The same thing always happens when I talk to people from the government. I get so flustered I begin to cry. Then I can't remember any English. The only words that come to me are in Yiddish. But everyone down there only speaks English or Spanish. So what should I do? Some nights I can't sleep at all, I'm so worried about what will happen if the pills I have now run out and I don't get another supply."

I couldn't answer her. Why, I wondered, did she have to come to me at all? Her nephews, the doctors, should have been able to get her the medicine she needed without any problem. But apparently, they had forgotten her completely. She was an invisible woman.

As I walked to the subway, I began to think of the scores of similar stories I'd heard over the past month. Almost all of them involved rifts between older people and their more prosperous, Americanized descendants.

Sometimes, elderly Jews like Moishe Kimmel preferred the threatening streets of the Lower East Side to the goyish suburbs where their children lived. They knew where to find kosher butchers, stores that observed Shabbos, Orthodox shuls. Modern American neighborhoods left them feeling depressed and disoriented.

Instead of respecting their elders, as they would have a century ago, the younger Jews seemed to treat them with disdain. Moishe Kimmel's daughter was only visiting him to drop off a pet cat. The woman who had been mugged in the Vladeck project begged me not to mention her name in print for fear that her son, a prosperous uptown lawyer, who was ashamed to visit her, would be so angry and embarrassed that he'd stop sending the weekly checks she depended on. Once I had visited a woman named Sylvia Rose, whose three rooms were particularly barren. The only prominent decoration in her apartment was a sign above her frayed brown couch instructing the person who found her remains to send them to a nephew, a chemical engineer on Long Island, who hadn't visited her for a decade. She was a difficult, demanding woman. I might have avoided her if I had been related to her, but still her gloomy sense of isolation was painful to see.

Naturally, the details varied from one story to another, but the quarrels I heard about often gave me some new insights into the one between Jacob Cohen and Louis Cowan. In that sense, their rift was much more typical than I'd imagined from my father's disparaging allusions to his father. In fact, Jake was better off than many of the people I was meeting on the Lower East Side. Although he was estranged from his son, Lou gave him financial support with no strings attached. Moreover, Jake lived among siblings who tolerated him and nephews and nieces who adored him, not in Rebecca Schwartz's total isolation.

In many Eastern European families, there had been a silent, secret war between *bubbe* and *zayde* (grandmother and grandfather) and Mom and Pop. The rifts began as soon as the immigrants left Ellis Island. No one was to blame for them. Yet, their consequences were shattering. They left many of the grandchildren, my contemporaries, orphans in history.

I still felt depressed as I got on the subway. What if I got Rebecca Schwartz her Medicaid prescription? There were thousands of people in the neighborhood I couldn't help—thousands that no one was helping.

But then, as I rode the F train uptown, I began to see her plight in a somewhat different perspective. For I realized that old people like Rebecca Schwartz used their complaints, real and painful as they were, to establish contact with people like me. Some of my contemporaries, relatively secure, Americanized Jews, could serve as surrogates for their inattentive children: we might do a little to heal some of the rifts that had multiplied through a generation.

I wanted to play that role. It was one way of healing the rift between my father and my grandfather. It was one way of coming home.

9

During the 1970s my job at the *Voice* gave me a chance to fulfill the journalist's fantasies I had harbored ever since I was a child, reading Steinbeck, Dos Passos, and Agee. For I could spend weeks or even months in new cultures I'd always regarded as appealingly mythical—among Mexicans in the border town of Juarez; or coal miners in Harlan County, Kentucky; or fundamentalist Christians in Campbell's Creek, West Virginia; and learn intimate details about the people who lived there without having to commit myself to them. Those stories, as a whole, represented a more introspective interlude than I realized when I was writing them. They were dialogues with experiences: ways of understanding my perpetual dissatisfaction with the highly mobile urban elite whose values had shaped me; ways of understanding my more recent dissatisfaction with the movement and with the narcissistic attitude people had begun to equate with radicalism. In the end, those excursions into American communities left me with a profound respect for the stability of religion, families, ceremonies—institutions I would have called bourgeois throughout the sixties. Those encounters with rooted cultures pushed me toward an increasingly deep personal interest in the Judaism I'd first seen on the Lower East Side.

In 1972 when I wrote "Jews Without Money, Revisited," I was still living on the turbulent periphery of the New Left, where virtually anything one said or wrote about blacks or women or left-wing political organizations was subjected to microscopic analysis, designed to detect any traces of sexism or racism or conservatism in one's thought. That nit-picking cantankerousness left me with a constant sense of uneasiness about much of my journalistic work. So it was especially rewarding to discover how much readers in general—

and especially Jewish readers—liked my series, even though it
contained explicit attacks on the Americanized generation that
had abandoned its parents and a very strong denunciation of organized Jewish philanthropies which, I thought, gave too much
money to Israel, too little money to America's Jewish poor. Scores
of people wrote friendly letters. Jewish organizations asked me to
describe what I had discovered. Since I had discussed my assimilated background in one article, their members often made me
feel like a prodigal son. In those years, my ego was so fragile that
the experience of being embraced by the Jewish community affected me almost as deeply and lastingly as did my experiences in
the Vladeck project.

Besides, the series actually did help people like Moishe Kimmel, and Rebecca Schwartz. Some readers sent in money so that
Mrs. Schwartz could buy her medication and the man in the
Vladeck courtyard could buy false teeth. More important, the articles accelerated a city-wide effort to assist poor Jews. In 1973
Mayor John Lindsay's administration helped inaugurate the United
Jewish Council of the Lower East Side. There Rabbi Joel Price and
a dozen of his counterparts assisted senior citizens who needed
housing, medicine, social security benefits. A few blocks away
from the council, in a building called the Educational Alliance, a
young, charismatic, Bulgarian-born Jew named Misha Avramoff
and some volunteers started an organization called Project Ezra to
work with the elderly Jewish poor. Down the hall, a man named
Fred Siegel—once a beatnik, now an Orthodox Jew—headed a
new multiservice center for the elderly, funded by the Federation
of Jewish Philanthropies. There was no way those organizations
could solve all the problems I'd heard about in the Vladeck. But,
once again, East Broadway was becoming a center of help for poor
Jews. And I was recognized as one of the people who had helped
bring that about.

At first, Rachel had a very tentative, ambiguous relationship to
my new Jewish persona. In those years, she was a freelance photographer. When I wrote about coal mining in Kentucky or busing

in Boston or truck drivers on Interstate 80, she took the pictures for my stories. But she didn't accompany me to the Lower East Side. While I was researching my piece, we both thought it was prudent to keep hidden the fact that we were an interfaith marriage. But I mentioned that fact when I wrote the articles. I didn't want to begin my involvement with the Jewish world under false pretenses, but Rachel and I also knew there was no guarantee that people who liked my journalism would approve of our private life. Rachel usually stayed away from my speeches about the Lower East Side because we were worried that some angry reader would see us together and accuse us of complying in cultural genocide. Many intermarried couples we knew had described experiences like that. But she was very much attracted to the world I had described.

In 1972 my involvement with poor Jews, my flirtation with the Jewish community, had much more effect on my consciousness than on my practice. In retrospect, though, I realize that I was already in a state of flux.

I remember, in mid-December 1973, I covered the truck drivers' strike that shut down America's highways for nearly a week. It had been a fascinating assignment, in which I learned the truck drivers' citizens-band lingo and the details of their free-wheeling lives. But it was dangerous too, since the drivers with whom I hitchhiked were often shot at by vigilante posses. I got home a few days before Christmas—the winter holiday Rachel and I had always celebrated. I felt a flood of satisfaction and relief, for I had a wonderful family week ahead of me and a wonderful story to write.

The day after I got home, Matt and I invented a rollicking game based on a television special. We were both bears who had come from Canada, in search of Christmas. In real life, I had an allergy to bacon—it gave me headaches and put me to sleep—so we incorporated that fact into our bear world: I attached an alarm clock to my foot in order to wake if some bad guys came along and fed me bacon. I described the game in a *Voice* article about my kids. Another staffer, a committed Jew, asked me angrily how I could reconcile it with the sentiments I had expressed in "Jews Without

Money, Revisited." But Christmas (not to mention non-kosher food) was a totally organic part of my life. In our apartment on the Upper West Side we always decorated our tree with some of the oldest heirlooms in the Cowan family—a cotton Santa Claus, a doughy wreath, a brightly clothed baker, a noble steed—with which my grandmother Lena Spiegel had decorated her tree in Kenilworth. My mother had hung them on our tree when I was a child. It never occurred to me, in 1973, that there might be a contradiction between the unexpected identification with Judaism I'd felt while writing the article on poor Jews and the celebration that my family enjoyed so much.

Nevertheless, during those months, we and our friends were constantly discussing Israel and Judaism. A year earlier—the week "Jews Without Money, Revisited" appeared—the PLO had murdered eleven Israeli athletes in Munich. The Yom Kippur War had occurred in October 1973. Why did so many non-Jews in the movement express indifference toward these tragic events? It turned out that dozens of Jewish friends of ours, who had always regarded themselves as radicals, shared that question. It made us introspective. What were *our* feelings about Israel? About being Jewish? What could we do to make sure that our children wouldn't grow up to be as ignorant and confused as we?

Rachel thought about such questions even more seriously than did most of our Jewish friends. Paradoxically, in those days, she cared more about Lisa's and Matt's Jewish identity than I did. Since she is a very practical person she decided to transform the free-floating emotions the rest of us expressed into some sort of durable institution.

At first, Purple Circle, the day-care center she started while I was covering the Catholic left, seemed an ideal base. Most of the parents were Jews who worried about Israel, worried about anti-Semitism, but who would never give their kids any sort of formal religious education. But in 1973—during the week I was covering the truck strike—Jerry Raik, a teacher there, with a strong Jewish background, an actor by training, had enthralled everyone at the Purple

Circle by telling the Hanukkah story. Rachel had been particularly moved. So, from then on, every Hanukkah and Passover, she organized celebrations where Jerry would come to our apartment and tell the stories of the Maccabees or the Exodus to about sixty fascinated adults and kids.

Rachel wanted something more substantial and durable for the children. So, soon, she and our upstairs neighbor, Judy Rosenberg Pritchett began toying with the idea of starting a Jewish school. It was a realistic notion, since the Purple Circle, the Riverside Park playground, and P.S. 75, where Lisa was in kindergarten, had created a network of friends who were suddenly interested in forging a brand of Judaism in which we could participate. None of us thought that could happen in a synagogue; those places, we believed, were too cold, too formal to nurture the kinds of classes and celebrations we wanted. But none of the parents—even those who had been to Hebrew school and had celebrated a bar mitzvah—knew enough about the Bible or Jewish traditions to teach the kids ourselves.

In our neighborhood, there was an organization called the New York Havurah (in Hebrew the word *havurah* means fellowship). It was a sort of Jewish counterpart to the New Left, composed of religiously knowledgeable people in their twenties and thirties who were searching for alternatives to a synagogue life. Most of us had been to the High Holy Day services they conducted, the Purim parties they organized, in a shabby, crowded apartment on Riverside Drive. So we knew that the New York Havurah didn't believe in rabbis. We had seen men and women—many of whom had studied at the Jewish Theological Seminary—conducting religious services without the sexual discrimination that existed in more traditional Jewish settings. Clearly, their style suited our needs.

So we asked members of the Havurah to help us start a school. Three of them agreed. Until then, they had taught in more traditional Hebrew schools where parents seemed indifferent to the content of what was taught. That was why they decided to take a chance that there was true commitment beneath our confusion. They insisted that the parents participate in shaping the curriculum—and in teaching. Like us, they wanted the school to be part of a community, not just a place where adults dropped off young Americans so that they could be processed into Jews. And they hoped that working with secularized people like us would help them re-examine their own faith.

Their gamble paid off. Soon the parents' meetings—and the school itself—became a forum for adults and kids to work out their ideas about Judaism.

The Havurah School, as we called it, began just after Passover 1974, with three teachers and twenty-one students between the ages of four and seven. Most of the parents were artists, academics, and professional people. There were two college professors, a psychiatrist, a social worker, an extremely successful professional photographer, a store owner who sold kitchenware, a potter, a secondary-school math teacher. Most, reared in middle-class Jewish neighborhoods like Forest Hills and Teaneck, New Jersey, had left home in the late fifties, and spent most of the sixties coupling professional training with a commitment to the New Left.

At first, our discussions about Judaism were permeated with the relativistic assumptions we'd developed in the movement. For example, one parent felt that the concept of Ten Commandments was too authoritarian. We should teach them as Ten Suggestions. Another thought we should devote part of the curriculum of our avowedly Jewish school to teaching alternative religions, like Buddhism. Some parents tried to forbid the teachers from describing the blessings. They wanted the very existence of prayer to remain a secret. Even the Bible, in its uncensored form, worried some adults, who wondered how children could cope with psychologically disturbing stories like Abraham's decision to sacrifice Isaac.

In the end, though, we decided that a Jewish school had to contain undiluted Jewish material and that the kids should be encouraged to explore issues that perplexed them through dramas, through drawing, through open-ended discussions.

Soon, the school—which met in the *havurah* apartment— became a sort of open-corridor *heder,* and one of the most cherished activities in the kids' week. I remember assisting on the day the binding of Isaac was taught. One of the teachers and I helped some kids improvise a play as a way of examining their reactions. Their most intense response, it turned out, concerned Sarah. How did she feel when Abraham told her about his discussion with the Lord? How could she remain calm when her husband and son were away? In the play, Lisa was Sarah. She made her into an active, combative woman who told Abraham he should refuse God's demand, and then marshaled her servants to follow him up the mountain to save her son if she had to. In that way, the kids took the text and gave it a psychological dimension—as countless Jews had done before them.

In the parents' meetings, I used to question the emphasis that Jews—and Jewish schools—had traditionally placed on the suffering of our people. That question was certainly woven into my life, for, valuable as my mother's emphasis on the Holocaust had been, it had made me regard Judaism as a remorselessly heavy ethical burden. Did I—did we—want to pass that feeling onto our kids? We didn't have to. As our Hanukkah parties and seders showed, the religion included innumerable opportunities for celebration. Why not blend them into the curriculum? Why not make the school a place where the kids equated Judaism with joy?

I tried to do that, when I was there, by helping them put out a newspaper, with serious articles about the land transaction between Jacob and Esau, with fashion items gleaned from the account of Isaac's marriage to Rebecca, with ads, by Matt, for products like Sarah's "rent a tent" or Abraham's longevity pills. After a while the newspaper turned into a Mary Tyler Moore-type news show, which was broadcast over an imaginary station the kids named WJEW.

We spent months wondering how the Diaspora should be taught, particularly life in the Eastern European shtetls, where most of the children's ancestors came from. Nothing seemed to work. There were no immigrant parents who could tell us stories about the old country. The kids had no interest in making family trees. Then, Paul Minkoff, a labor organizer who had two kids in the school, decided to end an afternoon with a story about Chelm, the fabled Eastern European village of fools. It was as if Isaac Bashevis Singer, who helped popularize the Chelm stories in America, had appeared in the flesh. By the spring of 1975, Paul's stories had become a weekly ritual. The kids got so involved with the imaginary village that they wanted to re-create it in the apartment on Riverside Drive. They used papier-mâché to build the synagogue, the *heder*, the blacksmith's shop, the house where Gimpel the Fool lived, and the streets that connected them all. Then, toward the end of those spring afternoons, the parents, teachers, and kids all gathered to hear Paul tell still another story of the Eastern European shtetl, or to make up a story of their own. It was an enchanted time.

That year, some of the children began to urge their parents to light candles and say the blessings which traditionally usher in Shabbos. That surprised us and threatened some of us, since most parents defined themselves as agnostics or atheists. We had hoped, somehow, to teach tradition without teaching religion. Now, suddenly, it looked as though we might be raising a generation of kids who believed in a God whose existence most of us denied. The mother who had wanted Buddhism included in the curriculum said, half jokingly, that if her son became a rabbi there would be an apparently unrelated string of assassinations around the world— and that we would be the victims.

Still, most parents were eager to analyze their intense negative reactions to what were, after all, very mild forms of observance. Soon our meetings became Jewish consciousness-raising sessions, where we re-examined our own childhoods in the 1950s.

Most of the parents in the school described childhood religious experiences that had left enduringly bitter memories. Most had worshiped in Conservative synagogues. They associated the synagogues with the High Holy Days, and the High Holy Days with tension over money. Those who had been relatively poor hated the fact that the price of tickets on Rosh Hashana and Yom Kippur had been scaled, and that they had been obliged to sit in the basement. Even the wealthier ones remembered the High Holy Days as a time when Jews flaunted their wealth: when women showed off mink shawls, which they jokingly described as their tallisim. Some of the parents, like our neighbor Judy Rosenberg Pritchett, had been quite religious as children. But as Judy grew increasingly political, she became disillusioned. Why, she wondered, did the rabbis, whose sermons were about morality and brotherhood, spend all their time worrying about sisterhoods and building funds instead of working for integration? Judy retained a deep attachment to the faith. But she began to see the place where it was practiced as a "chrome temple."

All of us acknowledged that we wanted to blend into America with no difficulty at all. As we discussed that feeling, some of the parents discovered that they identified all signs of being Jewish— from wearing yarmulkes to lighting Shabbos candles—with the slightly shamed sense of being different from the people whose world they longed to enter.

Those consciousness-raising sessions had a therapeutic effect on most of the parents in the school. For as each of us in turn confronted the fears and resentments we'd grown up with, we came away with the proud certainty that we had inherited something worth exploring and passing on.

One Friday night in the spring of 1975, Rachel and I asked Judy Rosenberg Pritchett and her son, Slim, to light Shabbos candles with us and Lisa and Matt. It felt like a bold step. I'd seen the ceremony on the Lower East Side and in Israel—but always as a spectator. I didn't feel as if I possessed the tradition. It was certainly alien to Rachel. But Judy knew the blessings and felt that they were part of her identity. So we all felt quite excited, and somewhat self-conscious, as we lit the candles, said kiddush, and placed our hands over the challah we had bought for the evening meal as we blessed God for the food that had come from the earth.

By the autumn of 1975, Rachel and Lisa and Matt and I had begun to light Shabbos candles almost every Friday night. It was the first

Jewish ritual we regularly observed as a family. In retrospect, I think we adopted it for our own distinct emotional reasons, and not for religious ones.

That was the year my work began to require traveling. Within twelve months, I had assignments that took me to Boston and Chicago; to West Virginia; to California; to Portugal and France. It was a marvelous time, but the steady barrage of fresh impressions—and the pressure to organize them into stories that were worthy of print—often distracted me from my inner life.

And, it turned out, the kids needed rituals too. For, in those years, the mid-1970s, the angry, self-centered emotions that had imperiled the New Left were beginning to destroy personal lives. Some combination of women's liberation and the sexual revolution was prompting parents to push ordinary fights into major eruptions; sometimes to shatter relationships that might have been salvaged. Many feminists insisted that marriage itself was a patriarchal trap. Men and women alike saw fidelity as an abridgment of personal freedom, a rein on psychological growth. In our cosmopolitan world, people argued for open marriage almost as if it were a theology. In my opinion, some had crossed the thin line that divides liberation from licentiousness. The victims, of course, were their children.

Lisa, seven, and Matt, five, had a kids'-eye view of the problem. They saw marriages falling apart for no apparent reason. Their good friends would come over for dinner, and suddenly begin to weep with grief because Mommy or Daddy had stormed out of the house that day. Had they—the kids—done anything wrong? Could they have saved the marriage? Who would they live with now?

Suddenly, the world seemed like a very unstable place to our two children. I realized that one night when they begged Rachel and me to promise not to get divorced. There was no reason to think we would. We had been through some rough times a few years earlier, when the strain of raising two tiny children seemed to sap our feelings for each other, but now that we were older that period of our lives seemed remote. In fact, between our journalism and photography and our evolving interest in Judaism we felt closer to each other than ever. But how could grade-school kids know that? How could they understand the vicissitudes of a marriage? They needed something firmer than a promise. Shabbos, with its rituals, its certainty of a full evening together, every Friday, watching TV or playing a game, seemed like one embodiment of stability, one steady way of quieting the kids' fears and drawing us closer together as a family.

Still, I hadn't quite recognized the conflict between my career and my private life—between my identity as a journalist who loved to travel and that of a family man who longed to make my increasingly Jewish home the center of my emotional life—until the *Voice* asked me to cover the revolution in Portugal during the weeks in September 1975 that included Rosh Hashana, Yom Kippur, and Sukkot.

Of course, I accepted the assignment. I was thrilled with the prospect of the adventure, and I loved the story itself, for Portugal was a beautiful country with friendly, candid people and a post-revolutionary political life that had as much intrigue as a political novel. As an American, I had a curious kind of access to that intrigue. My interpreter was the blond son of a missionary who'd been born in Brazil and worked as a Peace Corps volunteer in India. Often he and I traveled outside Lisbon, to the North of the country, the site of bloody clashes between Socialists and Communists. We'd sit in a bar or a main square and wait for pro-American Portuguese to seek us out. In town after town, they invited us to clandestine meetings at some merchant's house, and told us that they were secret right-wingers who were posing as members of the Socialist Party so that they could gain sympathy in Europe and the Americas when they provoked the Communists to attack them. They hoped that we were CIA agents so that we could help them in their struggle for freedom. In those conversations I remained as noncommittal as possible. It was clear to me that the encounters were adding up to a scoop.

But I remember going to Lisbon's main synagogue on Rosh Hashana and imagining Rachel, Lisa, and Matt on the Upper West

Side. They would be with the rest of the parents, teachers, and kids from the Havurah School, participating in a ceremony called *tash-lich*—a late-afternoon ritual where people put bread crumbs in their pockets, then walk to the nearest body of flowing water and throw the crumbs in the water as a symbolic way of casting out the year's sins. That Rosh Hashana, I knew, our long-haired, blue-jeaned group of men, women, and children would be wandering through Riverside Park, down to the edge of the Hudson. While I sat in the Portuguese synagogue, my family and friends would be gathered by the water, laughing and joking as they passed the Orthodox Jews who always seemed shocked by our appearance but were probably glad that we were keeping the tradition alive. Then they'd walk back through the tunnel on Ninety-sixth Street and up the hill to Riverside Drive, greeting everyone they passed with the traditional phrase *Le-shana tova*—Happy New Year.

To my surprise, I found myself wishing that I had turned down the *Voice's* assignment. I wanted to spend my newfound New Year with my family and community, not with strangers. Of course, my mood would change after the holiday, when I was back at work again, but still that momentary sense of loneliness taught me something new—something in my psychological equation had changed. For the first time in my life, my longing for home was immeasurably keener than my interest in a story. I would keep traveling on journalistic assignments, of course, but never on Jewish holidays, never for so much time. I no longer saw myself as a contemporary version of John Dos Passos or James Agee who would discover himself through his travels. From then on, my odyssey would be linked to my family and my community, and to my unexamined inner self.

In synagogue that Rosh Hashana I began to hear about scattered, isolated communities of secret Jews—Marranos, as they were called during the Inquisition, who still held fast to their version of Judaism. Their history fascinated me at once—I suppose because it bore an eerie resemblance to my father's and my own. When I asked about it I was told to talk with a Portuguese businessman named Ignazio Steinhardt, who had spent a great deal of time with them in the town of Belmonte, in the mountainous North of the country.

Steinhardt was used to serving as a conduit between the Marranos (or *conversos,* as they preferred to be called, since *marrano* is the Spanish word for pig) and the outside world. Some of his friends in Belmonte had allowed him to tape their prayers and their ceremonies. Once a few of them allowed an Israeli TV crew to film some interviews. Those machines, tape recorders and TV cameras, are products of an electronic age and carried no evil memories. But, Steinhardt told me, most *conversos* still forbid him to inscribe their words on paper. They still feared that a written record of their secret ceremonies might fall into the hands of the Inquisition.

Though they lived as Catholics, they quietly defied the church that forced them to convert or be killed. According to Steinhardt, they fused its forms with their inherited memories—they have a Saint Abraham, a Saint Moses, a Saint Job. In secret, generations of *conversos* have observed Shabbos, celebrated Purim and Passover, performed weddings and sat shiva (mourning the dead), just as their ancestors had. Living behind Portugal's remote mountains, completely out of contact with the outside world, they believed they were the last people on earth to do so.

For me, the Holocaust had always been the inferno of Jewish history. I had never realized what harm the Inquisition inflicted.

In Portugal, the Inquisition began in the 1490s. During it every book in Hebrew, including the Torah, was banned from the country, and anyone who was found reading or speaking the language could be executed. In fact, anyone who was circumcised, or refused to eat pork or shellfish, or refrained from going to church could be denounced as a heretic and killed. So, to preserve some shreds of tradition, Portuguese sages invented an elaborate system of subterfuges and translated much of the Hebrew litany into Portuguese jingles, which could be remembered and transmitted from one generation to the next.

As recently as sixty years ago, the *conversos* thought that all the Jews in the world had been killed in the Inquisition, and that they alone had survived by escaping to their barren, remote province and taking on the protective coloration of Christianity. Even though they now know that other Jews exist, they still fear the Inquisition. Their ceremonies must comprise one of the most durable underground religions in human history, since they blend open Christianity with rituals that hark back to the Judaism that was denied to their ancestors. For example, many of them are married in two ceremonies: in church and, later that same day, in the cellars of their own homes, where an old woman binds the hands of the bride and groom and weds them "according to the laws of Moses."

Most of them go to church. But, as they cross themselves and dip their hands into the holy water, they mutter an incantation of spiritual resistance—a rejection of idolatry—that bears some resemblance to the private contract Joel Cassel made with God every night in the Choate chapel:

> *I am coming into this house*
> *But you, God, know I don't believe*
> *In wood or stone.*

For the *conversos,* Purim, not Passover, is the major festival of liberation. Queen Esther has a special meaning for them. She, like the *conversos,* was a Jew who pretended to worship an alien God. She lived as a Persian until her cousin Mordecai warned her that Haman planned to exterminate all her people. Then she revealed her faith to the King, and persuaded him to send Haman to the gallows. The *conversos* knew that Esther fasted for three days before she sought to save the Jews. They follow her example. They call Purim the Fast of Esther.

They regarded her as an exemplar, as a special symbol of hope. She was their Saint Esther, and she plays the same powerfully mystical role in their lives that the Virgin Mary does for devout Catholics.

The outside world knew nothing of the *conversos* until 1917, when Samuel Schwarz, a Polish mining engineer, came to Belmonte. People there warned him not to trade at one of the local stores. It was owned by Jews. Of course, that warning whetted his curiosity. But when he attempted to establish contact with the *conversos,* insisting that he shared their secret faith, they didn't believe him. How could he have survived the Inquisition?

But they were curious about him. In Belmonte, their religion is a matrilinear one—possibly because the faith is centered in the home. When a girl reaches eleven she learns the secret prayers and ceremonies from her mother, and is warned not to share them with the outside world.

One summer evening, with much of the community present, Schwarz was moved to chant the ancient Hebrew prayer, *Shema, Yisrael, Adonai Elohenu, Adonai Ehad.* (Hear, O Israel, the Lord is our God, the Lord is One.) Though the people of Belmonte had never heard of a language called Hebrew, that prayer opened the door of trust. Adonai—God—was the only Hebrew word that had survived the Inquisition: the only trace of the holy tongue that remained in their Portuguese language liturgy. As soon as Schwarz uttered the word, the *conversos* covered their eyes. One of the oldest women among them recited a prayer. Then, weeping, she reached out her hands and touched Schwarz's face. "He is indeed a Jew," she said. "For he knows the name of Adonai."

Still Schwarz's visit didn't really change the *conversos'* attitude toward the outside world. To this day, they remain wary and clannish. In towns like Belmonte, they still preserve and protect the Shabbos and all religious ceremonies with secrecy. On Friday night while the women prepare a special meal, the men sit outside playing cards so that the neighbors won't suspect anything is amiss. Then, they bolt their doors, shutter their windows, and light their "Candle of the Lord"—the Shabbos candle—which provides the only light until it flickers out. They bless the dead and pray for the ailing members of the community.

Like all Jews, the *conversos* regard Passover as a plea for deliverance from their centuries of exile. So, for hundreds of years, the people who believed they were the only surviving remnants of an extinct faith preserved its rituals as carefully as possible.

Before the holiday, the *conversos* of Belmonte, like Jews all over the world, clean house. Then, for three days, they cease eating bread, in accordance with the Torah's injunction that any Jew who consumes leavening during the days of Passover will be cast out of the faith. They choose one of the families in the community to mix flour or cornmeal and water, and bake it on steaming bricks or in an oven. They don't know the word matzo, so they call the tortilla-like food *pao santo,* holy bread.

The act of baking is a community ceremony. Women put on white dresses. Men dress themselves in the white garments in which they will be buried. The floor of the house is covered with white linen. While the *pao santo* is baking, the *conversos* kneel—like Catholics— and pray. When it is finished they rise and kiss one another. Each family takes home a portion of *pao santo* wrapped in white cloth.

Once, during Passover week, small groups of believers meet for a picnic in the mountains or a meal in town. Afterward, they gather by a rivulet of water—a tiny stream or even a puddle. They carry olive branches, which they use to beat the surface of the water, hoping it will part as the Red Sea did for Moses.

Then, they cross it, to symbolize Moses' crossing out of Egypt. On the other side, they stand together and, still dressed in white, waving their olive branches, they chant their Passover prayer for freedom:

> *On the fourteenth day of the moon*
> *Of the first month of the year*
> *The people leave Egypt.*
> *Israel, my brother.*
> *The songs they sing*
> *And the land they bless.*
> *When will you bring us, Moses,*
> *Out of this empty land*
> *Where there is no bread,*
> *No wood,*
> *Where no cattle go?*
> *Let us praise the high Lord*

Who is our Lord.
Here comes Moses with his staff
And he beats it in a closed sea
And the sea has opened in thirteen places.
My people will surely pass.
My people have passed surely,
The way the Lord commanded.

As soon as I had described Portugal's aborted revolution in the *Voice*, I began to forget its labyrinthine details. But the *conversos'* story kept reverberating in my consciousness. It was a testament to the power of the faith that had been submerged in my family.

My father had sought to submerge his Jewishness because of the lures of the melting pot. He wanted to reach the pinnacle of this society, not escape the horrors of the auto-da-fé. But, as I was beginning to realize, the Louis G. Cowan, media executive, who got irritated when offices were closed for Rosh Hashana and Yom Kippur, was a transient being. His Jewish identity was so resilient that it began to flower as soon as he was forced out of the corporate world, as soon as he had time to grow at his own pace. He ceased being an American-style *converso*.

I called my father the day after I returned from Portugal. The revolution was still on the front pages of American newspapers, and I knew his moderate and liberal friends supported the Socialist Party which, I intended to write, was a Trojan horse for Portugal's right wing. I wanted to prepare him for my argument in advance, for he was always in the position of defending my radical views.

He was very interested in my story, and quite proud that his son, the journalist, had been assigned to cover it.

But he was eager to describe an important experience of his own. During the Jewish holidays, a friend of his had taken him to the Jewish Theological Seminary, where he ate lunch in the green-boughed sukkah. How beautiful it was there! How he wished I could have joined him. Well, he sighed, maybe next year.

I suppose aging, religiously committed Jewish fathers must talk to their ambitious, busy sons like that all the time. It was a new experience for me. I felt guilty, I suppose, but I liked the new sense of connection it gave us.

One night that winter I took out my pen and my reporter's notebook and asked my father to list his uncles and aunts on the Cohen side of the family. That was when he told me about Abraham Cohen, the alderman. But his voice literally shook as he divulged the information he regarded as dangerously compromising. What a difference there was between that frightened reaction and the joy that had been in his voice when he described the sukkah!

Shortly after Passover 1976, I was working on a profile of the singer Paul Simon for *Rolling Stone* magazine. I wanted the article to contain a scene on the Lower East Side, where Simon's parents had been married. Misha Avramoff, the head of Project Ezra, took Simon and me around the neighborhood. He made a point of introducing us to Rabbi Joseph Singer, sixty-two, born in Poland to a family of rabbis—a highly esteemed family, I soon realized. Rabbi Singer was the tenth-generation descendant of Gershon Kitover, who was the brother-in-law of the Baal Shem Tov, the founder of the Hasidic movement.

I can't remember what we discussed that day. But I do remember being fascinated with the fact that Rabbi Singer combined an intense faith that he seemed eager to share with a kind of lightheartedness that made you feel cheerful as soon as you met him. He made me feel as if I'd be welcome in his world. So I decided to learn more about it by writing a profile of him the next fall.

———•◆•———

10

It was 3 A.M. on the morning of November 18, 1976, when two policemen rang our doorbell to tell me that my parents had died in a fire. They had my father's middle name wrong. For a moment, I thought the visit might be a case of mistaken identity. I called the Hotel Westbury. The desk clerk said the fire had occurred. I remember walking back to our bedroom, wailing a single bellowing sentence—"Oh, shit, my parents are dead." I remember asking the policemen who were sitting in the living room, trying to comfort me, what practical things I should do next. And crying for a little while. And taking a huge gulp from a bottle of wine.

Then my mother's voice, the voice of stoicism, of farsighted self-discipline, began to run through my mind. Polly and Lou Cowan were prominent people. Their death was bound to be news. By now it was about 4 A.M. I had to call Geoff and Holly and Liza before they heard the story on the radio. I should call my parents' closest friends, too, to spare them the shock. Rachel, sobbing, telephoned her mother, Maggie, asking her to come to New York and help us.

The story was already on the radio when Lisa and Matt woke up. We had to tell them at once, before they heard about it from someone else. Matt, who was six, collapsed in my arms, shivering with fright. Lisa wept uncontrollably, except during the moments she tried to pretend the fire hadn't happened.

Suddenly, Rachel and I were living on the outskirts of death: at the morgue, at the funeral home, on the telephone with the hundreds of people who called to commiserate, planning a funeral that was a tribute to my parents. We had almost no time for our children or ourselves.

Those were the days when I discovered how dependent I was on the community that had formed around the Havurah School. Unlike most of my friends from the movement and from journalism, who didn't quite know how to react once they'd made a first phone call or visit, whose nervousness occasionally made me feel like the carrier of some unpleasant disease, the parents and teachers in the school were all acquainted with the Jewish rituals of mourning. They helped Rachel's mother cook and take care of the kids as if those tasks were routine matters of communal responsibility. They acted as if Rachel and I were following the age-old practice of sitting shiva: staying at home for a week, letting our grief ebb and flow. They treated us like mourners, not victims, and that gave us some room to mourn. Along with a few other close friends, they filled our house with love during those horribly bleak days.

How I wish I'd had the strength to lose control, to grieve openly as Rachel and Lisa and Matt could. But I'd spent most of my lifetime defining myself through my relationships with other people instead of dwelling in the still, small place where my inner feelings lay.

I'd always dealt with tumultuous feelings by writing. For about a month after the fire, I sat in my cluttered office, phoning people who had known my parents, interviewing them at great length, in meticulous detail, so that I could express my emotions in a very personal obituary. But I was overwhelmed by information. Temporarily, my sorrow was lost amid notebooks full of facts, amid the reams of typing paper on which I'd tried to make sense of them. I lost the little perspective I had on my parents and myself. During those few lonely weeks, I felt an increasing sense of claustrophobia and no sense of relief. I could help comfort my children; I could serve as a stand-in for my parents—at a poster exhibit my father had arranged, for example, or a civil-rights benefit my mother had agreed to co-sponsor; I could do a little bit to diminish their friends' sense of loss. But I didn't know how to find comfort myself.

Meanwhile, my father's two-year campaign to convince me to write about Orthodox Jewish craftsmen kept nagging at me. I found myself very eager to honor it, and to mingle once again with people on the Lower East Side, the one place in America that had seemed to ease my loneliness.

Though I had met Rabbi Singer only once, I was sure he would help introduce me to the *sofers* and the *shochets* (the scribes and ritual slaughterers) whom my father had wanted me to describe.

I had another objective. Since meeting Bert Lazarus at the funeral, I had been phoning elderly relatives to get more information about the Lidvinova rav, but none of them knew very much. Rabbi Jacob Cohen's Eastern European Jewish way of life had perished in the Holocaust. So the only way I could re-create that part of my ancestral past was by accompanying Rabbi Singer through New York's European-born Orthodox world, his home.

11

In the beginning, I had a literary, cosmopolitan idea of the story I hoped Rabbi Singer would help me find. I was curious about his world, even obsessed with it now that I understood its relationship to the Cohen family, but I had no experience, except the months I'd spent researching "Jews Without Money, Revisited," and its sequels, to suggest what I would encounter among the men in black garb who had frightened me for so long. So I began my research with a somewhat distancing, man-about-town pose that must have guaranteed me safety then but surprises me now. "The piece will be a Chagall painting, a wavy line of traditional Jewish life as it was transposed to the America of Christmas trees, Easter egg hunts and hearty ham dinner," I typed when I outlined the project to the editors of the *Voice*.

Attracted as I was to Rabbi Singer, I never imagined that this friendly man from a completely alien culture—whose observance of talmudic law was so strict that he couldn't tear paper on Shabbos or eat meat outside his own house for fear it wasn't kosher, or enter a synagogue where men and women sat together—could possibly become a force in my life. But he did, very soon. For the beliefs which made him sound old-fashioned or finicky or sexist when I described them to my liberal friends had endowed him with a raw spiritual power that I had never before encountered.

He had lost most of his family in the Holocaust, and yet his extremely strict form of Judaism radiated a contagious joy. Oddly, it was ` kind of enthusiasm I'd hoped the Havurah School could convey kids. But by its nature, the Havurah School was an experi- 'most secular institution, with a gusto for teaching Torah 'f-conscious reluctance even to suggest that the families involved incorporate ritual into their lives. Now, I was beginning to see the joy I'd talked about in so many meetings embodied in a human being who was totally committed to the Jewish laws that still seemed so strange to me. I began to think that, in some form, the religious Judaism that seemed to lift his spirits constantly might lift mine too.

Most weeks from December 1976 until May 1977, I spent several days with Rabbi Singer. Our conversations almost always took place as we hurried from one appointment to the next. For he was both a rabbi and a social worker at the United Jewish Council of the Lower East Side, the person who accepted the cases the rest of the Council staff deemed unimportant or impossible. I remember, soon after we met, taking a three-transfer subway ride to Coney Island so that we could help a crippled, half-demented mother and son find the comfortable mattresses which they believed would ease the emotional stress they always felt. After we left, I asked this descendant of the Baal Shem Tov's family, this talmudic scholar, whether he really thought that a mattress would help people who were so clearly psychotic. Secretly, I was marveling at the compassion that took a man in his early sixties on such long journeys—and wondering whether the journeys themselves were worthwhile. He didn't know about the mattress, he said. But he was sure that lonely people needed to know that someone else in the world was concerned about their well-being.

From Rabbi Singer's point of view, the trip was a mitzvah. From mine, it was the sort of concrete good deed that had once made the New Left seem so attractive. Didn't it involve the same leap of faith my partner Bill and I had made when we spent that summer in Chestertown, trying to teach the French language to a black child who was going to integrate the local high school but who barely knew English grammar? On the left, the impulse to do those good deeds seemed to have evaporated. Those mitzvahs could never disappear from Rabbi Singer's life. They were woven into the fabric of his faith. So, when I was with him, I felt able to help people in the way I had wanted to in the South and in the Peace Corps

Ironically, in his Hasidic milieu I often felt that I was back in the humane, compassionate atmosphere I'd missed since the mid-sixties.

Rabbi Singer not only helped me find a way to mourn my dead parents and relive my family's past. He helped me discover something new and precious in myself—and in Judaism. Outside of my parents, he became the most important teacher I have ever had.

During the first days of Hanukkah, nearly a month after the fire, I sought him out in his office at the United Jewish Council of the Lower East Side. As I approached his cubicle I saw him talking on the telephone to an elderly woman who refused to have her phlebitis checked at Beth Israel Hospital. His dark gabardine coat hung over his chair. He was pacing back and forth, shouting, joking, cajoling in a rapid mixture of Yiddish and English. He tugged at his beard and *payess* (the sidelocks tucked neatly behind his ears), told her it was her duty as a Jew to look after her well-being, and mentioned the tractate of the Talmud that contained that injunction. He called her a "grandmother-baby," with a soothing laugh. Finally, he convinced her to let someone from the Council take her to Beth Israel. Then he turned his attention to me.

I was never sure if he understood my plight or my project, since it took months for him to mention my parents' death or refer to the article I'd set out to write. But that didn't really matter. He saw through the mask of my mission to the heart of my need; to the fact that I was a spiritually parched Jew, in search of some deeper meaning for my life.

Joel Price, my longtime friend, had introduced me as Paul Cowan. But Rabbi Singer asked me for my Jewish name (most Jews are given one when they are born), and I said I had been called Saul Cohen in Israel. From then on, I was Sha'ul to him. He intoned my new name in such a fond, natural way that I never felt as if he was criticizing my old identity. He didn't treat Paul Cowan as an impostor or a heretic, the attitudes I'd feared most. Instead, he enriched my American identity with a special Jewish one.

That day he had to deliver a eulogy for an old Jew who had never been affiliated with a synagogue, but whose family wanted him to have a religious funeral. As we walked to the funeral home, five or six blocks from his office, he linked his arm in mine, instructed me to be very careful of the potholes on the Lower East Side ("This is a very holy neighborhood," he told me), and then began to tell me about how our forefather Moses had convinced the Pharaoh to let the Hebrew slaves rest on Saturday long before he received that commandment on Mount Sinai. He discussed that Midrash—that biblical legend—as if it had more importance to both of us than anything in our contemporary world.

There was a red light when we got to Grand Street. Rabbi Singer took my arm to prevent me from lunging ahead. He told me that the traffic light itself was a mitzvah, a reminder that it was a blessing to protect yourself. And, when you paused and said a *brachah,* a prayer, for small things, you reminded yourself to be thankful for the enormous, wondrous gift of life.

When we got to the funeral home, he told me his words would be brief and devoid of sorrow. "It isn't right to speak of mournful things on a happy time like Hanukkah," he said. But I didn't want to go to another funeral. I wanted to stay as far from death as I possibly could. So I told Rabbi Singer that I had to go back to the *Voice.*

He smiled at me, said something in Hebrew (a blessing, I later realized), and told me to give him a ring whenever I was in the neighborhood.

As I took the F train uptown, I realized that I hadn't thought about my parents for the two hours I had been with him. In fact, for the first time since the fire, I had almost been happy.

I had known very few rabbis in my life, but when the Havurah School parents were holding Jewish consciousness-raising sessions, I had begun to think that many of them were religious corporate executives, who had accelerated a generation's drift toward assimilation by emphasizing their congregants' pocketbooks, not their spirit. Rabbi Singer, born in Poland, nostalgic for Pilzno, the town his family had inhabited for generations, was the complete opposite of that image. He made faith seem like the most enviable gift a human being could possess. His passion for people ignored all price tags.

His shul was on Stanton Street, across from a rubble-strewn lot. Every winter day, at about 6 A.M. and 4 P.M., he went there to be sure that the congregants—former sanitation workers, bakers, rag vendors in their seventies and eighties—were comfortable. He would boil a large pot of water for coffee or tea, and place a bagful of cookies in the refrigerator. On an especially cold day the men came in early to warm themselves, to savor a cookie or two and a few minutes of fraternity. Then, Rabbi Singer and some of the congregants would gather around a spare table, to study a portion of the Talmud which concerned ethical issues—like the responsibility a businessman has toward his customers—or ritual ones—like the earliest moment in the morning when a person may begin to pray. In the back of the shul, the rest of the congregants would always continue to talk loudly—about the health of their children, the merits of a housing project or a race horse. One of them, a gaunt friendly man, always grew impatient and yelled at Rabbi Singer to start the *davening* so that he could get home in time for dinner. The rabbi always heeded the request. As he prayed slowly, with controlled dignity, the conversations continued. But Rabbi Singer never criticized the congregants. He was always teasingly gentle with them. He wanted them to feel that the shul was their home.

One bitterly cold morning in January, the synagogue's pipes broke. Rabbi Singer asked me to go with him to fix them. We hurried to the shul. He huddled inside his frock coat against the freezing Manhattan winter wind as we walked down Essex Street—past the shop where Moses Eisenbach, the scribe, was correcting letters on the flowing parchment pages of the Torah; past the tiny basement store where three women bent over sewing machines, making yarmulkes; past the cavernous old market where the *shochet* was honing his knife to be sure that the chickens squawking in wire cages would be killed quickly and mercifully, in accordance with Jewish law. Such people must have been part of Rabbi Jacob Cohen's world in Lidvinova. They were all Rabbi Singer's friends, just as they would have been in the *heim,* in Galicia, where he was raised. But he couldn't stop and talk with them now. He wanted the shul to be clean before anyone arrived for services.

Once we entered the synagogue we quickly began to mop the floors of the freezing bathroom. Then Rabbi Singer got a stepladder and held it while I replaced some bulbs in the vestibule.

As we worked I wondered aloud what I was doing there. I couldn't think of anyplace I would rather be than in that shul, performing that mitzvah. Why did I—so American—feel that way?

Rabbi Singer answered the question instantly. Sometimes, he said, when you have an ancestor who was a holy man or a scholar, his piety creates a spark that smolders through the ages until it burns again.

Several days later, while walking down East Broadway, I heard someone call the name "Sha'ul." I looked around. Rabbi Singer was hurrying toward me. "Did you really hear the name Sha'ul?" he asked. When I assured him I had, he said, "You see, that name is somewhere in your unconscious."

The night before, I'd had a long-distance telephone talk with my great-uncle Abe Cohen, who was once a Republican alderman in Chicago. He confirmed Bert Lazarus' story: his great-grandfather— my great-great-grandfather—was Rabbi Jacob Cohen from Lidvinova, though he didn't know much about the man. For the first time, I told Rabbi Singer about my ancestor. He beamed at me through his ginger-flecked gray beard.

So, I was Saul Cohen with Rabbi Singer and his friends, Paul Cowan in my own world. I liked the dual identity. When I was on the Lower East Side, among the Orthodox, I always wore a yarmulke. For a while I told myself I was doing so as a sign of respect, just as I had when I researched "Jews Without Money, Revisited." But that didn't explain the curious new sense of pleasure I felt when I pinned the skullcap to my head. It was no longer simply a piece of

cloth, an interviewer's convenience. It was a physical link to Rabbi
Singer's faith, to my own history. Sometimes, when I got off the subway on the Upper West Side, I would pause before I took my
yarmulke off. I was loathe to relinquish my new identity. I always
removed it, though, always emerged bareheaded. Uptown, I was
still Paul Cowan, still an assimilated journalist. It seemed uncomfortable and a little misleading to wear it. After all, I wasn't an Orthodox Jew. I didn't obey any of their rigorous laws. All I knew was
that I was still in flux, still launched on a journey whose destination was far from clear.

When Rabbi Singer and I took the subway to places like Coney Island, or walked the streets of the Lower East Side, I would tape his
reminiscences of life in Poland. He came from a long, proud line of
Hasidim, whose personal warmth and ecstatic religion was very
different from the cooler, more rational, more Westernized faith
that characterized most of the Jews who lived in the area of Lithuania that included Lidvinova. Still, I was sure that the life he led bore
some resemblance to the life Rabbi Jacob Cohen had led.

He loved to talk about the Europe of his youth, "where the air
was holy," where "a town without a rabbi was like a wedding without music." He talked about the Thursday nights he and his classmates stayed in *heder*, praying, fasting, so that they could study
harder, reading from the Torah so that their holy words would echo
through the night.

He had basked in the feeling of Friday morning, where everyone
went to market to buy fish or meat for Shabbos and the town
square was full of Jews from the country, come to get their chickens killed by the ritual slaughterer; when the tradesmen stopped
their work to go to the mikvah—the ritual bath—and then to pray;
when the entire town was already half-bathed in the amber glow
of Shabbos.

It was, he said, a world in which people "felt the way of the
Almighty in their souls. They felt that every little thing came from

the Almighty." And that spirit endured for centuries in Pilzno, a town about the size of Lidvinova, with about 250 Jewish families, about 1,000 Christian families, which was located on the Vistula River. To almost all the Jews who lived in the ramshackle wooden houses, Rabbi Singer's grandfather, Rabbi Gershon Singer, was a *tsadik,* an especially holy man, and his father, Rabbi David Singer, was a scholar, whose reasonable judgments could settle the most inflammatory disputes.

Rabbi Singer was the youngest son in a family of six boys and two girls. His father's house, on one of Pilzno's main streets, had two rooms. In one of the rooms a huge section of the floor was set aside for any traveler who needed sleep. It was always full of people.

During the day, the town's Jews formed a noisy line in the back of the room and waited to consult the rav. He would decide whether a tiny blister on a chicken's gizzard meant the animal was kosher or *trayf;* whether talmudic law instructed a pious man to respect his elders by keeping a mean-spirited mother-in-law in his house, or whether to preserve his marriage by banishing her; how to make sure a woman whose husband was drafted in wartime was guaranteed a divorce if he never reappeared.

Once when the rav was coming home from shul, he saw a child crying. Why was the boy so sad? he asked. Because an older man, a fisherman, had slapped him. The rav decided to see whether a wrong had been committed. When he got home he told the *shamess,* the sexton, to summon the fisherman. Then he bade the child and the adult to tell their versions of the story. After concluding that the boy was telling the truth, the rav fined the man ten guilders—money that was very important to the child, since he came from a poor family. "That story went all around in Galicia," Rabbi Singer said. "Everyone was impressed that my father gave so much attention to the boy."

In a way, Rabbi Singer's reminiscences helped me understand the unaccountable loneliness, the aimlessness, I sometimes felt in myself and even in my most ambitious friends. Of course, most people everywhere are aimless and depressed for some period of their lives. But these emotions had a distinctly American flavor. I was convinced that families like mine, whose ignorance of its specific history resembled the ignorance of most American Jews—of most Americans, for that matter—underwent profound emotional shocks when their life in this distant, open country caused them to be severed from their rooted pasts. No one has measured the effect those shocks have had on our collective psyche. But I believe it is immense.

When I reflect on the months I spent with Rabbi Singer, I realize that I was not only absorbing his passion for Judaism. I was influenced by his attitude toward the mental anguish and the ceaseless sense of displacement that he'd experienced during his difficult life.

He'd suffered in the wake of the Holocaust; so deeply, sometimes, that he didn't want to discuss it for fear of upsetting people who were dear to him. He'd been lonely. He bore scars that would last a lifetime. Still, as I listened to him and watched him, I realized that his grief had metamorphosed into a new source of spiritual strength.

As far as I was concerned, his attitude represented a wisdom that was far deeper than the brittle sophistication that usually passed for worldliness in the America I knew best. It was an attitude that said that no tragedy is terminal. Even after the Holocaust, life continued to unfold in unforeseeably sad or interesting or even miraculous ways.

I asked him often about the years during which his Europe perished. He talked about them freely.

Toward the end of World War I, the Singers, like many Jews in Pilzno, fled from the disorder that surrounded them. David Singer resettled in Kashow, an eight-hour train ride away. His health deteriorated. "He didn't eat the right foods. He didn't get enough sleep," his son said. In 1925, he died of lung problems.

In 1934, life in Pilzno seemed settled enough for one of Rabbi Singer's older brothers to return to resume his father's role as spiritual leader of the town. Rabbi Singer, twenty, accompanied him to serve an apprenticeship. He had never even contemplated another position. In Europe, his entire family consisted of "rabbis, not businessmen," he told me proudly.

But "as soon as Hitler took over Austria we were afraid." One day he and his brother went to Tarnow, a large city near Pilzno. It was noontime and they were walking down the main street, which was filled with Jews. Some gentiles started harassing them—jostling them, taunting them, knocking off their hats.

"That used to happen on side streets or late at night. But in broad daylight? In a town that was full of Jews? That was something new. We knew a terrible war was coming. The earth was not sure under us.

"Until then, the great rabbis had told us not to go to the United States. Too many Jews had lost their religion there. But in that time, before Hitler came to Poland, they said, 'Go, go.'"

In 1939 Rabbi Singer and one brother left for America. "We were the runners." But three brothers, all of them rabbis, and two sisters stayed behind. "I don't know where they were killed. Maybe at Auschwitz.

"I dream of those times always—about someone I knew, someone who got lost. I see him and I say 'You're alive? You're not alive. This is a dream.'

"How can I forget what happened? It was my memories, my childhood. I cannot forget."

His first years in America were disillusioning ones, for, despite the rabbis' warning about this impious land, he experienced some of the same surprises and conflicts that Moses Cohen's earlier generations of Orthodox settlers encountered. Before he left Poland he had planned to settle in a small American town—the equivalent of a shtetl—and be "an all-around rabbi. I don't like to rush, and I thought that in a village I could be a Jew in a European way. I'd be a rabbi. I'd be a scribe. If they needed a ritual slaughterer, I'd be a *shochet,* too."

But when he got here in 1939, he realized that it was impossible for him to settle in an American equivalent of Pilzno, since most

Jews who lived in those surroundings had grown so assimilated they had no use for a scribe; they didn't know what a *shochet* was. He had to stay in New York City and New Jersey, in the few Orthodox communities that existed in those years.

He became rabbi of a synagogue on the Lower East Side in 1940. Soon he began to hear stories which showed him how difficult it was for early immigrants to remain observant Jews.

"Jack, the *gabbai* (the manager of the synagogue), had been here for thirty, forty years," he recalled. "He was in the garment business. He had Jewish bosses, but he had so much trouble keeping Shabbos, I cannot tell you. He would criticize the bosses for working on Shabbos. And they would say, 'Get out of here. I'm a good Jew and I'm working on Shabbos.' Jack was a good cutter. Finally he got a job where he could be religious. On Friday afternoons, they let him go at 4 P.M. Summers it was okay. The days were long and he could get home in time for supper. But in the winter he had a terrible *tsouris*. The day was short. He *davened mincha* (afternoon prayer) in the shop. Then he walked home. When there was snow on the ground he'd get to the apartment very late. His wife had already lit the candles. She'd be waiting for him to make kiddush."

There was so much feeling in his voice when he told me that story that I wondered if such encounters, multiplied by the hundreds, interwoven with the Holocaust, helped account for the intense interest he took in people like me who seemed eager to return to the religion that had been snatched from their ancestors.

Rabbi Singer's own life was completely different from anything he or his forebears had imagined. "In Europe, a rabbi was a power. Here, your President is a power. A rabbi is on a much lower level.

"Besides, a lot of them don't care about religion. They care about making money."

So, like many immigrants from religious communities, he was disoriented and depressed during his first years in America. "In 1943 and 1944 there came a boom in diamonds. A lot of rabbis went to work in the diamond district. I did, too. I didn't give up my shul, but I made my living in the diamonds, as a cutter.

"Why did rabbis go in there? Because diamonds is a Jewish line. You have no trouble with Shabbos. Most of the work is on contract, so you can go in whenever you want. It is hard to be religious and punch a clock. If you want to go to the mikvah, or if you *daven* slow, you don't always have time for holiness, since you have to get to work by eight or nine in the morning. But in the diamonds, if I went to the mikvah and finished *davening* at ten o'clock, I could come in at ten. And if I wanted to I could work late, since there were always enough men to form a minyan."

After World War II, the boom in diamonds ended. Rabbi Singer abandoned his dream of settling in a small town. He decided to carry on his ancestors' tradition on the Lower East Side of New York.

One day, Joel Price glanced at the pink messages—some in English, some in Yiddish—that cluttered up Rabbi Singer's desk and filled a cardboard box on his floor.

"You think he's a holy man?" Joel asked. "He's really running a bookie joint." Rabbi Singer heard the joke and smiled.

But "each paper is a trouble," he says. And a mitzvah, echoing back through time.

It was nearly Passover, and Rabbi Singer was busier and more nostalgic than usual.

In Pilzno and in Kashow, before the holiday, ten or fifteen families would gather together in the rare house that had an oven and, according to Hasidic tradition, sing *hallel,* a series of psalms sung on Jewish festivals, while the men baked the matzo. As the holiday drew near, people would search their homes for *hametz* (leavening), the removal of which serves as a reminder of the Jews' hurried flight from Egypt.

Of course, Passover was an important holiday on the Lower East Side. But many of the "elderlies" Rabbi Singer worked with had forgotten the exact details of the faith that pervaded their parents' lives. Rabbi Singer felt a special responsibility for them. For years, he had used a modern, spacious synagogue near East Broadway to hold free seders for about two hundred of them.

He didn't trust anyone but himself to supervise the exhausting search for the *hametz*. During the days before Passover, he'd take off his black jacket, roll up the sleeves of his white shirt, mop the floor, scour every pan, and squat in front of the synagogue oven with an acetylene torch to make sure he'd burned away all traces of bread crumbs.

In 1977, I spent those days with him. And as I participated in the flurry of cleaning, which was completely alien to me, I could never quite believe that a man in his sixties, with so many responsibilities, could spend all his time doing what was, essentially, scullery work. Only from his point of view the scullery work was a holy mission, since the Torah says that anyone who eats *hametz* during Passover shall be cut off from the Jewish people. Still, much as I'd come to love the man, it was hard for me to see this particular job as anything but a form of fussiness.

He was very sensitive to my reactions, even my unspoken ones. "I know most of the people who are coming to the seder don't care about these things," he told me after two helpers and I had finished scrubbing an oven with Easy-Off. "But I do. I care for them and I care for me." There was more than a hint of yearning for the lost Europe, where *hametz* really mattered, in his wry remark.

Shortly before Passover, Rabbi Singer left the hurly-burly of the Lower East Side in order to perform a special personal mission in the more placid Orthodox milieu of Williamsburg. A Hasid he knew—a *rebbe* from Galicia—had promised to give him two of the especially pure, round, brownish *shemurah* matzos. Like the Jews in Pilzno—and in Lidvinova—the rebbe had planted and harvested the wheat that was in them. He had ground the wheat on a stone mill he kept in his basement, secure in his knowledge that no water or heat would cause fermentation, chanting prayers as he labored.

Children were playing tag outside the rebbe's house, their side-locks flying in the breeze. But inside the mood was solemn. The rebbe's wife and daughter, whose aprons enveloped their long, chaste dresses, were scrubbing the floor as they would have in Europe a century before. They told us the rebbe was upstairs in his study.

He must have heard our voices, for he summoned us to the room where the holy book he was reading lay open on a long wooden table. Moving slowly, he greeted Rabbi Singer, climbed on a chair, and reached to the top of a cupboard where some white boxes containing the special matzos were stored.

The old friends began to talk in Yiddish. Soon the rebbe, looking somewhat puzzled, began staring at my clean-shaven face, my tweed cap and my tan windbreaker.

"He wants to know how you came to me," Rabbi Singer said. "I told him our grandparents were connected."

Earlier that day he had described a place in Williamsburg where hundreds of Hasidic Jews would be baking *shemurah* matzos and chanting psalms. My religious imagination was still conditioned by the services I'd attended at Choate's chapel and, particularly, by the solemn hymns we had sung as Easter approached. So I visualized the Hasidim in a staid, solemn frieze—enacting a Good Friday in Yiddish.

Instead, the place was bustling, alive with throngs of men and women in traditional Hasidic garb, kneading dough at separate tables. It was all done very rapidly, since Jewish law insists that all matzo be baked within eighteen minutes of the time the water is added to flour, before fermentation begins.

Groups of yeshiva students kept arriving. Some stood in corners, while others elbowed their way through the crowd to find a spot where they could begin baking. Meanwhile, those who had been there for a while rushed from the oven to the main room, carrying boxes full of matzos high above their heads.

Some people standing near us chanted *hallel* as they worked, praising the Almighty as Rabbi Singer's ancestors had done when they baked matzos in Galicia. Once, my Cohen and Spiegel ancestors must have chanted the same words:

Open unto me the gates of righteousness, that I may enter through them and give thanks to the Lord.

More than two thousand years ago, the *Kohanim*—the priests in the Temple of Jerusalem—had chanted this same *hallel* on the afternoon before Passover, to commemorate the Exodus, the miracle that brought all the Jews, all our interconnected grandparents, to that hallowed place.

"Did you take it all in, Sha'ul?" Rabbi Singer asked me later. "You've had a little taste of Europe now."

He took my arm. As we walked toward the subway, people kept glancing at us. What an odd-looking couple we must have made!

Once we were on the train, he held the white box close to him so that the *shemurah* matzos—so sacred in themselves, so full of precious memories—wouldn't crack on the short, jarring journey back to the Lower East Side.

One afternoon during the intermediate days of Passover, Rabbi Singer and I were headed toward shul, when Frieda Provda appeared in the window of the Masaryk Cake Box near Grand Street. She rapped on the pane, summoning him urgently. Anna, a widow in a nearby housing project, had died of bone cancer the night before, and her only relative, a brother, lived in Los Angeles.

The Masaryk Cake Box had been Anna's second home during her last years. Most days at noon she'd leave her radio, her closest companion, and go down there to gossip with friends or take care of the customers' children. Now, Frieda Provda and her friend Betty Fried, feeling the responsibilities of surrogate kinship, had to arrange the funeral which, according to Jewish law, would occur the next day.

Frieda Provda was dressed for the 1970s. She didn't wear a wig or a long, modest dress like the women in Williamsburg. She was an Americanized businesswoman. "Be kind to the next person, that's my form of Judaism." But she'd chosen to work in a bakery where Shabbos was observed, and she had no question about her religious loyalties. "I'm not Conservative or Reform," she told Rabbi Singer proudly. "I think she should be buried as one of us."

So she had chosen an Orthodox funeral home and asked the director to comply with the age-old traditions: to make sure there were women from a *hevrah kadishah* (a burial society), to make a *taharah* (purify the corpse by cleaning it) and to watch it through the night. He didn't exactly refuse. But, she said, there was an unsettling hint of reluctance in his voice.

Passover was a busy season at the bakery. But Frieda was worried. What if the funeral director decided to save a hundred dollars by omitting the *taharah?* What if he was too busy to bother calling the *hevrah kadishah?* The widow's brother was coming to New York that day. What if the funeral director persuaded him to assuage his grief by purchasing an expensive coffin, not the simple pine box in which Jews are supposed to be buried. That would be a sacrilege!

What luck that she had glimpsed Rabbi Singer's gabardine coat as he rushed by! He would help her ward off the greedy bureaucrats of death.

This was a mitzvah he was glad to perform. He had hated the Jewish funeral business ever since he came to America—hated the morticians who cared more about today's profits than about the dead. For, traditionally, death has always been one of the most egalitarian aspects of Jewish tradition. Before a funeral, rich and poor alike are dressed in simple white shrouds—shrouds without pockets—to show that one's soul, not one's possessions, are important to the Almighty. All are buried in a simple pine casing, or a bed made with natural substances, so that the body and its casing can decompose naturally and return to the earth.

While Frieda Provda called the funeral director, Rabbi Singer raged:

"Who would have thought that Jews would make a chapel, that they'd take a fancy-shmancy custom—a non-kosher custom—a goyish custom—that they wouldn't make a *taharah,* but put a fancy-shmancy suit on the body—just to make money?"

"In Europe, a funeral was a holy thing. It belonged to the community. And if someone passed away, everyone helped out. Everyone knocked a nail in a coffin. Everyone pushed to do that. It was an honor, and a mitzvah, not a business. Who thought about business then?

"Well," he said, answering his own question, "sometimes a rich man passed away and then the *kehilla* (the community council) taxed his family. But that wasn't a business. The community used the money to pay the rabbi, pay the *shamess,* fix the shul, fix the mikvah, help the poor on Shabbos. When the community took money from such a person it was a hundred percent right to do so. But otherwise? A business! Bah! Here the chapel is a business. There, it was a sign of deep respect, of feeling, to go to a funeral, to help a family."

At last, the funeral director was on the phone. Rabbi Singer edged past the case of almond macaroons, of marble cake made of matzo meal—the sweets Frieda Provda was displaying for Passover—and transformed himself into a religious diplomat as he began to issue gentle, steely orders over a pay phone.

Of course, the funeral director would have a *hevrah kadishah.* Of course, there would be a simple pine box and a shroud. And he'd see that a few flecks of dirt—preferably dirt from Israel—was placed on the corpse, in conformity with the biblical injunction "ashes to ashes." The funeral was scheduled for nine the next morning? Fine. Rabbi Singer or his cousin, who had a synagogue in Washington Heights would be there . . . just to help out.

When Rabbi Singer hung up, he was smiling with relief. But he was still angry, still reminiscing about his past battles. "Once I had a funeral uptown. They wanted to sell the family a casket for fifteen hundred dollars or eighteen hundred. I told them, 'Don't take it, don't be meshugge. Buy one for a hundred and fifty.' The owners of the chapel were so angry they began to chase me. They wanted to kill me.

"Do you blame them? Do you know how much I cost them? Most chapels hate me like poison. If they could kill me, they would kill me. I spoil their business."

Rabbi Singer's campaign on behalf of the dead and their survivors—a campaign that could bring him no benefit, that grew out of the Torah and the Talmud and the egalitarian world he remembered from his childhood—gave me a microscopic view of the interdependence between text and tradition which was, I believed, the religious foundation for the ethical quality of Judaism that had been so important to my family. That discovery of that Jewish source for my political ideas answered one of the questions that had sent me from Harrisburg to the Lower East Side, from the Catholic left to the Jews without money, some five years earlier.

For almost a year after I met him, Rabbi Singer wanted to be written about pseudonymously. He wasn't publicity-shy. He believed that truly holy people refrained from taking credit for their own mitzvahs. But the better I came to know him, the more important it seemed to use his name. In the past, I'd written many articles filled with pseudonymous characters, and readers assumed I was creating composites. Now, I wanted them to see that the man I admired so much was a real, breathing person. Misha Avramoff and Rabbi Singer's son, David, agreed with me, and urged him to let his name be used. Despite his reservations, he said he would, largely to please us.

But he wanted me to understand why even the most charitable people could hurt others if they flaunted their good deeds. As he told me about his grandfather, Gershon Singer, the rabbi of Pilzno, who exemplified the qualities Rabbi Singer wanted to bring to the Lower East Side, I came to the rueful, haunting realization that those of us who had been in the Peace Corps and the civil-rights movement might have done our work better if we'd had some of his training in the social value of humility.

Every Thursday night, the rabbi of Pilzno would walk by all the Jewish houses in town, accompanied by his *shamess*. Their mission? To inspect the chimneys of the congregants. They looked for houses where there wasn't any smoke. Those families couldn't afford enough kindling to heat the Shabbos meal. So Gershon Singer would fetch a charcoal and a chicken for Shabbos.

But the mitzvah must never be discovered. The rabbi must remain anonymous. The people who received the food must never be embarrassed by the knowledge that he was aware of their poverty.

So, between 1 and 5 A.M., when all the Jews of Pilzno were asleep, the rabbi and the *shamess* would pile the chicken and the charcoal into a wheelbarrow and place them in front of the house. Then they would hurry away, before their goodness could be detected.

One Thursday night between Passover and Shavuot, Rabbi Singer asked me to accompany him to Brooklyn so that I could see a modern-day version of his grandfather's attitudes toward charity. First, we stopped for dinner at his apartment. After we washed our hands and said the *motzi* (the traditional blessing over the bread), we began to eat the lavish meal of chicken liver, matzo-ball soup, roast beef, kidney beans, and potato pancakes his wife had prepared. As we ate, he elaborated his grandfather's feelings—and, I realized, his own. "He didn't want to be a show-off. Of course, sometimes it is all right to be a show-off because if you give to others, they give too. But the highest point of charity should be anonymity. The taker shouldn't know who gave the gift and the giver shouldn't know who took it."

After dinner, he took me to a tree-lined residential street. Inside a large garage about fifty Hasidic men were filling grocery boxes with chicken, fish, wine, bread, and vegetables, and loading them into cars on the street outside. Soon they would distribute the cartons to needy Jews. They would drive away before the recipients could see them.

In one corner of the garage a stocky young diamond cutter had replaced his black suit with a blood-flecked butcher's apron and was cutting up carp. Three more Hasidim, still dressed in gabardine, wrapped fish in plastic bags and placed the bags in boxes. Then a young man whose father had died three weeks earlier came in. They'd been waiting for him before they *davened maariv* (the evening service); they would provide a minyan for him to recite the mourner's Kaddish.

All work stopped. Everyone picked up his *siddur* (prayer book), and, facing the eastern wall of the garage—symbolically facing Jerusalem—rocked back and forth in prayer. Then, in a few minutes, work resumed.

The organizer, middle-aged, European born, a civil servant, stood by shelves full of packages. Writing in Yiddish, he inscribed each box with the address of the people who would receive it. But not with the names. To spare the recipients any embarrassment, even the drivers who delivered the food would remain ignorant of their identities. My presence plainly made the organizer uncomfortable. Some of the younger people argued that publicity might help with fund raising, but he made me promise not to mention the organization's name—or even the area it worked in—because the anonymity meant more to him than the prospect of contributions.

Outside the garage, Jacob, twenty-five, an air-conditioner salesman, almost skeletally thin, with a teenager's wispy beard and sidelock, sat in his sleek new Mercury, testing the CB radio he would use that night when he and his friends made their surreptitious deliveries for Shabbos.

With Rabbi Singer and me jammed into the front seat, the food packed in the back, he tooled his Mercury down Brooklyn's streets. He hollered a greeting whenever he saw a friend. Once, he speeded up, then slowed down, to scare a man he had known at yeshiva. He congratulated the pedestrian on the birth of his new son.

He flicked the switch of his CB, and began to talk to a friend in a space-age patois. "Breaker, breaker," he began. "The handle here is Gumshoe." Then he switched to Yiddish, but his conversation was laced with trucker's phrases like "ten-four" and "negatory, guy."

Jacob was on a tight schedule, for the recipients knew just when the packages were due and what number to call if they were late. While Rabbi Singer and I watched, he hoisted a box out of the back seat, whisked it into the lobby of a building, and rang the apartment number that was on the package. Then he hurried down the street—a black hat and a wispy beard in a murky light—and gunned the car down the block, toward the neighborhood's main street, where he'd meet some friends outside a kosher pizza parlor.

Rabbi Singer had to leave. Every Thursday night he and his son David read the Torah and some commentaries together—just as Rabbi Singer's father and grandfather had done, over candlelight, in

Pilzno. This week, as Shavuot approached, he would sit at a table in David's comfortable Borough Park apartment, rocking his two-week-old granddaughter as she lay in her bassinet next to the *seferim* (holy books). He would read to his son from a commentary that discussed those mysterious days in the desert when Moses descended from Mount Sinai, and transmitted the Lord's commandments to the people who were still bewildered, still weary from their flight out of Egypt.

As we stood near the pizza parlor, waiting for a bus, Rabbi Singer bent forward to show me how his grandfather had looked when he pushed his wheelbarrow full of food through Pilzno's winding streets at 3 A.M., to make his clandestine deliveries.

Then the bus came and he hurried off to study Torah into the night.

Once a Hasid, a *tzadik,* was asked why Jews don't proselytize. He answered, simply, that a candle glows without making an effort to give off light. Religion should do that, too, he said.

Rabbi Singer never proselytized. If he had, I would not have listened. My experiences at Choate, then as an activist, as a journalist, had made me especially wary of any sort of exhortation. Instead, in the words of a gospel I loved in civil-rights days, he lived the life he sang about in his song. His Judaism, with its ethical and ritual demands, reached from the majesty of Sinai to the lower depths of the Lower East Side.

His example imbued the values my parents had passed on to me with a sense of history and an intensity of religious feeling that made them seem far more durable than anything I had found in the secular world. Moreover, he helped me get outside myself and my grief and feel that all of us—my parents, my brother and sisters, Rachel and me, Lisa and Matt—were part of something—call it a tradition or a faith—that was bigger and more mysterious than ourselves.

Occasionally, I had fantasies of living on the Lower East Side and becoming Orthodox. But I never felt the slightest realistic desire to abandon my world and enter Rabbi Singer's, as thousands of newly religious Jews in my generation were doing. I didn't want to cease being Paul Cowan—to renounce what my parents had given me and what I had become. I was too proud of those things.

So I continued to take off my yarmulke whenever the subway reached the Upper West Side. But I began to feel that I was taking part of Rabbi Singer's world home with me, and adapting it to mine.

12

In the months after the fire, while I was spending time with Rabbi Singer, I also tried to contact as many of my Cohen kinsmen as I could find. In Chicago I talked to Bert Lazarus, spent days with my great-uncle Abe Cohen, the former alderman, and my great-aunt Jen, a pawnbroker, and met my father's cousins—an accountant, a doctor, a furniture salesman, a nursing home owner, the proprietor of a very successful travel bureau.

Oddly, the only relative I failed to meet was the one I was most curious about: Lou's cousin, Saul Cohen. He was a busy executive who had been out of town whenever I was in Chicago. I'd talked to Saul on the phone, but our conversations were always cursory and unsatisfactory.

Then, in the summer of 1978, after my article on Rabbi Singer was published, Rachel and I had an assignment to describe the closing of some steel mills in Youngstown, Ohio. If Saul were going to be in Chicago, I figured we could make a side trip to see him. He did plan to be there, and he invited us to meet him at the Leeco Steel Company, the business that had evolved out of the scrap-iron yard my great-grandfather Moses Cohen had founded, that my grandfather Jake had nearly destroyed, that Saul's father, Leopold (the "Lee" in the company's Americanized name), had rescued. Because of my father's stories, I had never imagined that a branch of the Cohen family would be so prosperous.

When we arrived, Saul, lean and fit, in his early fifties, was sitting at his desk, talking about steel prices as he looked through his window at a large crane that lifted long, flat sheets of steel.

Since I'm not very good at small talk, I told him at once that I wanted to learn about the grandfather who had been a mystery to me. It turned out that Jacob Cohen was a second father to him. So, during the next hour he sketched a slightly sanitized verbal picture of his relationship to Jake. It was the flip side of my father's.

Except for Lou—fifteen years his elder—Saul was the oldest male in his generation of Cohens. As a boy, he had often accompanied his father and uncle Jake to their Orthodox synagogue. He respected Orthodox traditions because he felt a deep respect for his successful father and love for his ne'er-do-well uncle.

Like Lou, Leopold Cohen had loaned Jake tens of thousands of dollars. Saul had been the spendthrift's gofer, racing all over Chicago to pay the checks the would-be mitzvah man had kited. But Saul's family was on such solid economic footing that his uncle's fantasy-laden antics were no special threat to him. Saul, Jake's nephew, was amused and saddened by the traits that enraged Lou. After all, as Leopold Cohen's boy, Saul's name was never sullied in the way my father's was. From his point of view, it was a delightful indulgence to be related to a Jewish Robin Hood, who gave comfort to the poor and showered his nieces and nephews with outlandishly lavish gifts.

When Jake died, Saul said Kaddish for him. He was sure Louis Cowan would never do that.

Saul must have made a decision about me during that first interview, for he told me, quite openly, that he had harbored bitter feelings toward my family since Lou abandoned Jake. I asked Saul to look at the act from my father's point of view; as the only way out of a terrible economic trap; as a way of protecting himself from the cruel, sarcastic side of Jake that Saul might never have known; as a decision that caused a good man a lifetime of silent pain. He seemed to be as affected by my version of the story as I was by his.

After that exchange, I felt as if Saul had begun to see me as a cousin, not as an alien visitor from the other side of a family rift. When we parted he suggested that we meet a few days later. There were some things he wanted to give me.

That Sunday he and his wife took Rachel and me to their country club, just outside Chicago. We played two quick sets of tennis and then dawdled over our chicken salads as we exchanged details about each other's lives.

Toward the end of the lunch, Saul handed me a plastic bag with some of Jake's possessions in it.

There was the guest book the mourners had signed at his funeral. There were some condolence letters. There was a biography of Morris "Two Gun" Cohen, a distant relative of ours who had voyaged from Lidvinova to England, become a soldier of fortune, and wound up in China as a trusted adviser to the revolutionary leader Sun Yat-sen.

Finally, Saul gave me one of Jake's tefillin, the ritual objects that pious Jews put on their arms and head every morning when they say their morning prayers.

In appearance, it was just a battered black box and a maze of leather straps. But I saw it as a message from the past. I knew that, sooner or later, I'd have to decide whether to use it. The prospect frightened me. It would be my first serious commitment to Jewish ritual. Weakly, I tried to avoid it by refusing the tefillin.

"They're yours, Saul," I said. "You knew Jake. You loved him. You said Kaddish for him. I never met the man."

"No, Paul," he said firmly, as he placed the tefillin in my hand. "He was your grandfather. I've been keeping this at my house for twenty-five years, waiting for you to pick it up."

Quite deliberately, I kept the tefillin at the bottom of my suitcase when Rachel and I got back from Chicago, picked up Lisa and Matt at camp, and went to Martha's Vineyard. But once I was back in New York I was overwhelmed with curiosity. I told myself I wanted to know if the tefillin was still kosher—and if there was any way I could use a tefillin for my arm even though I didn't have one for my head. So I brought my grandfather's tefillin to Rabbi Singer for advice.

He called me up a few days later and announced he had a surprise for me. I should meet him in his cubicle at the United Jewish Council whenever I could. Of course, I went down there that day.

He had taken Jake Cohen's tefillin to Rabbi Moses Eisenbach, the scribe, he told me. Rabbi Eisenbach had examined the parchment inside, a quotation from Exodus which states: *And so it shall be as a sign upon your hand and a symbol upon your forehead that with a mighty hand the Lord freed us from Egypt.* The small scroll had decayed in the twenty-eight years since my grandfather last used it. So Rabbi Singer had bought me a new set of tefillin. "Sha'ul," he said as he gave them to me, "wear them wherever you go, even as far away as Lithuania."

I tried to tease my way out of the obligation I so plainly wanted to take on by reminding Rabbi Singer, with a nervous laugh, that I had no idea of how to use the strange object he had given me.

"So, I'll teach you. If your grandfather could do it, you can do it. You think he was so much smarter than you?"

The next thing I knew he had me standing erect while he sat on a chair. First he showed me how to attach the box that holds the parchment to my muscle, and how to wrap the leather strap around my forearm seven times. Then, for an hour, he worked with me while I practiced the difficult part, which involved looping the thong around my ring finger and my index finger, then bringing the remaining strand down the valley between my thumb and my forefinger and winding it once across my hand so that, eventually, the straps formed the Hebrew letters *shin, dalet,* and *yud,* one of the Lord's names. I remember feeling very tense and clumsy until Rabbi Singer eased my nervousness with a joke about how the maze of leather reminded him of a blood-pressure machine.

I knew at once that those tefillin represented a double blessing: an unexpected gift from the grandfather who had awakened my interest in Judaism, and a very intentional one from the teacher who had showed me its riches. How could I have refused to use them?

I always felt a surge of pleasure when I uttered the prayer that accompanies the act of weaving the thongs into the name of the Lord. *I will betroth thee to myself forever. I will betroth thee to myself in righteousness and in kindness, in justice and mercy. I will betroth thee to myself in faithfulness and you will know the*

Lord. Often, I had the feeling I was physically tied to my ancestors' history. Sometimes I felt a glimmering of the way genuinely pious Jews like Rabbi Singer must feel when they announce anew that they are wed to the Almighty.

And, most mornings, as I began to pray in my very disorganized study, amid my notes on the 1912 textile strike in Lawrence, Massachusetts, or my tape recordings of the people whose lives had been disrupted by the near meltdown at Three Mile Island, it seemed as if Jake Cohen's tefillin had broadened the pathway to the thing I had been seeking—a spiritual community whose faith echoed through time.

For most of that year, 1978, I made sure to put on my tefillin in the privacy of my study—not in my living room where guests or even my children could see my strangely Cyclopian appearance, not in synagogue where more practiced *daveners* were likely to be amused by my inexperience. By then, I was used to being a Jew in print, but not in person. For even though the article about Rabbi Singer had started a round of rumors that I'd become a Hasid overnight, I wasn't quite ready to alter my American self-image and enter a world of my contemporaries that was more assertively Jewish than that of the ambivalent parents at the Havurah School. In retrospect, I realize that I needed another dialogue with American experience to summon enough courage to clinch my claim to my birthright.

I had become fascinated with the textile city of Lawrence, Massachusetts, where about twenty thousand people, representing forty-five ethnic groups, waged a militant, successful strike against the mill owners in 1912—and where many of the insurgents' descendants voted for the reactionary politician George Wallace in 1976. When I spent time in the city I discovered that virtually no one there remembered the strike even though it had given rise to the phrase "Bread and Roses, Too," which was still a motto for much of the American Left.

Most of the strike leaders were Italian. In its wake, they were branded as un-Americans, as anarchists. Their militance had helped prompt Congress to keep America as ethnically sterile as possible by enacting the anti-immigration laws of 1924 and 1925. Many of them were blackballed at the mills. Some were chased out of town.

So the strikers had made a conscious effort to suppress their heroic efforts, and even their ethnicity, in order to help their children progress into mainstream America.

Of course, I felt a quick, keen sense of identification with them. For, just as "Jews Without Money" was a metaphor for Jake Cohen in my journalist's imagination, so the city of Lawrence was a metaphor for my father. Like him, its people had concealed a past which seemed shameful to them, which would be a source of pride for their offspring.

The strike contained a human-interest story that fascinated me. In 1912, a twelve-year-old Italian immigrant girl named Camella Teoli had been scalped when her hair got caught in a machine for twisting cotton. Just two weeks earlier, agents from the mill had come to her house, encouraging her to drop out of school and lie about her age so that she could work. She was hospitalized for nine months. The company paid her medical bills, but not her lost wages. No one tried to restore the educational opportunities she had lost.

The bitter strike ended shortly after Margaret Sanger, later a staunch advocate of birth control, arranged for about twenty insurgents to testify in front of the House Committee on Rules in Washington, D.C. She told her story and described routine details about the mills, like the fact that workers had to pay for every glass of water they drank. The next day the child was headline news all over America, especially because Mrs. William Howard Taft, the President's wife, was in the gallery that day and was visibly moved by Camella's plight.

Nearly seventy years later, I went to Lawrence to find Camella Teoli.

One of her cousins—whose name appeared in the phone book— told me she had died a few years earlier. But, he added, for the last decade of her life she'd lived with her daughter, Josephine Catalano, a store manager whose husband was a butcher. Josephine had a home in a nearby suburb. I called her up at ten o'clock one night.

At first she thought I was a crank—a late-night voice talking incomprehensibly about something that had happened in the vanished past. Then, I mentioned Camella Teoli's scalping. It was as if I'd unlocked some magic box of trust, furnished proof that there was a link between Camella Teoli and me. For the accident had left Camella with a permanent bald spot on the back of her head, a spot that was about six inches in diameter. Practically every day of her life, Josephine combed her mother's hair in a bun that disguised the spot.

Suddenly, she seemed eager to see me. She suggested that we have breakfast in a shopping mall the next morning.

As soon as we met I discovered why my unexpected phone call was so confusing. Without much pause for formalities, I began to ask questions about the 1912 strike. But Josephine Catalano knew even less about her mother's political past than I had known about my father's religious one. She knew nothing about her trip to Washington, nothing about Mrs. William Howard Taft's presence, nothing about the sensational impact her mother's testimony had made on America's consciousness. The Camella Teoli she knew was just a mill hand with an odd bald spot on her head, a sweet, silent lady who bought and cooked the traditional eels on Christmas Eve, who rarely missed a Sunday mass.

As we talked, though, some puzzling aspects about Camella Teoli's life began to seem clear. She had been an exceptionally gentle woman, her daughter said, who never complained about her job. But her supervisors often reprimanded her. They never promoted her. In fact, they often punished Josephine and her brother Frankie for brushing a braid over their mother's bald spot when the hair came loose. Evidently, Camella Teoli had been punished for her childhood act of boldness throughout her life.

No wonder she and her contemporaries called their children Josephine and Frankie and Paul, not Arturo or Dante or Nazone; no wonder they encouraged their young to Americanize their last names; no wonder they made a conscious effort to raise the children in English, to blot out their native language. That way they could be free from the past that had proved so threatening.

Still, as Josephine and I talked, I found myself musing about her in the same way as I so often mused about myself. What if she—and dozens of children like her—had been encouraged to see their own culture as a proud one? What if they had retained Italian as a language so that they could have access to writers like Dante, composers like Verdi, thinkers like Gramsci? What if they'd been allowed to feel that they weren't Italian versions of the "greenhorns," but heirs to a culture that was even finer than that of the Yankees who defined them as brutes?

That day in Lawrence I was carrying two books which contained accounts of Camella Teoli's testimony in Washington. Standing in a huge parking lot, Josephine Catalano read her mother's description of the old days at the mills. Then I drove her to the Lawrence Library, where there was a two-volume record of the 1912 hearing. She read her mother's testimony, enraptured.

"Now I have a past," she said. "Now my son has a history to be proud of."

That was how I felt when I met Bert Lazarus, when I became immersed in Rabbi Singer's world, when Saul Cohen gave me Jake's tefillin. The emotion—the joy one feels when one retrieves a shard of one's buried past—was, I realized, more American than any public sight one witnesses on Thanksgiving Day or the Fourth of July. For we are not a single people, but a nation of many nations. Most of us—Jews and Italians, Irish and Greeks, blacks and Hispanics—have sacrificed an enormously important treasure, our history, to become part of a melting pot that doesn't really exist. We have all amputated our histories; surrendered the memories that are intertwined with tradition—bright pebbles on a very familiar beach, things you love because you know them well.

In a way, Josephine Catalano—whose life was at least as remote from mine as Rabbi Singer—was my twin. Indeed, there must be millions of people like us scattered all over the United States. Once I realized that, I began to see that my clumsy, halting, sometimes ludicrous search for my very specific roots was one way of solving an endemic American problem—the unwitting suppression of scores of cultures—that has impoverished us all.

One Saturday in 1979, Rachel and Lisa and Matt and I were at Mohonk, a hotel in upstate New York, where you can skate or sled or go cross-country skiing. I don't like any of those sports. They make my body feel wet and cold. So I sat in my room, underlining passages in some novels I planned to incorporate into my article on Lawrence. It was a very pleasant activity.

But the themes I was emphasizing interfered with my work. I kept thinking, this is Shabbos, part of my specific past. Why not refrain from working and make its rhythms part of my life?

There wasn't much I could do that day except to observe the prohibition against writing on Shabbos by putting down my pen and dog-earing the pages I liked. It seemed like an absurdly small symbolic act. But I was unaccountably proud of myself for taking it.

Not, I knew, that I would become a complete Shabbos observer within a week—or even, most likely, within a few years. My life was too full of complicated competing commitments to make such a far-reaching decision. But I could begin the process by deciding to refrain from working, by turning down all Saturday assignments, no matter how strange my editors thought that was.

Now I see that the decision represented the most important single step into Judaism I could have taken. For it meant that one day every week I would relate to other Jews as *Jews,* and that I'd have to obtain more spiritual nourishment from my neighborhood than from the vicarious experiences I had in distant, rather exotic places like Portugal or even the Lower East Side.

13

I don't believe there are epiphanies in Judaism. Since it is a religion that insists on concrete deeds, not on blinding revelations of Divine Power, a newcomer like me who decides to become part of it has to do so slowly, one mitzvah at a time, in order to transform himself without losing himself.

I was lucky that Rachel was launched on a quest that was similar to mine. For dozens of marriages founder over these mitzvahs, which sound bizarre and abstruse at best, maniacally inconvenient at worst, to people who don't see them as the substance of God's law or as milestones on an inner odyssey. Couples fight bitterly over whether to have a kosher home, for example, or whether to turn Saturday into a Shabbos of sanctified time. For years, it is true, Rachel was loath to convert to Judaism, for she thought that might mean severing herself from the family she loved, from the New England past that had shaped so much of her character. And I was ambivalent about conversion, too. The word itself carried a worrisome reminder of my father's decision to suppress his past. So we rarely discussed conversion. We concentrated on learning about the religion, on trying to understand its rituals, on studying the Hebrew language.

Of course we were—and are—outwardly the same people—a journalist and a community organizer/photographer, a blond, WASPy-looking woman and an ethnically indistinguishable man—no matter what aspects of practice our inward journeys began to encompass. So we began to find ourselves in intriguingly incongruous situations.

During the intermediate days of Passover 1979, I wanted to cover the near meltdown at Three Mile Island and I asked Rachel, who was then working for an organization that supplied scientific information to lay people, to help me understand the story as well as photograph it. We asked the people in those rural Pennsylvania towns to describe the morning they thought the nuclear power plant would explode. Most of them relived the hysteria they'd felt just a few weeks before. They described hurrying to school, using newspapers or old coats to protect their children from radiation; sorting through a lifetime's worth of possessions as hastily as possible, then loading what seemed most precious into their cars and fleeing to a relative's house fifty or sixty miles away. They feared they might never see their own homes again. In the end, of course, catastrophe was averted. They all returned to their towns. The story had the eerie sound of a pogrom that never occurred.

In our own lives, Rachel and I had both decided to refrain from eating *hametz* during Passover. The act of giving up leavening enriched the story of the Exodus by incorporating a daily reminder of it into our lives. We brought our own matzos to rural Pennsylvania, and were careful about the foods we ate at restaurants. As we got to know the people in the area—devout Christians, who were extremely generous about inviting us into their homes—we found that they were glad to help us fulfill our dietary requirements. It turned out they couldn't quite understand Jews who weren't observant. Conversely, our explanation of the fact that we weren't eating leavening so that we could remember the hastiness of the Exodus paralleled their sacrificial period of Lent. It served as a bond, not a barrier. We might be big-city journalists, employees of an avowedly left-wing newspaper, but we had roots in something that was real to them, the Bible.

But in New York, we hadn't found a community in which we could explore our new, active attempts at observance with people who were like ourselves. That winter Rachel and Jerry Raik, who was now a teacher at the Havurah School, had organized a small *davening* group where about six friends recited psalms and prayers in English or Hebrew, then read the Torah at our own pace, pausing to discuss any questions or reservations that occurred to us. Sometimes those sessions grew quite intense. But they only occurred once every three or four weeks. We didn't know what to do in the interim. We were in a sort of no-man's land.

I remember one Saturday in October 1979, when I was tempted to cover the opening of the John F. Kennedy Library in Boston—an event that would keep Teddy Kennedy and Jimmy Carter, who would soon be locked in a dramatic primary battle, on the same stage all afternoon. A year earlier I would have assisted at the Havurah School on Friday afternoon, then spent Friday night with Rachel and the kids. After lighting candles, we would have eaten a special meal off my mother's Wedgwood plates, and played charades or board games, or read poems that appealed to us. I would have flown to Boston on Saturday morning.

But I decided not to go that day. I didn't want to compromise Shabbos. However, there was nothing spiritual about my weekend in New York. Our *davening* group didn't meet that Saturday. It had never occurred to Rachel or me to join a synagogue. In the past several years, the New York Havurah had spawned several minyanim, prayer groups of young, religious Jewish men and women. Although some of these people were friends of ours, although we were very attracted to their form of worship, we were still too uncertain of our ability to function on the alien turf of Hebrew-language Torah and prayer to ask if we could join them.

So, for the moment, the religious precept that seemed so promising—to heed the Sabbath and call it a delight—simply meant an idle Saturday, a time when I longed for sundown so that I could work again.

Just before Hanukkah, a new glossy magazine, *Jewish Living*, assigned me to go to Venice, California, a very hip seaside suburb of Los Angeles, to describe an Orthodox community that had developed there in the past two years—a place where young people combined traditional Judaism with an outwardly worldly life.

Its focal point was a synagogue on Venice's boardwalk, the Bay Area Synagogue, where screenwriters, lawyers, and doctors—

mostly in their thirties, many with as little religious background as I had—prayed alongside the elderly retirees who frequented the Israel Levin Adult Home—alongside an eighty-year-old tailor from Chicago, an eighty-seven-year-old chicken-market owner from East Flatbush, a seventy-five-year-old optician from St. Louis. The religious community existed in the midst of gaily dressed roller skaters, joggers, bicyclists, clowns, and former hippies who read Tarot cards. It was flecked with glamour. Michael Medved, the co-author of the extremely popular book and television series *What Really Happened to the Class of '65* was the president of the synagogue. His friend Barbra Streisand and her ex-husband, Elliott Gould had chosen to have their son Jason celebrate his bar mitzvah there. They had thrown a lavish, kosher-catered party for the community's residents. Streisand had endowed a day school in the community (the Emmannuel Streisand School, named after her father, a Hebrew teacher), which had attracted about one hundred children, mostly from non-religious homes.

Since the Jewish life I saw in Venice involved my contemporaries, my professional counterparts, I was forced to face questions that never quite presented themselves when I was in Rabbi Singer's enchanting, alien world. My Jewish development had been too unpredictable to rule out any future changes, but as I spent time with people at the Bay Area Synagogue, it became increasingly difficult for me to see how I could become Orthodox. I didn't like the *mehitza* (the curtain that separated men from women) at the Bay Area Synagogue, or the fact that, because the shul was Orthodox, women couldn't read from the Torah. (By contrast, the equality of sexes was the ideological foundation of the New York Havurah and the minyanim it had spawned.) And I felt uncomfortable with the hip Hollywood types who punctuated every sentence about their health or their work with the phrase that seemed so natural when Rabbi Singer used it: *"Barukh ha shem,"* "Blessed be the Name." (Thank the Lord.) Anyway, their newfound religious assurance troubled me in the same way as dogmatism had in the New Left. I distrusted any kind of certainty.

Still, the Venice environment was more hospitable than the one our friends in New York had managed to create. At the Bay Area Synagogue all newcomers were made to feel like welcome additions to any Shabbos table, not like people whose lack of Jewish knowledge slowed down discussions of Torah, whose ignorance of the community interfered with old friendships. Moreover, unlike the minyanim, the Bay Area Synagogue was resolutely multigenerational. It combined the rough-edged, slightly crack-brained Old World attitude I loved on the Lower East Side with the sophisticated blend of religion, intellect, and worldly interests that made Medved and his friends resemble people I'd met in the *havurah* movement. And, in Venice, the hunger for Jewish learning was incredible—especially when one realized that most of the young people there had only become interested in religion a year or two earlier. Every Thursday night, the synagogue's rabbi, Daniel Lappin, gave Torah classes for the seventy men and women who could cram into the house where it was held. Forty more people were on the waiting list. Each week, there were three Talmud classes, with about ten students apiece. There were courses on Jewish women, in beginning Hebrew, and on the book of Job. There was a seminar on kosher cooking, taught by a former *cordon bleu* student. And all this was happening among worldly people in Venice, California, not among Hasidim in Borough Park.

After I'd spent a week there I began to realize that Rachel and I were part of a widespread phenomenon. You saw it in the *baal tshuvah* yeshivas—places where newly observant Jews learned Torah and Talmud—which attracted thousands of spiritual seekers as students. You saw it in Manhattan's remarkable Lincoln Square Synagogue, where the charismatic Orthodox Rabbi Shlomo Riskin had involved hundreds of people, from secular and traditional backgrounds, in study groups, friendship groups, religious services. In a different form, you saw it in the New York Havurah, which was part of a nationwide *havurah* movement of several thousand people. You even saw it in the Havurah School, for all the parents' ambivalences. And I felt it personally in the scores of letters readers wrote when I published "Jews Without Money, Revisited," and then, again, in the even more intense letters I got when I wrote about Rabbi Singer.

Plainly, a completely unexpected, very pluralistic revival of religious Judaism—of a Judaism that combined learning and social service—was occurring in America. In an inchoate form the revival was spreading on the Upper West Side. After a week in Venice, I felt certain that it could be fused into the coherent, tangible community that hundreds of people like Rachel and me wanted to find.

That night I called Rachel from my brother Geoff's house, intending to describe what I had witnessed.

To my astonishment, she told me that she planned to convert. That day, she said, she'd talked with Steve Shaw, a Conservative rabbi we both knew, to find out how to do so. She said that she had been thinking about the idea for months, ever since she discovered that worshiping as a Jew released something inside her which enabled her to think about God, to feel, at rare moments, a faith whose intensity startled her. But she had to take the first step toward conversion herself to be sure that it stemmed from her own private decision to become a Jew, not from a residual wish to please me.

But there was a long distance between her decision to convert and her appearance before a *bet din,* a court of three rabbis, who would ask her questions about her beliefs and her Halachic commitments, and then accompany her to the mikvah, the ritual bath, where she would say the blessings that would make her a Jew. For she had to decide what kind of *bet din* she wanted, a relatively complicated matter. Steve Shaw felt that she should have an Orthodox conversion, because no one would question its authenticity. And, at first, Rachel agreed.

Steve, a remarkably energetic man, with scores of friends throughout the Jewish world, had his own list of potential rabbis. I wondered whether I should suggest Rabbi Singer to him. In the three years since I had met Rabbi Singer, he and Rachel had developed a great deal of affection and respect for one another. Indeed, she thought he was one of the most charismatic people she had ever known. But I didn't see how she—or I—could adhere to his strict religious standards, or embrace a view of women that made sense in his world but that was completely alien to ours. He knew that we were embracing new mitzvot slowly, knew that we believed in equality between men and women, and seemed to accept us wholeheartedly. But would he feel free to convert Rachel? I was afraid we'd offend him if we didn't ask him to be part of the *bet din*. But I was even more afraid that, if we did ask him, he'd make Halachic demands on the two of us that we couldn't accept—and that our attitude would rupture our friendship.

Early one very rainy winter morning, Rachel set out to meet an Orthodox rabbi whom Steve Shaw had suggested. He wanted to meet with her alone and I had a book review I had to finish, so I agreed to join them after they'd talked for an hour. But I'd written down the wrong address for his apartment. Panicked, I ran to every door in the five-block area of his building, asking doormen if they had heard of the rabbi. By the time I found the right building, Rachel was gone. So when I returned home, soaking, I was worried that I'd missed a crucial episode in our new Jewish life.

I hadn't. Rachel was calm but depressed. The rabbi was less concerned about the details of her Jewish observance—which were unpredictable anyway—than about the fact that the Jewish world that attracted us, the *havurah* movement with all its tiny minyanim, was so casual, so free-wheeling, that it might disappear. He was concerned that he would be converting her into limbo, when he believed that the very essence of Jewish life was its institutions, particularly synagogues, where the religious community gathered.

Rachel and I had always worshiped together in living rooms like Jerry Raik's, or in somewhat scruffy apartments, like the one the New York Havurah used for its High Holy Day services. It had never occurred to us that a synagogue in the neighborhood could be an interesting, welcoming place. But we had to admit that the rabbi had articulated a problem we had been reluctant to face.

Actually, there was a handsome yellow brick synagogue, Ansche Chesed, just a block away from our apartment. For years, the place had served our secular needs. Indeed, at times, it had been a second home for our kids. The Purple Circle, the day-care center that Rachel had founded, was located on the fourth floor of the educational building, and the Frog Pond, an afterschool program we'd both helped launch, was on the third floor. But as a religious center the place was in decline. Built in 1927, it had once claimed seventeen hundred members. By 1980, the congregation had dwindled to about one hundred. Dozens of people we knew saw the place as a potential community resource. Every year or two, members of the New York Havurah and the various minyanim held meetings to discuss ways of reviving it. But they always got stuck on the formal issues, like the best way of establishing a democratic decision-making structure.

Then one Saturday during the intermediate days of Passover, 1980, Rachel and I had lunch with Rabbi Wolfe Kelman, a neighbor, a noted teacher at The Jewish Theological Seminary, who loved sharing his knowledge with neophytes. Wolfe, whose liberal ideas had forced him to break, very painfully, with his Hasidic family, made Judaism come alive in words in very much the same way as Rabbi Singer did in deeds. He transformed the most casual conversations into exciting trips through the Talmud. He was able to explain all sides of every religious issue, to use his prodigious memory for Torah texts, Hasidic stories, his page-by-page knowledge of the Talmud, to help his guests discuss abortion or the West Bank or conversion as if we were all spanning four thousand years of tradition. In a way, he and his wife Jackie made their home, with its wonderful blend of gossip and theory, its delicious food, its emphasis on using books to track down every stray fact, a religious version of my parents' apartment.

Wolfe had read my *Jewish Living* article about the synagogue in Venice, California. After lunch, when Rachel and I said we were still searching for a place to pray in New York, that we missed a community that was committed to Judaism and receptive to people as open and ignorant and full of questions as we were, he mentioned the Bay Area Synagogue and said that you didn't have to be Orthodox to create the kind of environment I had described. We could do the same sort of thing at Ansche Chesed! That congregation consisted of old people. They needed younger, creative Jews to revitalize the place. Someone was even willing to give a quarter of a million dollars to help repair the synagogue's damaged boiler system and its flooded basement. Wolfe urged us to pursue the plan that had been raised and dropped so often: to urge people in the *havurah* movement to join the synagogue. If Wolfe was right, Ansche Chesed could provide a community for us. We decided to help revive it.

Over the next few months, Rachel and I grew increasingly close to the people in the minyanim whose knowledge had so recently threatened us. Most of them shared our political outlook. In high school and college, in their Jewish student movements and their synagogues, they had taken the same sort of risks to oppose the war and fight for civil rights as we had in the Peace Corps. They had used as many drugs, danced as much rock and roll, as most of our friends in SDS.

But most of them had been primarily identified as Jews, not as leftists. In their twenties and thirties now, they worked in the Jewish world or in the professions—as professors of Judaica or as Hebrew teachers, as architects or psychiatrists. They were caught in tensions that forced them to be creative. For example, they wanted to maintain some balance between their reverence for the past and the unassailable fact that they had been shaped by the forces that pervaded post-World War II America; between their love of Judaism and the Jewish people and their distrust of its traditional authority structure. These tensions had produced seminal works like the astonishingly popular *Jewish Catalog* (a *Whole Earth Catalog* of observance, which had sold 250,000 copies) whose editors, Sharon and Michael Strassfeld and Richard Siegel all lived within three blocks of Ansche Chesed. But the tensions had made them as loathe to create large institutions as their counterparts on the New

Left. For they—and we—were part of a generation that had never
worked out the proper balance between the individual and the
community. We were so terrified of losing our autonomy that we
had great trouble in reviving something like a synagogue—or creating a progressive political party—which might force us to adhere
to majority decisions or adhere to common standards of practice.

In the sixties the New Left and the *havurah* movement were
both ideal places to find one's political or religious identity. They
developed almost identical styles, which encouraged intimacy and
virtually outlawed authority. For instance, members of SDS and the
havurah movement sat in circles when they met, not in rows. Both
organizations insisted on a leadership that was rotated frequently,
arrived at all their decisions by consensus, not by votes or by the
decree of some central committee.

And both organizations provided specific outlets for their ad-
herents' social consciences—in the South or in antiwar demonstrations in the New Left; by working with elderly Jews or
supporting Soviet Jews in the Havurah.

But there was a crucial difference between the two movements,
which emerged clearly as idealism ebbed, as conflicts arose. The
fights within the Havurah were almost as bitter as those within the
New Left, but since everyone involved was a Jew with some commitment to religion, personal conflicts and power struggles—like
those between Stokely Carmichael and his white peers—couldn't
be confused with ethnic prejudices. Ironically, the *havurah* movement's strength lay in the very parochialism that sometimes made
it seem frustratingly narrow. It couldn't be Balkanized. It wasn't
even likely to become a hotbed of sectarian strife, since the disagreements were rarely ideological. Almost everyone had a dovish
view of Israel; the equality of women in Jewish life was part of the
havurah's creed. Still, no one really cared if a former member of a
minyan became Orthodox and chose to worship elsewhere, or if a
current one was becoming alienated from religion and ceased to
worship at all. So the intimate nature of the fights was undisguised.

Those quarrels could be painful, of course, but at their worst they led to the creation of another new minyan, not to the totally separate organizations for the women, the blacks, the gays, the white men whose inability to cooperate destroyed the New Left. For, on a fundamental spiritual level, the worst enemies in the *havurah* movement had to cooperate. They all said the same prayers on Shabbos. They all read the same portion of the Torah. They all observed the same holidays. So, because of Halacha and tradition, their generational rebellion would endure, in one form or another, as the New Left's had not.

But in what form? That was the question that perplexed Wolfe Kelman on the Shabbos Rachel and I had lunch at his house. His children, now adults, had all been part of the *havurah* movement and that was one reason that its fate concerned him so deeply. He knew that if its energy weren't channeled into something permanent, something adult, its influence might permeate the Jewish world, but the movement could die an unrecognized death. Its most talented members might leave a durable legacy, but there would be no structure, no coherent body of intellectual or liturgical work, no distinct change in ritual practice that would give permanence to the *havurah* movement. It would be recognized, if at all, as one of a dozen liberation movements that had flowered during the promising sixties, that had been fertilized by publicity during the novelty-hungry seventies, then faded when the intellectual climate of America proved to be chillier than any of us expected.

That was why Wolfe saw Ansche Chesed as such an important challenge. It would give focus to the diffuse Jewish groups that honeycombed the Upper West Side. It would oblige them to come into contact with one another, with unaffiliated seekers like Rachel and me, with kids like the ones in the Havurah School, and older people who still attended services at the synagogue. Those diverse forces would enrich the new Jewish culture and help it grow.

Rachel and I responded to Wolfe's idea because it promised to help us find the community we were seeking, and because our years in the New Left had convinced us that creative impulses can only be sustained through permanent institutions. But his words had more resonance for Rachel than he possibly could have known. For she had loved the yellow brick synagogue ever since we moved to the neighborhood in 1969, and she had felt a commitment to it ever since the Purple Circle began to occupy space there in 1975.

Within a few months, the prospect of reviving Ansche Chesed altered our Jewish world. It allowed us to feel that we were part of a spiritual community which was creating a movement and an institution, which was interested in social service and in art. Some Saturdays that spring, we would pray with people in the minyanim—or, rather, wrestle with our meager Hebrew while they prayed—and then discuss Torah or Talmud or Jewish history at lunches in their houses. One week that summer we went to the Havurah Institute in Hartford, Connecticut, where we studied prayer and post-Holocaust theology, the writings of Eastern European Jewish women and the Hasidic interpretation of the book of Genesis, went tubing on the Housatonic River, played tennis and softball, and had a full, peaceful Shabbos. It blended the best of college and summer camp.

Those encounters were always laced with discussions of Ansche Chesed. Sometimes we'd have to focus on mundane subjects, like pricing a new boiler for the building; we'd plan ways of moving a program that worked with elderly people into the synagogue; we began to plan a new day-care center, to devise community-wide forums on politics or literature which would attract people who weren't interested in religion; to fantasize about the concerts and theatrical events that would occur in the building once we had enough money to restore its ballroom and auditorium.

Often our new friends would discuss their own projects. Nessa Rapoport, an editor at Bantam Books, was just publishing a novel about love and friendship and faith, written from the point of view of a young, religious Jewish woman; Bill Aron was exhibiting his photographs of the Lower East Side and Jerusalem; Richard Siegel had organized a festival of ethnic Jewish music; now he and his wife, Jeanne, were opening a gallery of modern Jewish art in their apartment. Bill Novak and Moshe Waldoks were completing *The Big Book of Jewish Humor.* Jay Greenspan, a teacher at the Havurah School and a skilled Hebrew calligrapher, had just published a book describing his art. David Roskies, a professor at The Jewish Theological Seminary, had finished a movie called *The Shtetl in Fact and Fiction.* Nahma Sandrow had written a long book on Yiddish theater. Sharon Strassfeld had just completed writing *The Jewish Family Book* with her friend Kathy Green. All these people were part of a Jewish cultural renaissance. They all wanted to play a role in reviving Ansche Chesed.

In June, 1980, about a dozen Jews in the neighborhood called for a meeting in the synagogue's chapel to discuss its future. After a tumultuous discussion, everyone agreed that the place should become both a community center and a new sort of pluralistic religious institution, a display case of faith, where each kind of group, from *havurah* minyanim to some Orthodox women who wanted to *daven* together, to the synagogue's traditional congregation, whose average age was about sixty, would pray in its own way.

One Shabbos Rachel and I went to the traditional service in the synagogue's chapel. There were about two dozen people in their seventies and eighties, cheered by the sight of two relatively young newcomers. We were links to the future, signs that the religion that had been at the core of their lives would endure—and at the place where they had always worshiped.

There is a phrase in Hebrew, *tikkun olam,* which means repairing the world. Without knowing those words, Rachel and I had been trying to practice the concept most of our adult lives. We'd been doing it on a universal scale, in Mississippi, in Ecuador, in the antiwar movement. It was inevitable that our energy—that our generation's energy—would begin to ebb. For, when you try to rebuild the world for everyone, you don't rebuild it for anyone—least of all for yourself. So now we were starting once again, in our own home, in our neighborhood, in our place of worship, and hoping that from that very finite, concrete base we could reach out to all sorts of people everywhere—reach out in person and by example—and become what we'd always hoped to be: part of a force that had the practical wit and the spiritual will to repair the world.

By the summer of 1980, it was no secret that Rachel planned to convert. Her family was astonished that she had become religious at all but glad that she had decided to become a Jew, not a devout Christian. Secular Jewish friends—feminists, journalists, people we'd known in the New Left—couldn't understand her motives. Everyone in the Havurah School, including Lisa and Matt, regarded her step as an unnecessary formality since they perceived her as a *de facto* Jew already. Our new friends in the *havurah* movement thought she should convert with them, by taking the Halachically acceptable step of immersing herself in a body of flowing water— which is, by definition, a mikvah—while three people witnessed the process, heard her recite the blessings, and reported her actions to a rabbi.

But Rachel wanted a conversion that would be officially recognized. Throughout the spring, she discussed conversion with Rabbi Singer. From his own very religious point of view, he half agreed with the Havurah School parents. He thought that Rachel's commitment to Jewish law was the important thing, that a trip to the mikvah was a mere formality. Those conversations were always inconclusive. Then, one Friday morning, we went down to the Lower East Side to talk to him as frankly as possible.

As we walked down East Broadway, from his cubicle at the United Jewish Council to his synagogue—under the Pitt Street Bridge, past the kosher chicken market, past a graveyard for old cars—we began to talk about a favorite topic: Rachel's and my preference for an ethnically varied community like the Upper West Side as against his belief that Jewish children should grow up in a completely observant neighborhood like Borough Park. His way prevents kids from getting confused by different standards of Jewish practice, he said. Ours prepares them to live in a pluralistic country like America, Rachel answered. As we neared his shul, we passed the Masaryk Cake Box, where Frieda Provda always gives Rabbi Singer enough challah and cake to make kiddush on Shabbos. Frieda had become a good friend of mine since the fight with the funeral home, but she had never met Rachel. In fact, she had never realized I was married. "She's beautiful. No wonder you've been hiding her," she said, with a note of fond reproach in her voice. I was flattered by the familiarity of her words. I remembered the day, eight years earlier, when I had failed to wear a yarmulke in the yeshiva—the day I'd phoned Rachel, who had never seen the neighborhood, and watched, confused, while the religious Jews stared at me with an amusement I mistook for anger. Now the neighborhood was my second home.

When we left the Masaryk Cake Box I walked between Rachel and Rabbi Singer, happy that, on such a beautiful, early summer day, I was with two of the adults I loved most in the world.

We talked about Rachel's conversion for hours, sitting near the *bimah*, at the dark brown table where Rabbi Singer usually studies Talmud before he begins to pray. He barely looked at me while we talked. He engaged Rachel in a substantive discussion of *his* Halacha, *his* Torah.

It was Pilzno's religion; a Judaism of mysticism and revelation, not reason.

For example, when he talked about the dietary laws he didn't try to justify them with the familiar argument that Jews in biblical times somehow knew that pork causes trichinosis. From his point of view, that opinion represented an apology for the Torah: a retrospective effort to rationalize the irrational so that Judaism would seem palatable to post-Enlightenment gentiles. Kosher laws, he insisted, *were* irrational. What was logical about forbidding people to mix meat with milk? Indeed, it was the absence of logic that intensified the power of the laws. For they were part of the larger incomprehensibly intricate covenant the Almighty had made with the Jewish people.

That day, we talked about the religious laws we found most troubling—those that concern women and sex. It was a slightly

fragmented conversation since Rabbi Singer was constantly interrupted by old people who came to shul to complain about the
apartment he'd obtained for them, or to ask for help with some confusing portion of a social security form he'd given them. Then, once
their problem was resolved, they'd hover, lonely and fascinated, on
the periphery of our discussion.

First, he talked about his belief that synagogues should have
mehitzot to separate men from women because mixed seating can
cause one to flirt, to think about sex, not about the Almighty. And
he mentioned the conviction all Orthodox rabbis share, that
men—and men only—should be permitted to bless the Torah or
read from it. Those Halachic principles were so important to him,
he said, that he would never give any sort of speech (even a secular one about life on the Lower East Side) in a synagogue with
mixed seating. He felt that way even though he knew that such
talks could raise appreciable sums of money for his shul from suburban Jews. He didn't want to sanction what he regarded as a violation of the law with his physical presence.

Then, he began to talk about the laws of family purity, which demand that husbands and wives refrain from sex during the time of
the woman's menstrual period, and until she purifies herself in the
mikvah a week thereafter. Many Orthodox Jews often try to rationalize the laws on romantic grounds—insisting that it renews the
passion in a marriage every month—or on medical ones, pointing
out that Orthodox women have an unusually low rate of cervical
cancer. More poetically, they sometimes describe the laws of family purity as a pause to mourn for the life that fails to flourish each
time a woman has her period—and then a burst of celebration for
the prospect of a new life each time she begins the cycle again.

Of course, many feminists, including Jewish women who keep
kosher and observe Shabbos, see the laws of family purity as a sexist statement that women with their period are unclean.

Rabbi Singer mentioned the medical argument and the romantic
one, but only in passing. He said that family purity forced people to
discipline themselves in their lives. In doing so, it helped establish

a pattern that disciplined them in their prayers. That might open them up to the Almighty.

But even that argument was too rational for him. He was absolutely convinced that the laws of family purity contained more mystical importance than any human being could possibly understand, and that men and women who heeded them, who saw monthly trips to the mikvah as a source of holiness, achieved a degree of spiritual elevation that he would not describe.

Now Rachel, a third-generation feminist, is sensitive to any remark that denigrates women even slightly. She can drive and hike, fix a car, and pitch a tent better than most men, and rages at women who become helpless and flirtatious whenever they have to function in what most people define as a man's world. The only time she and I had gone to an Orthodox service she was overcome with rage—and sorrow—at the fact that women were segregated from men, and from the Torah. She felt a steadfast certainty that she had exactly the same right to religion as I did. And I agreed with her—or, to put it more honestly, even though I loved the experiences that were available to men in Rabbi Singer's world, I knew I'd feel a constant mournful guilt if I embraced a kind of Judaism that made her feel excluded and angry.

As Rabbi Singer talked, I tried to read Rachel's face for clues to her emotions. For the first time, I felt embarrassed about this teacher; worried that his attitude toward women, his explanation of family purity, would fill Rachel with depression or dismay. Two hours ago I had been ecstatic. Now I was terrified that I'd feel torn between them.

He asked Rachel her opinion of his ideas, but the synagogue phone rang before she could answer. He had an emergency, he said—a woman who lived nearby had locked herself out of her apartment and he had the only other set of keys. We should forgive him for leaving such an important conversation. But he would be back in a few minutes.

As soon as he left, Rachel and I began to talk. She might have been angry with him, she said, if she'd read his words in a book—

but in his presence even an idea as alien as family purity seemed to possess an emotional logic. For he had attained the degree of spiritual elevation he was describing. What if obedience to the Torah's laws, not our compromised version of Halacha, was the thing that enabled a person to exude such joy, such unreserved passion and compassion?

But the question itself was unrealistic and hypothetical, for there was no way in the world that Rachel or I could follow Rabbi Singer's route and wind up with his force. He was rabbinic aristocracy from a very specific milieu; it had taken centuries of Eastern European Hasidic Judaism to create him. His American counterpart hadn't yet been born—we, the Jews, hadn't been in this country for a long enough time for that to happen. An American Rabbi Singer could only grow out of an indigenous movement—a *havurah* movement, perhaps, if it dug in and endured—that allowed Torah and Talmud to merge with the realities of this age just as the early Hasidim had let the Holy Books merge with the realities of theirs.

Besides, if Rachel converted with Rabbi Singer, he'd cease to be a friend and become a religious conscience. Inevitably, we'd feel a degree of guilt toward him that would undermine the relationship that had been at the core of my religious odyssey. So, to protect that friendship, to make sure that our evolving religion remained a source of joy, not guilt—to make sure, indeed, that we took on new mitzvot for ourselves and not for Rabbi Singer—we decided that the most practical step was for Rachel to have a Conservative conversion in the fall. But we were both scared to tell Rabbi Singer that we had made that decision.

By the time he returned to the shul, Rachel had figured out a tactful way to describe her feelings. She planned to dwell on one crucial aspect of the truth: that she wanted to be a Jew, but she wasn't ready to take on all the mitzvot; that she didn't want to feel she'd betrayed Rabbi Singer every time she violated a commandment.

Rabbi Singer had guessed at those feelings, just as he'd always sensed that Rachel would convert.

"Do you think you have to be as observant as me?" he asked teasingly. "I gave Sha'ul his tefillin. Do you think I'm going to give you a wig—so that you can settle in Borough Park?"

Then, more seriously: "You wouldn't be betraying me, Rachel. What you do is on your conscience. It's a matter between you and the Almighty."

In response, Rachel summoned all her courage and told Rabbi Singer that observance wasn't really the main issue for her. It was her own participation in religious life. She knew that he believed, with all his heart, that the Orthodox way was the Almighty's way, and that Orthodox women were even more profoundly rooted in Judaism than Orthodox men. That was probably the case in his world. It wasn't in hers. Her spirit would only flourish when she felt fully accepted as a Jew and as a woman.

When she finished talking, Rabbi Singer remained silent for a moment. "I think I know how you feel, Rachel," he said. "I respect it. Only do me this favor. Don't close your mind. Don't be sure you've gone as high as you can go. Maybe in five years you'll agree with me."

Then he blessed her.

He walked us to the street outside his synagogue, in keeping with the talmudic injunction that a host must walk his guest past the door sill to the point of departure. Then he smiled at both of us, and thanked us for coming down to see him. He wished us a good Shabbos. As always, he made us promise to give him a ring the next time we were coming to the neighborhood.

By late October 1980, when Rachel converted, Ansche Chesed was already a bustling synagogue. Nearly a thousand people had prayed there during the High Holy Days. Hundreds more ate potluck dairy suppers under a rooftop sukkah, which one of the minyanim had fashioned. On the festive Simchat Torah, the celebration of the giving of the Law, about six hundred jubilant people had come to the evening service, to pray and to dance with the Torah. Soon, they were dancing outside, on 100th Street.

The longing for some sort of Jewish center was even more widespread than any of us had realized. In less than six months, Ansche Chesed had become home for several minyanim, for the Havurah School, for the older people who had wondered whether the synagogue would survive, for hundreds of unaffiliated Jews who had a new curiosity about religious life. Together, those people formed the rudiments of a community. Some of them were present the night Rachel converted.

That afternoon she had gone alone to a *bet din,* at Rabbi Wolfe Kelman's house. After a forty-five-minute discussion, she and Dorien Grunbam, a friend who had spent eighteen months of her childhood in Bergen-Belsen concentration camp, who was almost like a sister to Rachel, had gone to the mikvah with the three rabbis. While the men stood outside the door, Rachel immersed herself in the water and recited the blessings that made her a Jew.

There was no salaried rabbi at Ansche Chesed—we didn't have enough money for that. So, that evening, Jerry Raik agreed to *daven maariv.* Rachel sat on the *bimah,* wearing a deep purple shirt and a brown leather skirt that had belonged to my mother. She was covered by a tallis, woven by David Weiderman at the Munkaczer Tallis Factory, and she held a siddur between her hands, which rested on her lap. Her mother was in the congregation, still confused that she had a religious daughter, but very proud. Lisa and Matt and I sat near the *bimah* so that we could open the ark that held the Sefer Torah, which Rachel would hold while the congregation prayed.

Soon she began to lead the congregation in prayer. She held the Torah against her shoulder. Then, with a calm expression on her face, she opened her siddur and began to read the central words in the Jewish creed: *Shema, Yisrael, Adonai Elohenu, Adonai Ehad.* Hear, O Israel, the Lord is our God, the Lord is One. When she finished the three sections that comprise the Shema, she put aside her siddur and began to speak in her clear, direct voice.

"To me, this is a very important moment, a moment of passage, but one that is part of a continuum. I used to think that conversion meant that you stopped being one thing in order to become another, and therefore I resisted it. But the Israeli Rabbi Adin Steinsaltz gave me a more organic metaphor. Conversion, he said, is like marriage. You are joined to a new community, but you bring to the union the strengths and the values that have been your foundation all your life.

"My conversion officially marks a love I've already experienced very deeply.

"That love started as a respect which my parents taught me for the Jewish people. They taught me and my sisters, Connie and Peggy, and my brother, Richard, always to speak out against anti-Semitism and racism.

"When I fell in love with Paul seventeen years ago, I began to identify with the Jewish people. Over time, I have felt that identification broaden from him to his parents, Polly and Lou; to my friends here tonight and the larger Jewish community; and to the country Israel. It has become increasingly important to me not just to identify with Judaism, but to be a Jew. I have always been proud to be a Yankee from New England. Now I'm proud to be a Jew.

"Today marks an important step for me, a step in the search we all share to lead lives that are meaningful to ourselves and useful to each other. I feel strengthened in that need by my husband, my parents and siblings, and by my friends.

"I also feel strengthened by affirming publicly that an important step in being the person I want to be is being Jewish."

For years I had thought I was completely indifferent to Rachel's religious decisions. She was the wife I loved, no matter what she chose to call herself. But now I knew that I felt stronger because Rachel was one of us, too.

14

When Rachel talked about being a Yankee and a Jew in her conversion speech, I began to focus on a paradox I'd been ignoring in my own life. For, although I was always emphasizing the need to retrieve one's ethnic past, the fact was that when I told my story to friends or to formal audiences I often obscured more of my family's history than Rachel did of hers. As late as 1980 I minimized the importance of my mother's German-Jewish ancestors, or discussed them as material for satirical anecdotes, not as human beings. I knew that my mother's dislike of those people had made her life especially difficult. Until I learned more about them, they would remain a problem for me, too.

Shortly after Rachel converted, I asked my uncle Modie Spiegel to take us to Ligonier, Indiana, where my grandmother's family, the Straus family, had begun to make their fortunes. It was a way of seeing the American roots of the prosperity that had made my mother and me feel such strange shame all our lives. And it was a way of understanding my uncle. Even in the sixties, when I saw him as the embodiment of the capitalist system I was fighting, I had always felt a fondness for him. I sensed a gentleness completely at odds with his public image as a tycoon, a trace of a poet who wondered if his very private dreams had been squandered in the boardroom battles he had to fight in order to do his duty and provide for his entire clan.

I'd had five or six long conversations with him since my parents' death—first to research this book, then because I'd developed a strong attachment to the eighty-year-old man. I think he was surprised and gratified that the two of us had formed such an unexpectedly close friendship.

I knew he'd be pleased to go to Ligonier, for he loved the family past and always regretted the fact that his brothers and sisters and their children seemed indifferent to it. His feeling had no direct connection to Judaism. He'd drifted away from the religion when he was a boy and his parents became Christian Scientists and now, at eighty, was so devoted to the Unity Church that he carried a prayer book in his jacket and read from it eight times a day. He couldn't imagine why Rachel had "gone Jew," as he put it. As we set out for Ligonier, he told her, musingly, that he and she "were like two ships passing in the night." Nevertheless, as we began our voyage to our ancestors' well-preserved homes, he admitted, in his wistfully poetic voice, that "I guess I'm a roots man, just like both of you."

Ligonier is a freckle of a town, near Amish country, about forty miles from the nearest city, Fort Wayne. On an autumn day, the rich, flat land looks like the heart of Christian America. Then, suddenly, just past a cornfield, a sign with a green star of David announces, "You are now entering Ligonier, Indiana, historic Jewish community." The small old gray stone Carnegie library, a mile down the road, contains a Jewish reading room, full of clippings of the Strauses and the dozens of other Jewish families who had once made that generation of German refugees refer to Ligonier as "America's Jerusalem."

There were about three hundred gentiles, mostly farmers, living in Ligonier when my great-grandfather Frederick William Straus had settled there in 1853. A year earlier, he had arrived in New York from the Rhineland town of Laufersweiler, but the city was too crowded for him so he decided to voyage West. In Auburn, Indiana, he met a landsman, a hardware-store owner named Joseph Stiefel, who taught him some English and advised him to use it in Ligonier, where the Northern Indiana Railroad soon would lay tracks. Actually, Stiefel was wrong—the railroad chose another town—but Frederick Straus stayed in Ligonier anyway, and sent for his brother Jacob to help him run a general merchandise store.

As soon as they arrived in Ligonier they began to hear the farmers, their customers, discuss their need for new buggies. So they learned to construct the wagons, or to repair them, and then to loan the farmers money to buy them. Since they were scrupulously honest businessmen, they won their customers' trust. So, if a farmer needed money to make improvements on his land, he would come to the Strauses for a loan. By 1880, less than thirty years after they had arrived in America, the family had developed a prosperous bank and farm mortgage business in Ligonier.

Though they Americanized themselves in order to do business with the gentiles, they continued to take their Jewish life very seriously. In the 1850s, before there were enough Jews to form a synagogue in Ligonier, they went to Auburn or Fort Wayne for the High Holy Days. By 1868, once ten Jewish families had come to town, the Strauses helped form Ahavos Sholem, a congregation that met in their homes until they found a larger building to house services. They were completely unapologetic about their faith. Most families had kosher homes until the late 1880s. Anyone who traveled through Ligonier on a Friday night in the late nineteenth century would see candles flickering in most of the fifty-five Jewish households in town. On Saturday mornings, traditionally the most lucrative business hours in a farm-oriented community, even the merchants closed their stores and went to synagogue.

Apparently, the town's gentiles respected the Jews' pride; they befriended them on their own religious terms instead of making complete Americanization the price of acceptance. In September 1889, Ahavos Sholem—by then a Reform congregation—moved to a spacious new building, and most citizens of Ligonier participated in the celebration, according to the Ligonier *Banner*. That Friday afternoon, the congregation's two oldest members carried the Torah scrolls through Ligonier's streets in a procession—with music by the Ligonier military band—that included Jewish and gentile adults. When the townspeople arrived at the new building, dozens of Jewish children were there to greet them, to give the synagogue keys to Jacob Straus, the president of the congregation.

That Saturday, the German-language services were led by Rabbi Isaac Mayer Wise, the president of the Hebrew Union College and the most prestigious Reform Jewish leader in America. Then, after sundown, hundreds of Jews and gentiles gathered at the town's new B'nai Brith Lodge for a kosher dinner. When they were finished eating, they walked over to city hall for an elegant dance.

My uncle Modie was delighted by the saga of Ligonier's Jews. The town was his mother's home, a vivid part of his past. He wanted me "to get a little taste of it," as Rabbi Singer might say. Though he had some trouble walking, he was eager to visit the former synagogue—now a Baptist church—which was a few blocks from the library. He insisted on driving to the cemetery where the Strauses were buried. He seemed as disappointed as I was when the owner of Frederick Straus's former home told us we couldn't enter because the place was being repaired.

By 1890, Ligonier, with its population of 2,200, was the second-richest small town in the United States. But in this peculiarly American story it was prosperity, not pogroms, that drove the Jews away from the rural village where they nourished their faith to Chicago where they shed it. Families like the Strauses discovered they could double or triple their annual incomes by relocating their banks or stores to large commercial centers. Their children went to Dartmouth or Yale and could never again accept the constraints of small town life. By 1980, there wasn't a single Jew left in Ligonier. There was just the sign, the room in the library, and a Jewish cemetery to memorialize the past.

I learned some facts on that beautiful autumn day—but, more important, I surrendered some crippling prejudices. Once I was able to imagine my German-Jewish ancestors in the American town where they had first settled, I found myself admiring them in a way my mother never could. When I was in Ligonier, I read the ethical will Frederick W. Straus had composed for his children. "I hope you will never cease to do good acts and be upright to your friends and relatives and everyone you deem worthy. Never accept thanks or reward for your good deeds, and do not be proud except upon your character." I found myself liking the man behind the fortune. He must have coupled his morality with an intelligent, self-possessed, and self-disciplined character—a character which allowed him to preserve his faith and lay the foundations for his prosperity during his first disorienting years in this new land. Besides that, he must have displayed an unusual generosity of spirit, for it would have been hard for anyone who addressed small-town Americans in a foreign accent, who spoke to his friends in a foreign tongue, who observed unfamiliar holidays in a highly visible way, to gain the trust of his neighbors by financial skill alone. He must have had the same respect for himself, and for the citizens of his adopted land, that Rabbi Singer did.

That day, I saw my remote ancestor as a mirror for my own as-pirations, for I wanted my Judaism, like his, to enhance my appre-ciation for my country—to deepen the love for diversity I'd tried to convey when I wrote about Lawrence—to form a bond with non-Jews, like those who lived in Harrisburg or Ligonier, by letting my pride in my faith intermingle with their pride in theirs. Freder-ick Straus's history intensified my own conviction that the religion my father had belatedly transmitted to me, that my friendship with Rabbi Singer had intensified, which now had a home at Ansche Chesed, would deepen my roots in my native land.

Still, as I sat in the Ligonier library reading the one-hundred-year-old documents, I found myself brooding about the difficult voyage my mother's family had made. From Laufersweiler to Ligonier. From Ligonier to Hyde Park. From Hyde Park to Kenilworth. From Kenilworth to Glencoe or New York. Five or six way stations, each of which seemed to be home, in only one hundred years. How could they possibly have retained a cohesive culture, a cohesive set of values, during such a long and varied trip? How could they feel completely comfortable with the new cultures, the new values, that allured them along the way?

I wished my mother could have accompanied Uncle Modie and me to Ligonier in the same way as I wished my father could have accompanied me to Rabbi Singer's Lower East Side. Perhaps, then, she could have appreciated the strength her mother's parents pos-sessed, and seen that strength as her legacy. Maybe she would have

been able to declare a truce in her lifelong war with her immediate past. She might have recognized herself as the product of thousands of years of history, not of a relatively difficult set of parental
relationships. She might have accepted herself as a human being
and a Jew and found the peace she sought so desperately. That
would have been a lovely thing for her to possess, and a lovely gift
for her to transmit to her children.

15

When Rachel converted, Lisa, twelve, wasn't at all sure of what she wanted to do about a bat mitzvah. There had already been three bar or bat mitzvahs at the Havurah School, all in June 1980. The children, two boys and a girl, had learned to recite the blessings over the Torah and read a few lines of Hebrew. One of them had written a lively, moving poem about King David; a second had given a speech about Jewish mysticism; the third had read eight verses from the Torah. Lisa felt that if she had a bat mitzvah at all, she wanted her own tutor, a woman, and thought the affair should be a spare, personal ceremony in our apartment.

I tried to keep our conversations about the subject tentative and low-key, even though I secretly cared about Lisa's bat mitzvah with the same depths of feeling that I cared about Rachel's conversion. With more feeling, perhaps. For my truth was that, despite all the spiritual richness I'd found in Rabbi Singer's world, despite the community Rachel and I had helped to create at the Havurah School and the new one that was flourishing at Ansche Chesed, my deepest emotions were still rooted in my very private search through my parents' Jewish past. Unlike Rachel, who had finally converted because she fell in love with the religion, I felt my Judaism was inextricably linked to my complicated heritage; to my desire to understand the rifts that had plagued our family, and heal them if I could. I suppose I saw Lisa as my collaborator in this spiritual project. Already, I could imagine my father and Jake Cohen bursting with shared pride when their tough, savvy, Americanized descendant decided to fast on Yom Kippur or Tisha B'Av, when some strong sense of family and tradition convinced her to give up hametz for Passover. And I could imagine my puzzled mother, my desperately embarrassed Spiegel grandparents, slowly re-examining the traditions they'd discarded as they realized that not only Rachel and I, Holly and her husband Seth, but our children found some meaning in Judaism, too. Of course, I knew that I was casting Lisa in a role that was too difficult, too demanding for any child to play. My father's ambition for me—the ambition that sent me so unwillingly to Choate—made me acutely aware of the dangers of making any youngster the repository of one's own unattainable hopes. So with some frustration, some pain, I realized that I had to trust Lisa's judgment about a highly emotional subject like a bat mitzvah; try to influence her feelings within her own frame of reference; but not impose any of my new, somewhat mystical sense of the sweep of tradition and community on her.

I felt that especially strongly because the family history I'd learned as I was researching this book kept echoing through our daily life. For what was our story—the Cohens', the Spiegels', even Rachel's and mine—except the relentless saga of children, born in America, who had renounced their parents' faith. Plainly, my father's uneasy rejection of Jake Cohen and his form of Judaism formed a subtext of the ambition that led to his very public, very American success—and, later, to his undying sense that he'd been permanently disgraced by the quiz-show scandals. He was most comfortable with himself when he finally decided that his professional home should lie somewhere at the crossroads of academia and organized Jewish life. Similarly, my mother's inability to accept her family's secularized, mercantile form of Judaism—or to see their Christian Science as part of a real spiritual quest, not a nutty burden they'd inflicted on her and her brothers—intensified her abiding sense of isolation from the past.

What if Rachel's and my growing pleasure in Judaism had a similar effect on Lisa and Matt? What a paradox that would be!

As most parents do, I suppose, I kept projecting my own life story on the very different screens of my children's minds. So, despite myself, questions that seemed irrelevant from any rational point of view would disturb me for days. For example, Rachel's mother and sisters played an infinitely larger role in Lisa's and Matt's life than Jake Cohen had played in mine. Her father, who came with the dust and went with the wind, was a real if evanescent presence. Indeed, after the fire, we saw much more of the Browns than we did of my relatives. But what if the desire to discover Rachel's half-hidden Protestant past kindled the same inexpressible yearnings in Lisa's or Matt's imagination that Jake Cohen's almost tangible, invisible presence did in mine? What if the kids found the same meaning in the Episcopalian Church, in the arcane writings of Cotton Mather and Jonathan Edwards, as I found in Rabbi Singer's shul, in my increasingly detailed study of Torah and Talmud? I'd have to accept it. But the curse of the rift would still plague my family.

There was, of course, no way that Rachel and I could disguise the fact that we were observant Jews. We were proud of the choice. The kids had helped prompt it when they were little, and participated in it as they grew older, though they sometimes found the increasing intensity of our involvement unsettling. But we didn't know how the substance of the Havurah-style Judaism we'd adopted would mingle with the shadows of the faiths they had seen us reject—the shadows of the Orthodox Judaism I loved when I was with Rabbi Singer; of my mother's secular messianism, which still flickered through all my discussions about politics; of the left-wing atheism Rachel's family espoused; of the Episcopalianism that had both attracted and frightened me at Choate. We tried to describe what was best in all those creeds. Certainly, in becoming, we had tried to maintain contact with what we had been. Still, these were all rejected possibilities. How would they reassemble themselves in the substratum of Lisa's and Matt's beliefs?

Of course, it would be decades before we knew the answers to those questions; decades during which we kept changing ourselves. I understood that rationally. But I was a father in love with his children, not a detached observer of a family in flux. So I was emotionally convinced that Lisa's decision about her bat mitzvah would suggest how much she cared about our present. But I didn't want the choice to be a family loyalty test. So, for months, I hoped, almost wordlessly, a little desperately, that she herself would decide to assume a place within the tradition Rachel and I had rediscovered.

She did.

She had just graduated from P.S. 75, our multi-ethnic neighborhood grade school and entered Fieldston, a predominantly Jewish private school in New York. A few parents there were quite religious. Others had enrolled their children in Hebrew school when they were seven or eight for the instrumental reasons we had rejected when we founded the Havurah School; to memorize their *alephs* and *beths,* not puzzle out their feelings about the binding of Isaac, so that they would be prepared for the bar or bat mitzvahs. I recognized contemporary versions of my 1950s friends at Dalton among the friends Lisa brought home, and the parallel gave me a respect for the kind of Hebrew school education I once would have scorned. There hadn't been a single bar or bat mitzvah in our seventh- or eighth-grade class. Though most of us were Jews, there was nothing at all to give us any collective awareness of that fact. At least the Fieldston kids were asserting their religious identities in their early teens. Most likely, the bar and bat mitzvahs, which demanded considerable study, which were the hub of their social life for a year, would imbue many of them with a measure of pride in their Jewishness that would stay with them forever.

In any case, after Lisa had been to three or four of her classmates' bar and bat mitzvahs she decided to have one of her own. Now she wanted to learn Hebrew and chant the Haftorah—the weekly passage from the prophets—from the *bimah* of the main sanctuary of Ansche Chesed.

We had bought a Hebrew-language version of Dr. Seuss's *Cat in the Hat* and, in the winter of 1981, Lisa decided to learn the language by studying the simple words in the children's book. Sometimes, early in the evening, I'd stand in her cluttered room with its collection of Oz books that had been handed down from my mother and Laura Ingalls Wilder books that had been a present from

Rachel's mother and listen, enraptured, as she and her tutor, Peggy Brill—a lively, perceptive twenty-seven-year-old Midwesterner whose predominantly German-Jewish background was as full of contradictions as mine—labored over simple sounds or giggled over silly rhymes. I couldn't imagine how my daughter could learn an entirely new language, and an unfamiliar form of cantillation in just nine months. I was proud beyond words when I saw her trying.

By summer, I found myself looking forward to the event with a degree of anticipation which made me wonder if I was confusing her coming of age with mine.

I remember the evening, late in August on Martha's Vineyard, when Rachel and I asked Lisa to chant her entire Haftorah for us. Though we couldn't teach her Hebrew, we could both read the language well enough to evaluate what she had learned. So, for nearly an hour, we sat in the brightly colored living room that had remained unchanged since my parents' death, on the island where I had courted Rachel, where Holly had married Seth, where Lisa was born, where my parents were buried, listening to her sing the marvelous verses from the prophet Isaiah. She made some mistakes, of course—plenty of them—and complained continually about how dull it was to keep studying those same twenty-seven verses for an hour every day. But it was clear that she would soon master the passage. Some hidden reserve of will, some symbiosis between parent and child had enabled her to poise herself to take a proud step into the tradition her forebears in America had ignored for so long.

No one had been more emotionally involved in Lisa's progress toward her bat mitzvah than my sister Holly. Holly is a more intellectual, more organized person than Rachel or I. She has always thought that I was giving way to a romantic impulse by searching out the Eastern European roots which, from her point of view, were a very minor part of our legacy. So we pursued very different paths toward Judaism. Nevertheless, we kept arriving at similar points. For example, in the year after Rachel's conversion and Lisa's decision to have a traditional bat mitzvah, Holly finally convinced her husband and three children to let her kasher their home. In July she began to learn a Haftorah herself, so that she could read it on a Shabbos in January 1982 and have the bat mitzvah she had wanted as a child.

She was eager to arrange a family gathering on the eve of Lisa's bat mitzvah. So she and Geoff and Liza reserved a room in a West Side restaurant and arranged a dinner with kosher wine, dairy food, challah, and Shabbos candles. My uncles John and Modie were there. To my surprise, they had accepted my invitation to come to the bat mitzvah. They traveled from Boston and Chicago to participate in a religious ceremony that neither of them had ever witnessed. Of course, Rachel's mother, sisters, and brother, and their children came to New York for the occasion.

It was a disparate array of people. As Holly and I tried to figure out how to include them all in some comprehensible version of the Shabbos blessings I experienced a strange series of flashbacks. Actually, these adults, the Spiegels, the Cowans, and the Browns, had been together at two family events—Rachel's and my wedding and my parents' funeral. But I associated gatherings of each clan with Christmas. As children, Geoff and Holly and Liza and I used to take an enchanting train ride through the snow-blanketed Midwest so that we could spend the holiday in Kenilworth with the Spiegels. As teenagers, the four of us always trimmed the tree and listened to my father's self-conscious reading of *A Christmas Carol* at our apartment in New York. In the sixteen years since Rachel and I had been married, we had only failed to spend one Christmas with her mother. So this Shabbos dinner, this foretaste of Lisa's bat mitzvah, was the first time Rachel's gentile family and my assimilated one had ever been together for an uncompromisingly Jewish event.

After the blessings, Holly, engagingly intense in private, extremely shy in public, got up to deliver a toast—or, rather, a special blessing—which put the event in perspective.

"There is a traditional prayer called a *shehechiyanu*," she began, "which we recite, as Jews, when we reach a new season—a new season in the world, in nature, or in our lives. We are here to share in Lisa's arrival at a new season in her life, for she has reached the Jewish age of majority. So, to help her celebrate the occasion, I want to recite the blessing.

"*Barukh Attah Adonoi, eloheinu melekh ha-Olam, shehech-iyanu v'kimanu v'higianu lazman ha zeh.* Blessed art thou, Lord our God, King of the Universe, who has granted us life and suste-nance and permitted us to reach this season.

"The blessing, the *shehechiyanu,* seems to me especially mov-ing because Lisa's bat mitzvah is the coming of a new season in sev-eral ways.

"She is the first member of our family to celebrate her bar or bat mitzvah—and not only to be called to the Torah but to chant the Haftorah—in two generations.

"She is the first woman ever to do so in our family.

"She represents a new season for her family, one in which Jew-ish traditions have become a central part of their lives.

"So it seems to me especially fitting that the Haftorah she will re-cite tomorrow is from Isaiah. For Isaiah believed that among the Jews there would be a saving remnant—a part of the community that would stay within the fold and preserve it for all other Jews and non-Jews.

"As the first Cowan to be called to the Torah in two generations, and the first Spiegel to be called to the Torah in far more than that, Lisa is playing the role of the saving remnant: restoring the parts of the tradition that have meaning to the Cowan/Spiegel family.

"Still, although Lisa's being called to the Torah has meaning for all of us, her bat mitzvah is first and foremost her event—a tribute to her decision and her bravery. It is her celebration.

"Mazel tov—congratulations."

Then Liza got up to augment Holly's toast with a gift. After the fire, she had combed my parents' apartment for any reminder of them that might be preserved. To her astonishment, she had found a necklace, with the initials LGC, that Tillie Smitz and Harry Smitz had given to my father for his surreptitious bar mitzvah.

"I've always felt as if I was the custodian of this," she said, as she handed the necklace to Lisa. "It's yours now. Wear it at your bat mitzvah."

Lisa took the necklace, one of the few physical links between the generations that seemed to be very distant, put it around her neck, and wore it proudly the next day as she recited her Haftorah.

It was misty and warm on the morning of Lisa's bat mitzvah, and I savored the very short walk to Ansche Chesed. It put the ceremony in perspective: as one event—albeit a very important one—in the rooted lives Rachel and I had chosen back in the days when our community of friends was still the New Left, when peace demonstrations, not Shabbos suppers, were the most important rituals we observed.

By 1981 we had lived on the same block for nearly thirteen years. Every morning since 1973, when Lisa started kindergarten at P.S. 75, we had joined the parade of parents who walked down hilly West End Avenue, past Ansche Chesed, past the apartments that housed the day-care center and food co-ops, the political cells and minyanim which gave our neighborhood its raffishly cooperative, freewheeling character, to the very integrated public school where, we hoped, our kids would experience democracy instead of hearing about it in private school civics classes.

In those days, when Lisa was five, I used to hoist her on my shoulders and carry her to her classroom. When I deposited her, back then, I'd kiss her very lightly on the lips. Later on, when Lisa was eleven and Matt was nine, I'd walk down the hill to school with them, chatting about books or TV shows, about the Gene Kelly films Lisa loved or the encyclopedia's worth of baseball statistics Matt had memorized. When we parted—on the street corner, now, not in school—Lisa would make sure I kissed her on the forehead, not the lips. Matt would get embarrassed if I kissed him at all. He always said good-bye by waving his hand in a shy, rapid arc.

The image of those walks lingered in my mind on the morning of Lisa's bat mitzvah. For their mundane, slightly inconvenient nature had given me an anchor in the kids' reality, forcing me to notice their growth, month by month, year by year. They allowed me to rejoice in the fact—once so terrifying—that I was an adult, maturing as my kids matured, growing with them. From the point of view of our decade in their neighborhood, Lisa's bat mitzvah didn't seem like a terminal event, a conclusion of our family's journey, but a happy way to begin her adolescence and my middle age.

Rachel's mother, Maggie, had spent Friday night with us. Now, she was holding Lisa's hand as we all walked to synagogue.

It still amazed me how easily she accepted the rituals of our religion, how gladly she welcomed Rachel's conversion. On Rosh Hashana 5742, she had written us a card saying, "This is surely the time to be celebrating the New Year. There is so much feeling of exhilaration everywhere—of a new beginning—which is certainly not true of the atmosphere and climate of January first. From now on, I intend to begin my year with you, and eliminate New Year's (January 1) from my calendar."

In her own way, I knew, she was as proud of her granddaughter, the bat mitzvah girl, as I was.

We got to Ansche Chesed at about nine-thirty, in time to see the first trickle of our family's friends mingle with the regular worshipers—the *daveners,* as my father had described them to Joe Berkenfield on the morning of his clandestine bar mitzvah. Most of the *daveners* were over sixty—the oldest, Hilda Lesser, was ninety-six. That morning I noticed Mr. Maurice Benzaken, a very religious Egyptian Jew who chanted Haftorah every few weeks in flawless, beautiful Sephardic Hebrew, with intriguing Arabic intonations. I'd never exchanged more than a few words with the man. He was simply someone with whom I prayed. Yet, his solid presence gave me a fresh sense of the ceremony in which Lisa was about to participate.

I realize that I have been writing about her bat mitzvah in very individualistic terms—as if it were a private statement of faith. In fact, by tradition, it is a completely public occasion. Among many

Orthodox Jews, like some in Rabbi Singer's milieu, it is a relatively routine occasion, since it represents nothing more complicated than acknowledging one's adulthood by receiving an *aliyah* to the Torah on one of the three days it is read—Monday, Thursday, or Saturday—and reciting a blessing you've known from your earliest childhood in a language you've been able to read all your life. "I'll tell you the difference between people like your friends and people like mine," an Orthodox rabbi from Israel once teased me. "We make a big thing of a wedding, since we assume it's the last time we get married. You make a big thing of a bar mitzvah since you assume it's the last time you'll be in a synagogue."

The joke was harsh. Its message resounded in my mind. I thought of it as I put on my tallis in time for the *borkhu* (the call to prayer), whose concluding blessing reads *Blessed art Thou, Lord our God, King of the Universe, who formest light and createst darkness, who makest peace and createst all things.* This bat mitzvah that had been preoccupying us for so long—what was it, really, but one part of a routine Shabbos service: a service that included Shaharit, the morning prayer, the Torah and Haftorah portions—which were determined by the liturgical calendar, not individual tastes—and the additional Musaf service.

In most synagogues, skilled congregants—not rabbis—lead the prayers and read from the Torah. For her bat mitzvah, Lisa had asked Jerry Raik to lead the *davening*; Jerry, the son of first-generation immigrants from Lithuania who had owned a laundry in Astoria, Queens; once a Peace Corps volunteer, once an actor, a marathon runner, and an avid Yankee fan; Jerry, who had whetted our family's appetite for Judaism when he told the Hanukkah story at the Purple Circle Day Care Center in 1972; who'd presided over all the sprawling communal seders in our house since 1975; who'd taught Matt since he was two, and Lisa since she was three; who had led the *maariv* service the night Rachel became a Jew.

He was beginning the Amidah, the benedictions pious Jews repeat daily. Lisa, looking cool and poised in her blue dress, was sitting beside Rachel and Maggie, glancing first at the prayers, then at the Haftorah. In an hour, when she was called to the Torah, she would be embarking on a pathway that linked her to Jewish communities everywhere; to people everywhere who now, like us, were finishing the Amidah, beseeching the Almighty to let our eyes behold *Thy return in mercy to Zion;* communities that would protect her if she was a stranger, celebrate with her in moments of triumph, support her in a moment of extreme difficulty. She would be her independent self, free to believe what she chose, to question what she chose, in a world that spoke a common language of history and ritual and prayer.

By now, dozens of people were arriving at the synagogue: some of my parents' dearest friends, people Rachel and I had known in school and in the movement, at the *Voice* and in the neighborhood; adults and kids from the Havurah School; people who were involved in reviving Ansche Chesed; Lisa's friends from summer camp and Fieldston and P.S. 75. Some, of course, were not Jewish. Many of the Jews were not religious. But most of them, I knew, hadn't simply come because they were fond of us. Many hoped to get something for themselves or their families out of Lisa's bat mitzvah. What if the occasion kindled some inexplicable yearning in a few of them, encouraging them to pass the knowledge of Judaism on through their families, as our small, embattled tribe of people had been doing for five thousand years. *You shall teach these words to your children, speaking of them when you are sitting at home and when you go on a journey, when you lie down and when you rise up.* Earlier, Jerry had read those words in the Shema. In the long run, what aspect of Judaism was more important than that—than the commandment to keep the religion alive? But it had to be made accessible to those who craved it: in this age, Judaism could only be spread by invitation, not by intimidation.

Rachel was now Ansche Chesed's program director. I watched her walk around the sanctuary, making each guest feel welcome. I began to realize that it would take all her social worker's skill, her convert's zeal, to help guide the revitalization of the synogogue. It was an important task.

For the vessel of tradition which had once held all Jews to-gether had been cracked by the enlightenment, by immigration, by the attractions of assimilation. It could only be repaired if people whose attitudes and experiences were as different as those who filled Ansche Chesed on the morning of Lisa's bat mitzvah treated each other with openness and patience.

The Torah is the vessel of the tradition that has always linked Jews. The act of reading it is the center of the Shabbos service. Yet, ironically, though there are many holy rituals that pertain to the Torah as an object, there is nothing very spiritual about the read-ing itself.

Whenever the Torah is removed from the ark, the synagogue's dignitaries carry it to the congregants, so that anyone who wants can touch the covered scroll with a finger, a prayer book, the fringe of a tallis. If the Torah is dropped, those who are responsible must fast. If it is destroyed, it must be buried like a person. When a reli-gious Jew like Rabbi Singer talks about having a Torah in his home or in his shul, it is as if the parchment with the holy words pos-sesses its own independent life, its own precious personality.

But the act of reading from the Torah is a relatively routine one—a form of communicating with people, not praying to God. It was designed primarily as a means of making sure that all Jews hear all the stories and laws from all five books of Moses between one Simchat Torah and the next.

But during it, there are at least seven holy moments: the *aliyahs,* when a congregant walks to the *bimah,* kisses a tallis and places its fringe on the Hebrew word that begins the next reading. The congregant blesses God for giving us the Torah, waits while a specified number of verses are read, and blesses God again. Once that is done, dozens of people in the synagogue shake the congregant's hand and offer congratulations, in Hebrew, for the honor he has received, and wish him strength to keep learn-ing and to perform good deeds.

In that way, every Shabbos most people in the synagogue have the sense that they possess part of the Torah—part of God's word.

For her bat mitzvah, Lisa had asked Michael Wolf, another teacher in the Havurah School, to read the Torah portion.

I had suggested that Holly make the first *aliyah*, for, in fact, she was the Cowans' saving remnant, the one member of the family who had felt committed to Judaism ever since she was a child. In a way, she was my spiritual twin; the person whose focused search kept my helter-skelter one in rein, whose steady commitment to her religious principles allowed me to feel that my more random, romantic yearnings were part of my family's fabric, not some mad aberration from its norm.

She walked up to the *bimah* and sang out the blessing in her clear, self-confident voice. A few minutes later, it was Geoff's turn. He strode up to the Torah for the first *aliyah* of his life, and recited the Hebrew words he had just memorized in his forceful lawyer's voice. Then, Uncle Modie, frail but eager to participate in the family occasion, made his *aliyah*, reading the completely unfamiliar Hebrew words in an English transliteration. He looked proud of himself when he was done.

My sister Liza had telephoned Holly the week before the bat mitzvah. She wanted to alter the language of the *brachah* so that she could change the gender of God. So she blessed Malka ha-Olam, the Queen of the Universe, in a transposition so startling that Wolfe Kelman, who was serving as rabbi, referred to the Almighty as He or She throughout the service.

Rachel and I had purposely chosen to make the next-to-last *aliyah* so that we would still be at the Torah when Lisa's turn came. Standing on the *bimah,* staring out at my daughter and son, my brother and sisters, my uncles and aunt, my in-laws, I felt as if I were on a shuttle through time.

In a minute my daughter would chant an entire Haftorah in Hebrew. I remembered how overwhelmed I felt when she learned to read English. It was the fall of 1973, and we were spending Thanksgiving at the house in Maine my mother-in-law had rented. One night, sitting at a hardwood table, Lisa's Aunt Connie taught her how to sound out simple rhyming words: B-A-T, C-A-T, H-A-T. I tried to describe my feelings in the *Voice:* "I can't imagine myself as the father of a girl who reads, of a first or second grader who goes to school by herself and stays overnight at friends' houses. It makes me realize that the boy-man I still am will have to find the resources to help guide a daughter who is growing up into the dense world of words and books and conflicting ideas."

Lisa was putting on her creamy white tallis, looking far more self-confident than I would have felt. As she started to walk toward the Torah, my mind filled with a dozen images. There was the baby I had been afraid to diaper, the four-year-old girl who dawdled with me on a field in Martha's Vineyard so that we could find the quiet moment when she asked me not to stay away so long on journalistic assignments. There was the eight-year-old who, in mid-November 1976, comforted Mary, a sick adult friend, who was now sitting in the third row at Ansche Chesed, with a poem that compared Mary's pain to the snarls in Lisa's hair. The next morning Lisa awoke to the news that her grandparents had died in a fire.

There, too, was the tough, sassy ten-year-old who threatened to sit-in if she weren't allowed to play in a boy's softball league, and who organized the first kids' disco party in the neighborhood. There was the eleven-year-old, who reached the apex of her grade school career with a meditative performance as Sonia in a P.S. 75 production of Chekhov's *Uncle Vanya.* The next year, in sixth grade, she spent miserable months wondering why a clique of kids in school had decided to ostracize her. Then, suddenly, she was a twelve-year-old private school girl gazing into her mirror so that she could achieve the right look for the Fieldston School she loved. Still, in her two worlds, at Fieldston and on the Upper West Side, it was clear that she retained vivid memories of the grief that had seared her for years after the fire, of the loneliness she had felt in sixth grade, and used those memories to make people feel proud, not belittled, to spread her version of thoughtful joy instead of inflicting her inner suffering on the world.

As she walked to the *bimah,* she looked astonishingly mature in her blue dress, with her thick brown hair falling over her shoulders.

There was a peaceful, expectant smile on her face as she stood over the parchment scroll, touched with the corner of her tallis the Hebrew word Michael had just read, and recited the blessing. Still poised, she stood near Rachel and me, near Jerry and Wolfe Kelman, while Michael read the last words of the portion— "observe, therefore, the words of this covenant, and do them, that ye make all you do prosper." Then, she concluded the Torah reading, as Jews always have and always will, by blessing "God, King of the Universe, who has given us a Torah of truth and planted everlasting life in our midst."

Spontaneously, the congregation began to sing "Simon tov and mazel tov"—traditional words congregations use to greet proud events like a bat mitzvah—until finally, Wolfe Kelman, who was afraid the service would run for too long, quieted everybody by saying, "There will be plenty of time for celebration later."

Then, all the adults who had surrounded Lisa sat down. Looking calm, but suddenly quite lonely and vulnerable, she took the sheaf of Hebrew pages she had been studying since March, placed them carefully on the podium, and began to recite Isaiah's prophecy.

I could see tears in Rachel's eyes as we sat listening to her. Matt, who had remained his bemused, wise-cracking self during his sister's months of study, suddenly began to smile with pride as he realized how much Hebrew Lisa really knew. I suppose I was smiling too—my old friends told me they had never seen me so happy— although I remember feeling momentarily distracted by the sudden realization that it would be much harder to guide this newly mature thirteen-year-old girl-woman through a world mined with drugs and alcohol than it had been to guide her five-year-old self into the dense world of words and books and competing ideas.

Lisa's voice was unfaltering as she recited Isaiah's beautifully embroidered tribute to the Almighty:

> *Who are those that float like a cloud,*
> *Like doves to their cotes?*
> *Behold, the coastlands await me,*
> *With ships of Tarshish in the lead*

To bring your sons from afar
And their silver and gold as well—
For the name of the Lord your God,
For the Holy One of Israel who has glorified you.

As I listened to those sumptuous words, I found my worries about the future vanishing. For the truth was that Rachel and I, strangers in the land of 5743, had created a world for our children that made far more sense than those we'd known as adolescents. The poised young woman on the *bimah,* the golden-haired boy sitting next to me, both possessed a pride in themselves—as people, as Jews—that I'd never felt. With luck, they would never experience the kind of confusion that paralyzed so many of us as the movement disintegrated. If they had enough self-respect to avoid those emotional perils, then the institutions through which Rachel and I had tried to fortify their sense of identity would seem like successes.

Now Lisa was reading the passage of her Haftorah I liked the best:

Instead of copper I will bring you gold
Instead of iron I will bring you silver;
Instead of wood, copper;
And instead of stone, iron.
And I will make your government be peace,
And righteousness your magistrate.
The cry of violence
Shall no more be heard in thy land.
Nor desolation nor destruction within your borders.
But thou shalt call thy walls salvation
And thy gates praise.

Those words made me think of my mother. For what was her Judaism but an effort to embody Isaiah's prophecy—that thy government shall be peace, and righteousness thy magistrate—in her own actions. The Holocaust had been her metaphor for her unapologetically Jewish form of secular messianism—for the core of ethics that governed our family's life. Nothing could dilute my pride in those ethics. Only I wanted to convey them to my children, and my children's children, through the substance of Judaism, not the memory of oppression. I wanted those values to come from the joyous voice of the spirit, not the painful throbbing of the conscience.

Now, as Lisa approached the end of her portion, her voice was slowing slightly. She almost sounded introspective as she chanted Isaiah's last extraordinary prophecy:

> *Your days of mourning shall be ended*
> *And your people, all of them righteous,*
> *Shall possess the land for all time;*
> *They are the shoot that I planted*
> *The handiwork in which I glory.*
> *The smallest shall become a clan;*
> *The least a great nation,*
> *I, the Lord, will speed it in due time.*

The first line of the verse, a prophecy for Israel, was a revelation for me. For, at last, my days of mourning had ended. At last, I felt free to possess the spiritual land which had seemed so alien for so long.

I missed my parents, of course; more deeply, on this day, than ever. I missed my father's raw, enveloping sentimental love, and my mother's tough façade of wisecracks and skepticism, the worried absorption in the details of physical appearance and family harmony, which, I knew, would have disguised her gushing pride in Lisa, one of the very few people in the world she loved unconditionally. I missed them as they were, for their flaws as much as their strengths. But I no longer mourned them. In the five years since they died, I had brooded about them constantly. Paradoxically, I had removed myself from the fascinating, omnivorous present in which they had raised me so that I could find my roots in the more stable, communal world of 5743, the hidden source of their values. Now I felt free to re-emerge. I felt as if I embodied the best of their spirit, as if I could live the ethical life they always preached in America, our land, precisely because I had seen the shoots that were planted in the past, because I had discovered my Jewish self.

An end to mourning. For decades I had felt a silent, inexplicable raging grief over the feeling that I was an orphan in history, a dazed member of a lost tribe. I was the descendant of *conversos,* American-style, free to call myself a Jew, bereft of the memories that brought tears to one's eyes at the mere mention of the word Adonai. I was on a lifelong journey to find faith: a journey through the land of the ancients; through Beersheba's shantytowns, built on the caves which Abraham inhabited; through the pawnshops in Chicago's ghettos; through the courtyards, shuls, and restaurants of the Lower East Side, the places that could have been Jake Cohen's haunts; through Rabbi Singer's New York, where Weiderman, the tallis maker and Eisenbach, the scribe, could have been Rabbi Jacob Cohen's neighbors in Lidvinova. Now, as I sat in our synagogue, I realized I was no longer an orphan in time, but a wandering Jew who had come home.

Lisa was finished with the Haftorah, reciting the final blessings with Rabbi Kelman. Matt, his blond hair a flag under his white yarmulke, was walking toward the *bimah.* With a shy smile that radiated through the room, he waited until his sister was finished and it was time to open the ark, where the Torah would be replaced. When the two of them sat down, next to Rachel and me, Matt, a born clown, hugged Lisa tightly, and in an overripe voice that was designed to conceal his genuine sense of pleasure, he kept repeating, "I'm so proud of you."

As they were embracing, Rachel and I held hands. Then Wolfe, still on the *bimah,* asked the three families—the Cowans, the Spiegels, and the Browns—to stand and recite the *shehechiyanu,* the blessing that had been the centerpiece of Holly's toast the night before. So now, Maggie and Uncle Modie, Holly and Uncle John, Geoff and Liza, and Connie and Peggy and Richard joined the rest of the farflung family in words which, I'm sure, would have made my parents cry, thanking the Lord "who has granted us life and sustenance and permitted us to reach this season."

Not so long ago, I had been obsessed by the rift between my father and my grandfather. Curiously, that obsession, which could have been resolved by simple genealogical research, had launched me on a path which, by some inexplicable alchemy, had transformed my worldly, powerful, mysteriously vulnerable father into a spiritual partner. The path led beyond myself, beyond my generation, into the world of my ancestors, which stretched all the way back to Moses and Mount Sinai. So, when I sought to understand the rift between Jake Cohen and Louis Cowan I found myself thinking about revelation. What had united this people, my tribe, for so long? Why did any prospect of its dissolution fill me with such despair? Why did the mission of extending knowledge of Judaism—revelation—into the future seem so glorious to me?

As Jerry Raik offered his tribute to Lisa by quoting the Talmud's Rabbi Hanina, who once said, "Much have I learned from my masters, still more from my colleagues, but I have learned the most from my students," she and Rachel and Matt and I encircled each other in a hug. Soon we were embracing brothers and sisters, cousins, uncles, and aunts. In the back of the shul, two religious women who barely knew each other—a retired Hebrew teacher named Emma Gordon and a young calligrapher named Betsy Teutsch—were sitting next to each other, shivering with emotion, as they saw our family, which once seemed lost to Judaism, take a very traditional stride back toward the faith.

Later on, Wolfe Kelman showed me the very last lines of the prophetic texts—lines from the book of Malachi—which put the primal horror I felt about the rift between my father and grandfather into two powerful verses that provided the context for the journey I'd been on for so long—a journey I'd always been reluctant to make, whose next steps I could never see, which had still brought us to this joyous day:

> *Lo, I will send the prophet Elijah to you before the coming of the awesome, fearful day of the Lord. He shall reconcile fathers with children and children with their fathers so that, when I come, I do not strike the whole land with utter destruction.*

Afterword

Rachel Cowan

Paul Cowan died of complications from leukemia on September 26, 1988, five days after his forty-eighth birthday. It was also the first day of Sukkot, in the Jewish year 5749. He was buried and wrapped in a white linen *kittel*—the Jewish burial shroud—in a plain pine coffin. His grave is in the small New England cemetery on Martha's Vineyard in which his parents are buried. One of the few comforts in that mist of pain was that he was buried just the way his Grandfather Jake had been buried, and Moses Cohen before him, and Rabbi Jacob Cohen before him, back in Lidvinova. I knew Paul would have wanted it that way. I felt grateful that his life's path had brought him back to his spiritual home.

In the beginning of *An Orphan in History,* Paul wrote, "Until 1976, when I was thirty-six, I had always identified myself as an American Jew. Now I am an American and a Jew. I live at once in the years, 1982 and 5743, the Jewish year in which I am publishing this book. I am Paul Cowan, the New York-bred son of Louis Cowan and Pauline Spiegel Cowan, Chicago-born, very American, very successful parents; and I am Saul Cohen, the descendant of rabbis in Germany and Lithuania."

Paul continued to live as an American and a Jew. Friday night for us was the beginning of Shabbat—we always lit candles and had a special meal with our kids, their friends, our friends. On Saturday mornings we'd go to services in the Chapel Minyan at Ansche Chesed; in the afternoon we'd read and take long walks. Paul was a regular at the daily morning minyan too, arriving with a cup of hot coffee which he gulped down before beginning his prayers. He helped lead the reshaping and revitalizing of Ansche Chesed.

Paul stayed very close to Rabbi Singer, his friend and teacher. He never left on a trip without talking to him and would usually call as soon as he got back to discuss whatever he had seen and learned.

He also took great interest in my studies at Hebrew Union College-Jewish Institute of Religion, and was proud that I would become a Reform rabbi. He hated the factionalism that plagues the Jewish community and believed that Jews in Israel and America should honor the widest range of ideas and people.

Becoming an observant Jew never diminished Paul's interest in the secular world of journalism, politics, sports, and culture. He read widely, followed political and intellectual debates, and wrote articles for *The Village Voice.* He tried to bring his two different areas of interest together whenever he could.

In the mid-eighties, he and I wrote a book called *Mixed Blessings: Marriage Between Jews and Christians.* We had traveled across America interviewing couples who were involved in interfaith marriages or relationships, and talking with their parents and their children. Paul wrote a personal afterword to *Mixed Blessings,* in which he said, "*An Orphan in History* has allowed me to meet thousands of Jews in America. I feel as if I have become part of a large, warm, contentious family that extends from Maine to Oregon. . . .

"But we are still part of the secular world we come from. That is why our work with interfaith couples engages us so deeply. The fact that people from so many different backgrounds can explore their religious and ethnic feelings so freely is a tribute to the American openness we were both raised to treasure. The discussions always teach us something new about America, religion, and ourselves."

Paul's funeral reflected that mix. The synagogue was filled with mourners. Rabbi Singer spoke; Paul's brother Geoff, my sister Connie, and our children Lisa and Matt gave loving eulogies. Friends from childhood, from *The Village Voice,* and Ansche Chesed added their words. Another friend chanted the Twenty-third Psalm, and at the end all the mourners stood and sang "We Shall Overcome," all of us strengthening each other in our sorrow and our fear at confronting death.

Perhaps the most important thing to remember about Paul is the quality that infuses *An Orphan in History*—his honest, passionate love of life. He described it best in the conclusion of a *Village Voice* piece he wrote on living with his leukemia:

"I've always wondered how strong I'd be if I were tested. I still don't know. There may be many difficult tests ahead. But I have discovered that I am stronger than I realized. I've learned that I can need love and be self-reliant at the same time. I've learned that I can keep loving and laughing and working in the face of relentless fear.

"I've learned a more important lesson—one I hope stays with me. Dreading death, I've discovered I can still affirm life."

About JEWISH LIGHTS Publishing

People of all faiths and backgrounds yearn for books that attract, engage, educate, and spiritually inspire.

Our principal goal is to stimulate thought and help all people learn about who the Jewish People are, where they come from, and what the future can be made to hold. While people of our diverse Jewish heritage are the primary audience, our books speak to people in the Christian world as well and will broaden their understanding of Judaism and the roots of their own faith.

We bring to you authors who are at the forefront of spiritual thought and experience. While each has something different to say, they all say it in a voice that you can hear.

Our books are designed to welcome you and then to engage, stimulate, and inspire. We judge our success not only by whether or not our books are beautiful and commercially successful, but by whether or not they make a difference in your life.

We at Jewish Lights take great care to produce beautiful books that present meaningful spiritual content in a form that reflects the art of making high quality books. Therefore, we want to acknowledge those who contributed to the production of this book.

Stuart M. Matlins

Stuart M. Matlins, Publisher

PRODUCTION
Tim Holtz, Martha McKinney & Bridgett Taylor

EDITORIAL
Amanda Dupuis, Polly Short Mahoney,
Lauren Seidman & Emily Wichland

COVER DESIGN & INTERIOR TYPESETTING
Bridgett Taylor

COVER / TEXT PRINTING & BINDING
Versa Press, East Peoria, Illinois

Spirituality

The Dance of the Dolphin
Finding Prayer, Perspective and Meaning in the Stories of Our Lives
by *Karyn D. Kedar*

Helps you decode the three "languages" we all must learn—prayer, perspective, meaning—to weave the seemingly ordinary and extraordinary together.
6 x 9, 176 pp, HC, ISBN 1-58023-154-3 **$19.95**

Does the Soul Survive?
A Jewish Journey to Belief in Afterlife, Past Lives & Living with Purpose
by *Rabbi Elie Kaplan Spitz*; Foreword by *Brian L. Weiss*, M.D.

Spitz relates his own experiences and those shared with him by people he has worked with as a rabbi, and shows us that belief in afterlife and past lives, so often approached with reluctance, is in fact true to Jewish tradition.
6 x 9, 288 pp, Quality PB, ISBN 1-58023-165-9 **$16.95**; HC, ISBN 1-58023-094-6 **$21.95**

The Gift of Kabbalah
Discovering the Secrets of Heaven, Renewing Your Life on Earth
by *Tamar Frankiel, Ph.D.*

Makes accessible the mysteries of Kabbalah. Traces Kabbalah's evolution in Judaism and shows us its most important gift: a way of revealing the connection between our "everyday" life and the spiritual oneness of the universe. 6 x 9, 256 pp, HC, ISBN 1-58023-108-X **$21.95**

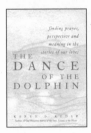 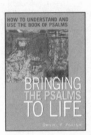   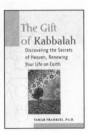

God Whispers: *Stories of the Soul, Lessons of the Heart*
by Karyn D. Kedar 6 x 9, 176 pp, Quality PB, ISBN 1-58023-088-1 **$15.95**

Bringing the Psalms to Life: *How to Understand and Use the Book of Psalms*
by Rabbi Daniel F. Polish
6 x 9, 208 pp, Quality PB, ISBN 1-58023-157-8 **$16.95**; HC, ISBN 1-58023-077-6 **$21.95**

The Empty Chair: *Finding Hope and Joy—*
Timeless Wisdom from a Hasidic Master, Rebbe Nachman of Breslov **AWARD WINNER!**
4 x 6, 128 pp, Deluxe PB, 2-color text, ISBN 1-879045-67-2 **$9.95**

The Gentle Weapon: *Prayers for Everyday and Not-So-Everyday Moments*
Adapted from the Wisdom of Rebbe Nachman of Breslov
4 x 6, 144 pp, Deluxe PB, 2-color text, ISBN 1-58023-022-9 **$9.95**

Or phone, fax, mail or e-mail to: **JEWISH LIGHTS** Publishing
Sunset Farm Offices, Route 4 • P.O. Box 237 • Woodstock, Vermont 05091
Tel: (802) 457-4000 • Fax: (802) 457-4004 • www.jewishlights.com
Credit card orders: **(800) 962-4544** (9AM–5PM ET Monday–Friday)
Generous discounts on quantity orders. SATISFACTION GUARANTEED. Prices subject to change.

Spirituality—The Kushner Series
Books by Lawrence Kushner

The Way Into Jewish Mystical Tradition
Explains the principles of Jewish mystical thinking, their religious and spiritual significance, and how they relate to our lives. A book that allows us to experience and understand the Jewish mystical approach to our place in the world.
6 x 9, 224 pp, HC, ISBN 1-58023-029-6 **$21.95**

Jewish Spirituality: *A Brief Introduction for Christians*
Addresses Christian's questions, revealing the essence of Judaism in a way that people whose own tradition traces its roots to Judaism can understand and appreciate.
5½ x 8½, 112 pp, Quality PB, ISBN 1-58023-150-0 **$12.95**

Eyes Remade for Wonder: *The Way of Jewish Mysticism and Sacred Living*
A Lawrence Kushner Reader Intro. by *Thomas Moore*

Whether you are new to Kushner or a devoted fan, you'll find inspiration here. With samplings from each of Kushner's works, and a generous amount of new material, this book is to be read and reread, each time discovering deeper layers of meaning in our lives.
6 x 9, 240 pp, Quality PB, ISBN 1-58023-042-3 **$16.95**; HC, ISBN 1-58023-014-8 **$23.95**

   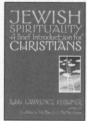 

Invisible Lines of Connection: *Sacred Stories of the Ordinary* AWARD WINNER!
5½ x 8½, 160 pp, Quality PB, ISBN 1-879045-98-2 **$15.95**

Honey from the Rock: *An Introduction to Jewish Mysticism* SPECIAL ANNIVERSARY EDITION
6 x 9, 176 pp, Quality PB, ISBN 1-58023-073-3 **$15.95**

The Book of Letters: *A Mystical Hebrew Alphabet* AWARD WINNER!
Popular HC Edition, 6 x 9, 80 pp, 2-color text, ISBN 1-879045-00-1 **$24.95**; *Deluxe Gift Edition, 9 x 12, 80 pp, HC, 4-color text, ornamentation, slipcase, ISBN 1-879045-01-X* **$79.95**; *Collector's Limited Edition, 9 x 12, 80 pp, HC, gold-embossed pages, hand-assembled slipcase. With silkscreened print. Limited to 500 signed and numbered copies, ISBN 1-879045-04-4* **$349.00**

The Book of Words: *Talking Spiritual Life, Living Spiritual Talk* AWARD WINNER!
6 x 9, 160 pp, Quality PB, 2-color text, ISBN 1-58023-020-2 **$16.95**; HC, ISBN 1-879045-35-4 **$21.95**

God Was in This Place & I, i Did Not Know: *Finding Self, Spirituality and Ultimate Meaning*
6 x 9, 192 pp, Quality PB, ISBN 1-879045-33-8 **$16.95**

The River of Light: *Jewish Mystical Awareness* SPECIAL ANNIVERSARY EDITION
6 x 9, 192 pp, Quality PB, ISBN 1-58023-096-2 **$16.95**

Because Nothing Looks Like God
by Lawrence and Karen Kushner; Full-color illus. by Dawn W. Majewski
11 x 8½, 32 pp, HC, Full-color illus., ISBN 1-58023-092-X **$16.95** For ages 4 & up

Spirituality

My People's Prayer Book: *Traditional Prayers, Modern Commentaries*
Ed. by *Dr. Lawrence A. Hoffman*

Provides a diverse and exciting commentary to the traditional liturgy, helping modern men and women find new wisdom in Jewish prayer, and bring liturgy into their lives. Each book includes Hebrew text, modern translation, and commentaries *from all perspectives* of the Jewish world.

Vol. 1—*The Sh'ma and Its Blessings*, 7 x 10, 168 pp, HC, ISBN 1-879045-79-6 **$23.95**
Vol. 2—*The Amidah*, 7 x 10, 240 pp, HC, ISBN 1-879045-80-X **$23.95**
Vol. 3—*P'sukei D'zimrah* (Morning Psalms), 7 x 10, 240 pp, HC, ISBN 1-879045-81-8 **$24.95**
Vol. 4—*Seder K'riat Hatorah* (The Torah Service), 7 x 10, 264 pp, HC, ISBN 1-879045-82-6 **$23.95**
Vol. 5—*Birkhot Hashachar* (Morning Blessings), 7 x 10, 240 pp, HC, ISBN 1-879045-83-4 **$24.95**
Vol. 6—*Tachanun and Concluding Prayers*, 7 x 10, 240 pp, HC, ISBN 1-879045-84-2 **$24.95**

Six Jewish Spiritual Paths: *A Rationalist Looks at Spirituality*
by Rabbi Rifat Sonsino
6 x 9, 208 pp, Quality PB, ISBN 1-58023-167-5 **$16.95**; HC, ISBN 1-58023-095-4 **$21.95**

Becoming a Congregation of Learners
Learning as a Key to Revitalizing Congregational Life by Isa Aron, Ph.D.;
Foreword by Rabbi Lawrence A. Hoffman, Co-Developer, Synagogue 2000
6 x 9, 304 pp, Quality PB, ISBN 1-58023-089-X **$19.95**

Self, Struggle & Change
Family Conflict Stories in Genesis and Their Healing Insights for Our Lives
by Dr. Norman J. Cohen 6 x 9, 224 pp, Quality PB, ISBN 1-879045-66-4 **$16.95**

Voices from Genesis: *Guiding Us through the Stages of Life*
by Dr. Norman J. Cohen 6 x 9, 192 pp, Quality PB, ISBN 1-58023-118-7 **$16.95**

Ancient Secrets: *Using the Stories of the Bible to Improve Our Everyday Lives*
by Rabbi Levi Meier, Ph.D. 5½ x 8½, 288 pp, Quality PB, ISBN 1-58023-064-4 **$16.95**

The Business Bible: *10 New Commandments for Bringing Spirituality & Ethical Values into the Workplace*
by Rabbi Wayne Dosick 5½ x 8½, 208 pp, Quality PB, ISBN 1-58023-101-2 **$14.95**

Being God's Partner: *How to Find the Hidden Link Between Spirituality and Your Work*
by Rabbi Jeffrey K. Salkin; Intro. by Norman Lear **AWARD WINNER!**
6 x 9, 192 pp, Quality PB, ISBN 1-879045-65-6 **$16.95**; HC, ISBN 1-879045-37-0 **$19.95**

God & the Big Bang
Discovering Harmony Between Science & Spirituality **AWARD WINNER!**
by Daniel C. Matt 6 x 9, 224 pp, Quality PB, ISBN 1-879045-89-3 **$16.95**

Soul Judaism: *Dancing with God into a New Era*
by Rabbi Wayne Dosick 5½ x 8½, 304 pp, Quality PB, ISBN 1-58023-053-9 **$16.95**

Finding Joy: *A Practical Spiritual Guide to Happiness* **AWARD WINNER!**
by Rabbi Dannel I. Schwartz with Mark Hass
6 x 9, 192 pp, Quality PB, ISBN 1-58023-009-1 **$14.95**; HC, ISBN 1-879045-53-2 **$19.95**

Children's Spirituality

In Our Image
God's First Creatures   AWARD WINNER!

For ages 4 & up

by *Nancy Sohn Swartz*
Full-color illus. by *Melanie Hall*

A playful new twist on the Creation story—from the perspective of the animals. Celebrates the interconnectedness of nature and the harmony of all living things. "The vibrantly colored illustrations nearly leap off the page in this delightful interpretation." —*School Library Journal*
9 x 12, 32 pp, HC, Full-color illus., ISBN 1-879045-99-0 **$16.95**

God's Paintbrush   AWARD WINNER!

For ages 4 & up

by *Sandy Eisenberg Sasso*; Full-color illus. by *Annette Compton*

Invites children of all faiths and backgrounds to encounter God openly in their own lives. Wonderfully interactive; provides questions adult and child can explore together at the end of each episode. 11 x 8½, 32 pp, HC, Full-color illus., ISBN 1-879045-22-2 **$16.95**

Also available: A Teacher's Guide: **A Guide for Jewish & Christian Educators and Parents**
8½ x 11, 32 pp, PB, ISBN 1-879045-57-5 **$8.95**

God's Paintbrush Celebration Kit 9½ x 12, HC, Includes 5 sessions/40 full-color Activity Sheets and Teacher Folder with complete instructions, ISBN 1-58023-050-4 **$21.95**

In God's Name   AWARD WINNER!

For ages 4 & up

by *Sandy Eisenberg Sasso*; Full-color illus. by *Phoebe Stone*

Like an ancient myth in its poetic text and vibrant illustrations, this award-winning modern fable about the search for God's name celebrates the diversity and, at the same time, the unity of all people. 9 x 12, 32 pp, HC, Full-color illus., ISBN 1-879045-26-5 **$16.95**

What Is God's Name? (A Board Book)

For ages 0–4

An abridged board book version of award-winning *In God's Name*.
5 x 5, 24 pp, Board, Full-color illus., ISBN 1-893361-10-1 **$7.95** A SKYLIGHT PATHS Book

The 11th Commandment: *Wisdom from Our Children*

For all ages

by *The Children of America*   AWARD WINNER!

"If there were an Eleventh Commandment, what would it be?" Children of many religious denominations across America answer this question—in their own drawings and words. "A rare book of spiritual celebration for all people, of all ages, for all time."—*Bookviews*
8 x 10, 48 pp, HC, Full-color illus., ISBN 1-879045-46-X **$16.95**

Life Cycle & Holidays

The Jewish Family Fun Book: *Holiday Projects, Everyday Activities, and Travel Ideas with Jewish Themes*
by *Danielle Dardashti* & *Roni Sarig*; Illustrated by *Avi Katz*

With almost 100 easy-to-do activities to re-invigorate age-old Jewish customs and make them fun for the whole family, this complete sourcebook details activities for fun at home and away from home, including meaningful everyday and holiday crafts, recipes, travel guides, enriching entertainment and much, much more. Illustrated.
6 x 9, 288 pp, Quality PB, Illus., ISBN 1-58023-171-3 **$18.95**

The Book of Jewish Sacred Practices
CLAL's Guide to Everyday & Holiday Rituals & Blessings
Ed. by *Rabbi Irwin Kula* & *Vanessa L. Ochs, Ph.D.*

A meditation, blessing, profound Jewish teaching, and ritual for more than one hundred everyday events and holidays. 6 x 9, 368 pp, Quality PB, ISBN 1-58023-152-7 **$18.95**

Celebrating Your New Jewish Daughter: *Creating Jewish Ways to Welcome Baby Girls into the Covenant—New and Traditional Ceremonies*
by Debra Nussbaum Cohen; Foreword by Rabbi Sandy Eisenberg Sasso
6 x 9, 272 pp, Quality PB, ISBN 1-58023-090-3 **$18.95**

The New Jewish Baby Book AWARD WINNER!
Names, Ceremonies & Customs—A Guide for Today's Families
by Anita Diamant 6 x 9, 336 pp, Quality PB, ISBN 1-879045-28-1 **$18.95**

Parenting As a Spiritual Journey
Deepening Ordinary & Extraordinary Events into Sacred Occasions
by Rabbi Nancy Fuchs-Kreimer 6 x 9, 224 pp, Quality PB, ISBN 1-58023-016-4 **$16.95**

Putting God on the Guest List, 2nd Ed. AWARD WINNER!
How to Reclaim the Spiritual Meaning of Your Child's Bar or Bat Mitzvah
by Rabbi Jeffrey K. Salkin 6 x 9, 224 pp, Quality PB, ISBN 1-879045-59-1 **$16.95**

The Bar/Bat Mitzvah Memory Book: *An Album for Treasuring the Spiritual Celebration* by Rabbi Jeffrey K. Salkin and Nina Salkin
8 x 10, 48 pp, Deluxe HC, 2-color text, ribbon marker, ISBN 1-58023-111-X **$19.95**

For Kids—Putting God on Your Guest List
How to Claim the Spiritual Meaning of Your Bar or Bat Mitzvah
by Rabbi Jeffrey K. Salkin 6 x 9, 144 pp, Quality PB, ISBN 1-58023-015-6 **$14.95**

Bar/Bat Mitzvah Basics, 2nd Ed.: *A Practical Family Guide to Coming of Age Together*
Ed. by Cantor Helen Leneman 6 x 9, 240 pp, Quality PB, ISBN 1-58023-151-9 **$18.95**

Hanukkah, 2nd Ed.: *The Family Guide to Spiritual Celebration*—The Art of Jewish Living
by Dr. Ron Wolfson 7 x 9, 240 pp, Quality PB, Illus., ISBN 1-58023-122-5 **$18.95**

Shabbat, 2nd Ed.: *Preparing for and Celebrating the Sabbath*—The Art of Jewish Living
by Dr. Ron Wolfson 7 x 9, 320 pp, Quality PB, Illus., ISBN 1-58023-164-0 **$19.95**

The Passover Seder—The Art of Jewish Living
by Dr. Ron Wolfson 7 x 9, 352 pp, Quality PB, Illus., ISBN 1-879045-93-1 **$16.95**

Women's Spirituality

The Women's Torah Commentary: *New Insights from Women Rabbis on the 54 Weekly Torah Portions* Ed. by *Rabbi Elyse Goldstein*

For the first time, women rabbis provide a commentary on the entire Five Books of Moses. More than twenty-five years after the first woman was ordained a rabbi in America, these inspiring teachers bring their rich perspectives to bear on the biblical text. In a week-by-week format; a perfect gift for others, or for yourself. 6 x 9, 496 pp, HC, ISBN 1-58023-076-8 **$34.95**

Moonbeams: *A Hadassah Rosh Hodesh Guide*

Ed. by *Carol Diament, Ph.D.*

This hands-on "idea book" focuses on *Rosh Hodesh*, the festival of the new moon, as a source of spiritual growth for Jewish women. A complete sourcebook that will initiate or rejuvenate women's study groups, it is also perfect for women preparing for *bat mitzvah*, or for anyone interested in learning more about *Rosh Hodesh* observance and what it has to offer. 8½ x 11, 240 pp, Quality PB, ISBN 1-58023-099-7 **$20.00**

Lifecycles In Two Volumes **AWARD WINNERS!**
V. 1: *Jewish Women on Life Passages & Personal Milestones*
Ed. and with Intros. by Rabbi Debra Orenstein
V. 2: *Jewish Women on Biblical Themes in Contemporary Life*
Ed. and with Intros. by Rabbi Debra Orenstein and Rabbi Jane Rachel Litman
V. 1: 6 x 9, 480 pp, Quality PB, ISBN 1-58023-018-0 **$19.95**
V. 2: 6 x 9, 464 pp, Quality PB, ISBN 1-58023-019-9 **$19.95**

ReVisions: *Seeing Torah through a Feminist Lens* **AWARD WINNER!**
by Rabbi Elyse Goldstein 5½ x 8½, 224 pp, Quality PB, ISBN 1-58023-117-9 **$16.95**;
208 pp, HC, ISBN 1-58023-047-4 **$19.95**

The Year Mom Got Religion: *One Woman's Midlife Journey into Judaism*
by Lee Meyerhoff Hendler 6 x 9, 208 pp, Quality PB, ISBN 1-58023-070-9 **$15.95**

Ecology

Torah of the Earth: *Exploring 4,000 Years of Ecology in Jewish Thought*
In 2 Volumes Ed. by *Rabbi Arthur Waskow*

An invaluable key to understanding the intersection of ecology and Judaism. Leading scholars provide a guided tour of Jewish ecological thought.
Vol. 1: *Biblical Israel & Rabbinic Judaism*, 6 x 9, 272 pp, Quality PB, ISBN 1-58023-086-5 **$19.95**
Vol. 2: *Zionism & Eco-Judaism*, 6 x 9, 336 pp, Quality PB, ISBN 1-58023-087-3 **$19.95**

Ecology & the Jewish Spirit: *Where Nature & the Sacred Meet* Ed. and with Intros.
by Ellen Bernstein 6 x 9, 288 pp, Quality PB, ISBN 1-58023-082-2 **$16.95**

The Jewish Gardening Cookbook: *Growing Plants & Cooking for Holidays & Festivals*
by Michael Brown 6 x 9, 224 pp, Illus., Quality PB, ISBN 1-58023-116-0 **$16.95**;
HC, ISBN 1-58023-004-0 **$21.95**

Spirituality & More

The Jewish Lights Spirituality Handbook
A Guide to Understanding, Exploring & Living a Spiritual Life
Ed. by *Stuart M. Matlins, Editor in Chief, Jewish Lights Publishing*

Rich, creative material from over fifty spiritual leaders on every aspect of Jewish spirituality today: prayer, meditation, mysticism, study, rituals, special days, the everyday, and more.
6 x 9, 456 pp, Quality PB, ISBN 1-58023-093-8 **$18.95**; HC, ISBN 1-58023-100-4 **$24.95**

The Story of the Jews: A 4,000-Year Adventure—A Graphic History Book
Written and illustrated by *Stan Mack*

Through witty cartoons and accurate narrative, illustrates the major characters and events that have shaped the Jewish people and culture. For all ages.
6 x 9, 304 pp, Quality PB, Illus., ISBN 1-58023-155-1 **$16.95**

The Jewish Prophet: Visionary Words from Moses and Miriam to Henrietta Szold and A. J. Heschel
by *Rabbi Dr. Michael J. Shire*

This beautifully illustrated collection of Jewish prophecy features the lives and teachings of thirty men and women, from biblical times to modern day. Provides an inspiring and informative description of the role each played in their own time, and an explanation of why we should know about them in our time. Illustrated with illuminations from medieval Hebrew manuscripts.
6½ x 8½, 128 pp, HC, 123 full-color illus., ISBN 1-58023-168-3 **$25.00**

 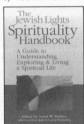 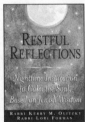  

The Enneagram and Kabbalah: *Reading Your Soul*
by Rabbi Howard A. Addison 6 x 9, 176 pp, Quality PB, ISBN 1-58023-001-6 **$15.95**

Cast in God's Image: *Discover Your Personality Type Using the Enneagram and Kabbalah*
by Rabbi Howard A. Addison 7 x 9, 176 pp, Quality PB, ISBN 1-58023-124-1 **$16.95**

Mystery Midrash: *An Anthology of Jewish Mystery & Detective Fiction* AWARD WINNER!
Ed. by Lawrence W. Raphael 6 x 9, 304 pp, Quality PB, ISBN 1-58023-055-5 **$16.95**

Criminal Kabbalah: *An Intriguing Anthology of Jewish Mystery & Detective Fiction*
Ed. by Lawrence W. Raphael; Foreword by Laurie R. King
6 x 9, 256 pp, Quality PB, ISBN 1-58023-109-8 **$16.95**

Sacred Intentions: *Daily Inspiration to Strengthen the Spirit, Based on Jewish Wisdom*
by Rabbi Kerry M. Olitzky & Rabbi Lori Forman
4½ x 6½, 448 pp, Quality PB, ISBN 1-58023-061-X **$15.95**

Restful Reflections: *Nighttime Inspiration to Calm the Soul, Based on Jewish Wisdom*
by Rabbi Kerry M. Olitzky & Rabbi Lori Forman
4½ x 6½, 448 pp, Quality PB, ISBN 1-58023-091-1 **$15.95**

Embracing the Covenant: *Converts to Judaism Talk About Why & How* Ed. by Rabbi Allan Berkowitz & Patti Moskovitz 6 x 9, 192 pp, Quality PB, ISBN 1-879045-50-8 **$16.95**

Wandering Stars: *An Anthology of Jewish Fantasy & Science Fiction* Ed. by Jack Dann; Intro. by Isaac Asimov 6 x 9, 272 pp, Quality PB, ISBN 1-58023-005-9 **$16.95**

Israel—A Spiritual Travel Guide: *A Companion for the Modern Jewish Pilgrim* AWARD WINNER!
by Rabbi Lawrence A. Hoffman 4¾ x 10, 256 pp, Quality PB, ISBN 1-879045-56-7 **$18.95**